Feeling the Stones

'... crossing a river feeling the stones with your feet' — Deng Xiaoping

'摸著石頭過河' —— 鄧小平

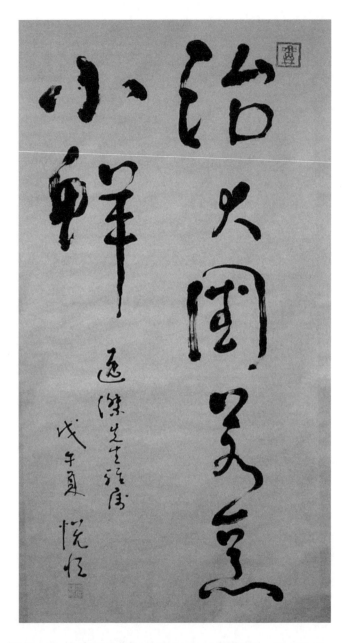

'Ruling the country is like cooking a small fish' — *Dao De Jing*
'治大國若烹小鮮' ——《道德經》

Feeling the Stones

Reminiscences by
David Akers-Jones

香港大學出版社
HONG KONG UNIVERSITY PRESS

Hong Kong University Press
14/F Hing Wai Centre
7 Tin Wan Praya Road
Aberdeen
Hong Kong

© Hong Kong University Press 2004
First published 2004
Reprinted 2004

ISBN 962 209 655 7

British Library Cataloguing-in-Publication Data
A catalogue record for this book is available
from the British Library.

Secure On-line Ordering
http://www.hkupress.org

Printed and bound by United League Graphic & Printing Co. Ltd. in Hong Kong, China

For Jane

Jane in 2002 just before she passed away.
We had been in Hong Kong for 45 years.

Contents

Contents

Foreword

The Rt. Hon Lord Wilson of Tillyorn

ong Kong has been very fortunate in its civil servants, both Hong Kong Chinese and expatriates. They form one of the pillars of the phenomenal success of the territory since the end of the Second World War. Another even more substantial pillar has of course been the sheer energy and drive of the Chinese people of Hong Kong, both those born there and those who came from Mainland China at times of political upheaval north of the border.

Allowing vigour, determination and the urge to better one's lot to take a productive course is a key attribute of good government. "Ruling the country is like cooking a small fish" is the wording of a fine piece of calligraphy with which this book opens. It is a good choice for the story of a man who knew in his bones just what that meant and who understood also another ancient Chinese text: "The way to govern a country is first to make the people prosperous".

From his first arrival in Hong Kong in 1957, David Akers-Jones made it his business to understand and get to know the people of Hong Kong, their culture, their history and their ambitions. He must rank as one of the last of that great breed of District Officers who knew intimately the people and the area for which he was responsible. He never lost his enthusiasm for listening to the views of younger generations, as anybody lucky enough to have attended his informal discussion dinners will remember well.

For anyone who wants an understanding of how Hong Kong has

changed, and the role played in this by dedicated and knowledgeable expatriate civil servants, this book on the life led by David Akers-Jones, backed in her life-time by his equally involved wife Jane, is a first-rate and fascinating introduction.

Perhaps one of the most unexpected facts to emerge from the book is that it was not until 1973 that David Akers-Jones visited Mainland China and, even then, he was one of the first Hong Kong civil servants after the Communist victory in 1949 to be allowed to do so. Such was the gulf, until relatively recently, between Hong Kong and Mainland China. How things have changed since then! But change is the life-blood of Hong Kong. That Hong Kong rode change with such skill owed a great deal to the dedication, wisdom and love for the territory and its people of those like David Akers-Jones.

Preface

This book is not a history of post-war Hong Kong; it is an account of experiences of and reflections on living and working in Hong Kong on the doorstep of mainland China from 1957 until, as a Special Administrative Region, we crossed the threshold of the new century. It is an account of some of the challenges I faced as a member of the government, and, because I found politics of such absorbing interest, inevitably it contains much about political development and logs aspects of the march of events leading to the return of Hong Kong to China. It also contains descriptions of untoward events and ground-breaking decisions which I hope are of more general interest.

It is often said that Hong Kong suffers from a border mentality and prefers to think of the present boundary between Hong Kong and the mainland as a protective barrier. My wife and I crossed the border, as it was called then, into China many times: first in 1973 when the violence of the Cultural Revolution had abated but the country was still in the grip of its harsh and frequently violent theories of reform of thought and attitude. A few years later, following its opening to the world, we saw how throughout the land China was stirring, and how far removed it was from many of the available descriptions. To give the book more balance, I have included among these pages an account of some of these visits.

The record is incomplete because my memory is incomplete. It is not an autobiography, a chronology of our lives, but a record of things which stand out most in the memory. There will be those who will say 'Oh, but it was not like that', and I ask their forbearance.

I hope it will be read by a wider audience than simply those who have lived or are living in Hong Kong, and that they will find occasional delight and enjoy reading about how Hong Kong, this special small place of crowded pavements, skyscrapers, giant ships, mountains, seascapes and forests, has managed, without natural resources, to survive and flourish.

Today, government is more challenged as it strives to find its identity within the governing embrace of China, and there is tension, strain and effort as Hong Kong struggles with unexpected and unfortunate challenges. Of course there are now no expatriates recruited directly into the administrative service, although, perhaps surprisingly to the unbeliever who would think that these last vestiges of colonialism had been swept away at the moment of reunification, there are still a number of British administrative officers with a good knowledge of Chinese in senior positions left over from the colonial era and staying on. That said, there are now opportunities throughout Hong Kong for those from around the world who look for the rewarding empathy of living and working among the people of China.

We stayed on after retirement because we scarcely knew anywhere else and because in Hong Kong we have so many friends and so much involvement. There was work to be continued in many voluntary organisations. Retired in England, we would have been like the sad old man in the Chinese poem who left his native village so long ago his whiskers are white, and when he returns the children laugh at him although he speaks like one of them they don't know who he is.

Would we do it again? Yes, and with the knowledge now gained, I hope would do a better job of those things left undone which we ought to have done. A member of the administrative service in Hong Kong had so much opportunity to uncover ideas, sow seed and watch them grow. The government never seemed short of money to back a good idea, to knock it into shape, and within a few years literally to turn it into concrete or a change of policy. Papers on policies and projects did not gather dust: government was a living, bubbling thing and needed these spontaneous injections of both ideas and energy to keep pace with the challenge of the need, without any significant natural resources, to provide a livelihood for the swelling population, and to keep stoking the fires of burgeoning prosperity.

We have had wonderful, rewarding lives in Hong Kong and our thanks go out to so many colleagues and friends who have shared these years.

David Akers-Jones
2002

Prologue

I n January 1945 I left the woods, the quiet villages, the soothing curves of the South Downs, seventeen years old, still a schoolboy self-conscious in a handsome gold-buttoned bridge coat which reached below my knees. The train rattled and swayed through the cold, bleak night, passing through the dim orange gloom of stations with names removed to fool invading armies, until with the coming of day we arrived, tired, at grey, wintry, war-time Hull.

I had grown up in a quiet country village in Sussex and attended the local church primary school. As the clouds of war gathered, my father lost his lifetime employment at the local brickworks, the fires in the kilns were put out and he spent the war years, until retirement, in the Civil Defence organisation. My mother, who trained the church choir, ran the Women's Institute and supported many village activities, returned to teaching for her war work but, sadly, died while I was still a boy.

When invasion threatened the south coast I was evacuated with the rest of the Worthing Boys' High School to Newark in the Midlands. After several months the school straggled back and classes resumed, but even then school was often interrupted by hours spent in the air raid shelters which fringed the school sports ground. When freed from school, an added boyhood excitement was to cycle and tramp the Sussex Downs to the wreckage of German aircraft shot down duriing the air raids of the Battle of Britain. For war work we joined in the haymaking and harvesting. At school I had risen to be the leading cadet in the Army Cadet Corps, and as my call-up for military service approached the obvious thing seemed to be to join the army. But in 1944, with the war coming to an end, military service would not have provided a very broad experience or opportunity to travel. A friendly retired Merchant Navy Captain suggested joining the Merchant Navy, and helped me to apply to the British India Steam Navigation Company.

Service at sea counted equally for military service, and fifty guineas indentured me for four years as an apprentice in the 'B.I.', as it was affectionately known. The money was repaid in small amounts, month by month, until after four years it would be expended. It was augmented by 'danger money' paid to merchant seamen in wartime, which curiously doubled if you survived six months at sea.

My uniform had been made in Leadenhall Street, London, by the practised hands and quiet sympathy of Miller, Rayner and Haysom, who had fitted out generations of young men, supplying them with the brown and white topis, white drill tunics, shirts and shorts, caps and cap covers, packed in a steel trunk. In Hull, this bruising, sharp-cornered trunk was borne on the shoulders of Indian seamen in red-sashed, blue smocks and white, round caps, up the long gangway and ladders of the ship, to be left between the bunks in a crowded cabin, home to four apprentices.

The *Mantola* made no claim to beauty. She was a solid, straight up and down 9,000 tons with cargo holds fore and aft and, amidships, a three-deck box structure of cabins. In peacetime she had a black-painted hull with a white stripe and two white bands around a black funnel, all now reduced to the ranks beneath an unidentifiable and protective grey. The British India Company had a long history and its many ships were a familiar sight in all ports east of Aden. It lingered on for some time after the war, succumbing eventually to the container revolution of the seventies.

Two days in Hull were spent in a 'dome', a concrete igloo with dive-bombers projected onto its ceiling, learning the rudiments of gunnery — knowledge which was precious little use later, when the convoy was intercepted by lurking E-boats down the cold reaches of the North Sea, flashes and explosions filled the night air, and I was in a gun turret with a gun about which I knew nothing.

The next four years were spent around the coast of India, on long hauls to Australia, to Burma and Thailand, shuttling between Singapore and Bangkok with rice and kerosene, west along the equator to Seychelles, and to Mombasa, Zanzibar, Lindi, Dar-es-Salaam, Tanga and Mikindani, carrying fuel for the tanks of the giant tractors of the soon-to-be-abandoned groundnut scheme.

We moved from ship to ship — cargo liners, troop ships, steam ships and coasters — across sea so calm it mirrored the stars, mountainous seas that sent the ships groaning, reeling and staggering, or with the sea hissing at the bow, climbing the long, pillowing, silken swells of the Indian Ocean, brown with dust from distant shores. I experienced the pleasure of sighting another ship on the wide expanse of ocean and the delight of sighting whales and flying fish; I saw phosphorous stars in the lavatory flush and the mirage of approaching coastline.

Disjointed memories of those years surface in the mind: crews from Gujerat, carpenters from China, Malays, Goans, Indians, Muslims and Hindus; and a veteran quartermaster on the troop ship *Nevasa* , Frank Huntley, who had joined the ship at her launching shortly after World War I and had remained on the ship since then, now a small figure with a red swollen nose reputed to drink a bottle a day (he died, I believe, when the ship was scrapped). I remember the thrill of keeping watch, swinging at a buoy on the wide cocoa-cream waters of the Irrawaddy with the passenger taxi boats skimming across the river and the donging of the prayer bell from the gleaming spire of the Shwedagon rising above the sleeping city. I remember coaling in Calcutta, watching the continuous stream of men and women in blackened loincloths and saris, mounting a long swaying and bouncing plank with quick steps and deftly dumping a basket of coal through the rising dust into the bunkers below; and then the sweating firemen in the choking heat of the engine room, heaving, with long swings, coal into the white-hot furnace. I remember being hove-to in a violent gale in the Australian Bight, with stalls of valuable racehorses among the cargo on deck. I remember scraping across the muddy bar to Bangkok on the M.V *Kola*, and then the thrilling journey of a big ship surging though brown estuary water between narrowing palm-fringed river banks and stretching paddy fields. And I remember being strike-bound for weeks in Sydney, tied up behind *Lawhill*, one of the last four-masted grain ships.

So the days and four birthdays passed without a holiday and without return until we buffeted our way, in a gale, slowly through the Straits of Gibraltar on *Durinda* .

Sunderland was cold. The dockworkers, gaunt men, trudged the iron decks speaking a strange tongue. Departure from the ship and the sea is as unceremonious as arrival. It is not that sailors are unfriendly, but it is a life of arrival and departure, of welcome and goodbye — better not to become too attached. After all that had passed in those four years, there was just a simple 'Well then, cheerio, all the best!' At this moment of parting I had now to choose between a life at sea or the continuation of an education interrupted for four years by the demands of war. I chose Oxford.

Britain remained impoverished. Clothes, meat, sugar, butter and petrol were rationed. After four years away at the other side of the world, I was a stranger. Those next years have an air of unreality, a bubble in time, in which in 1951, I met and married my wife, Jane, much to the disapproval of her parents, who had higher hopes than a penniless Oxford undergraduate struggling to make ends meet on an insufficient government grant. To pay for this bold venture, I worked in the long vacation as an engineer on a Salters river steamer, three men in a boat carrying our load of trippers up and down the Thames, tying up at night alongside the water meadows. One evening, leaning on the lock gate at Marlow, I struck up a conversation with a man walking his dog, which led to me becoming a lifelong member of the Royal Central Asian Society (now the Royal Society for Asian Affairs) and, although I did not know it, presaged a return to Asia.

At Brasenose, I learned something of the origins of the English language, sound changes in the dialects of Anglo-Saxon, Old French and Old English Paleography. Then, armed with a degree in these obscurities and precious little else, the Oxford University Appointments Board suggested I apply for work as trainee manager in a second-hand jute bag factory in the Mile End Road, or in the petroleum, soap and chemical industries!

The great smog of 1952 had just cleared from the London streets. On a winter morning I visited the jute bag factory, where gnome-like women with a sack for apron, a sack for cloak, a folded sack for hood, worked at giant, clacking sewing machines, and huge vacuum tubes reached down from the roof to carry the gunny dust away. My courage and my knowledge failed these tests.

My four years spent growing up in the Merchant Navy east of Suez had left me with a desire to return. But at that time, commercial firms were not recruiting married young men, especially those with no business experience, to start their careers in the East. The Colonial Office was more relaxed.

Not wanting to join the government, I had used the back of the first application for the colonial service as a shopping list. We applied for another form, and armed with my experiences of the Far East, a smattering of Eastern languages, and a reading of *A Pattern of Islands* by Arthur Grimble, I passed the scrutiny of a board of colonial veterans. I was handed on to the venerable Dr Brunel Hawes, who pronounced me fit to return to the Far East as a cadet in the Malayan Civil Service.

There followed almost a year of waiting for Jane and me, the spring filled working as a housemaster and housemother at a boy's preparatory school in Sussex. The headmaster, Mr Mowll, brother of the much-loved Archbishop of New South Wales and visiting bishop to South-West China, was a member of the Magic Circle and could quell welling tears of homesickness by suddenly producing an egg from behind a small boy's ear. The summer we spent teaching at Gordonstoun. It was the last term of Dr Kurt Hahn, founder of the schools at Salem and Gordonstoun and the Outward Bound training school at Aberdovey, and this began our long association with Outward Bound.

Then there were a few short weeks at the School of Oriental and

African Studies, ostensibly to learn Malay. Since I had already some Malay from working for a year with Malay seamen, I began a lifetime of learning Chinese.

We look back on our three years in Malaya with delight. As though there was no thought of looming Independence and the end of a career before it had scarcely started, and as if there was all the time in the world, instead of being put to work I was to learn Hokkien, an obscure and complicated Chinese dialect spoken in the former Straits Settlements of Penang, Malacca, and Singapore, which many centuries before had been settled by immigrants from Fujian province in China. Other Chinese recoil from the complexities of Hokkien, with its strange words and tones which change from their original tonal value as you talk, and in which pronunciation of the written word character retains its centuries-old sound and is different again. As Sir Gerald Templer said curtly, but not unkindly, to me when he asked to see his new recruits, 'That will fix you'.

Jane worked for a while for Lady Templer, and one morning heard Sir Gerald shouting 'Does anyone here know anything about Outward Bound?' We did, and thus began our involvement with the setting up of the first Outward Bound School in Malaysia and, later, in Hong Kong.

The Chan Family Ancestral Hall, at the end of Petaling Street in Kuala Lumpur, stands to this day. It had been rented by the government for the language school where we would-be scholars sat for two years beneath the eaves of the verandahs, under zooming swallows and whirling fans, while unperturbed family members brought offerings of flowers and fruit and lit joss sticks before the tablets of their ancestors. At the end of two years we could hold a conversation, write simple sentences and slowly read a newspaper. My teacher, a poet and writer, chose my Chinese name by taking the Hokkien pronunciation of Jones as Chiong [鍾] and Akers as Yek Kiat [逸傑]. So, for the rest of my life, I became Chiong Yek Kiat 鍾逸傑, pronounced differently by speakers in various dialects: 'Zhong Yat Kit' in Cantonese, the prevailing dialect of Hong Kong. The name can be translated in many ways; 'modest or serene hero' is probably what my teacher wished for me.

I was sent to be District Officer in Alor Gajah in the Malacca settlement. There were paddy fields at the end of the lawn and, in the lallang grass behind the house, two untended headstones marking the graves of ensigns killed in the Naning wars of the nineteenth century. (I wonder, are they still there?)

The house was open to the winds, with wide verandahs home to many bats, and up the slope past the tennis court were the swing doors of the District Office, through which villagers and goats wandered at will. There were scattered kampongs of stilted houses with curved attap roofs, some with blue delft-tiled steps from an earlier Dutch coloniser; there were a few small, sleepy country market towns with their Indian shopkeepers and Chinese *towkays* (owners).

There were eerie, silent regiments of rubber trees, wide paddy fields, rain forest on the hills and long stretches of golden sanded coastline lined with indolent palms, a Portuguese fort, aboriginal settlements, New Villages into which had been corralled Chinese squatters collected from the fringes of the jungle, veteran Scottish planters, and in the jungles, terrorists who kept a record of our journeys around the district and whose lurking presence in the jungle made driving at night, swishing past the lines of rubber trees, a creepy business. As we entered, lights had to be dimmed at the gates of fenced-in villages. Gurkhas with loaded weapons boarded our small Morris Minor, and at the other side of the village closed the gates behind us, leaving us to drive on into the black night and enclosing trees.

We had only a year in Alor Gajah before Merdeka, Independence, but we had been in Malaya long enough to grow a lifetime of liking. We had to leave. Merdeka came, and we were offered either a short stay in another colony in Africa, also approaching independence, or a transfer to Hong Kong. My four years at sea had taken me no further east than the Gulf of Thailand. Now was the chance to see China.

This book, then, is about Hong Kong, about China, about journeys taken from Hong Kong; it is about Hong Kong's efforts to prepare itself for life after 1997 when the colony would be returned to China's sovereignty; it is about good deeds and dirty deeds. It is not a diary, but rather a series of chapter-essays recounting a journey that has lasted more than fifty years.

1

Arrival

My wife and I and our baby son arrived in Hong Kong one blazing hot summer morning in 1957, after a three-day flight from England which ended with the plane skimming over the hills of Kowloon, swooping swiftly down to the runway and bumping past traffic waiting at a level crossing for the plane to land. We crossed the harbour by launch and saw for the first time the steep hillsides, the mountains, the blue waters of the harbour and the greying buildings of the city. Hong Kong was struggling twelve years after the war to adjust to the fate that had left it as lonely as it had been when occupied by the British a hundred years before, isolated on the coast of southern China.

The founding of the People's Republic in 1949 and the changes in China's political and economic landscape had a profound effect on Hong Kong. Although it was the last left of the nineteenth-century Treaty Ports, it was no longer an entry port to China. China was virtually closed to Hong Kong and to the outside world. The population had swollen in the aftermath of war from five hundred thousand to more than two million, with half living in an amazing and ingenious architecture, a straggle of wood and tin-sheet-covered rooftops stretching up the hill slopes and hiding among trees along stream courses.

From our apartment in Mid-Levels we could see the solemn, undistinguished building of the Commerce and Industry Department where I worked among the many office buildings along the waterfront. We lived in one of that band of houses and apartments halfway between the waterfront and the skyline homes of senior citizens on the Peak. Although we were not paid much, it was enough to employ two amahs in white buttoned-across tunics and black trousers. We looked across the harbour with its ever-changing crowd of merchant ships turning at buoys, at sampans, launches and barges threading their way among the ships, and junks from China making their way nonchalantly through the bustle, taking a shortcut through the harbour of capitalist Hong Kong before sailing northwards up the coast to communist Swatow. On the far side of the harbour were the grey tenements of Kowloon, ringed by range after range of mountains fading into the blue of China.

Although it received a plentiful supply of cheap vegetables, pigs and other supplies from China, Hong Kong was ready for the worst to happen, ready for supplies to be cut off, ready for a siege. I became part of the team which ensured that we had several months' supply of rice in warehouses, stockpiles of firewood for cooking, soya beans for essential vitamins and corned beef for protein. I had, too, to control and keep out of the hands of the communist bloc, strategic chemicals used by tin-shed factories to make enamel pots and pans and coating for gas mantles to light the lamps of the third world. I learned how to buy soya beans on the world market, about the danger of blown cans in bully beef past the 'use-by' date, and how to buy and sell black cords of mangrove timber from Borneo, which were chopped and, before the advent of bottled gas, sold by grocers for cooking rice in the kitchens of Hong Kong.

The rice trade was dominated by the Chaozhou, a close-knit community making up one-fifth of Hong Kong's population, who come from the marches of Fujian and Guangdong in southern China. Because of emigration in previous centuries, the rice merchants of Thailand also come from Chaozhou. They speak a nasal dialect into which they can switch as their private world, unintelligible to other Chinese. Most rice for Hong Kong is imported by these merchants and sold at silent auctions in which only the seller can see the bid made by the buyer who comes forward to move a bead or two on the auctioneer's abacus. No one speaks; a nod of the head and business is done. Rice is bought and sold in an interlocking train of relationships where each in the chain seems to be in debt to the other: farmers to exporters, importers to exporters, wholesalers to importers, retailers to wholesalers and housewives to shopkeepers. Money passes down the chain from kitchen to paddy field, with a few days or weeks between payments. Behind the simple process of buying and selling was a ricochet of social, ethnic and economic relationships, all of which had to be kept in balance, stretching from the crowded streets of Hong Kong to rice farmers in the fields of Thailand.

My first two years in Hong Kong among the merchants and shopkeepers and the raw material of life and industry were a useful background for what was to follow.

Hong Kong was stirring, beginning to find its post-war identity, left to its own devices by Whitehall and Westminster. It was putting aside its colonial status, developing a sense of responsibility and self-reliance, realising the need to make a start on housing the millions who had arrived following the end of the China's civil war; realising a need to bring order out of disorder; realising, more keenly than in the pre-war years, that it was a place with people who had their rights. Hong Kong had not been included in the post-war reappraisal of Britain's imperial role and the status of its colonies. It had briefly toyed with introducing a more representative municipal government and then, overwhelmed by the flood of immigrants from the mainland, moved cautiously towards its terminal date of 1997.

This slower pace was dictated by political reality. There was none of the haste of other colonies to introduce elections because of looming independence. Hong Kong recognised that the uncertain future would last until it was known what would happen when the lease of most of the colony, the New Territories, expired. This was to give Hong Kong time to develop socially and economically, to build a great dynamic city and to become one of the wonders of the world. The 'huddled masses', the millions who sought refuge in Hong Kong, brought with them machines, money and skills to start up industry in ramshackle sheds. The government responded by building grey, barrack resettlement blocks, one room to a family, with kitchens and lavatories shared between the blocks. Children, always amazingly clean and neatly dressed, loaded with school bags clambered upstairs to rooftop schools. Hawkers, selling everything a family needed, filled the space between the blocks. Rent was low, food from China plentiful and cheap and life hard. Uncomplaining families spent years in these cramped rooms driven by the desire to lift themselves and their children out of poverty.

The first tender roots of Hong Kong's cultural life were slowly extending. The Sino-British Club, whose members included academics and professionals from the Chinese, British and Portuguese communities, had among its members the gentle and distinguished poet, Edmund Blunden, a professor at that time at the University of Hong Kong. I became its secretary. The club played a seminal role in promoting the building of a new City Hall, which had been lacking in Hong Kong since the early years of the century when the place of the old colonnaded City Hall was taken by the Hongkong and Shanghai Bank. It played a major role in the formation of the Hong Kong Philharmonic Orchestra and arranged the first rudimentary Arts Festival in the newly completed pier of the Star Ferry. After scouring Hong Kong for musicians who could play Chinese instruments, as far as I know the first public concert of Chinese music was held in 1958 in the elegant hall of the Club Lusitano. Now Chinese orchestras and concerts of Chinese instrumental music are everywhere to be heard.

The city of Victoria, on the island of Hong Kong, and Kowloon were separated by more than the harbour. Kowloon was a different place, a different society, a necessary place to pass through on the way to the golf course. There was no need to risk a journey to Kowloon, as all the comforts of life could be had in Hong Kong, and in any case it involved a tiresome crossing by ferry. The business and professional life of international Hong Kong took place on the island. This had been so since the nineteenth century, and even to this day many islanders know little of Kowloon, although three tunnels now link the two sides. We were soon, with all our belongings, to cross on the ferry to this other world, for almost a lifetime of work in what was, in 1959, the rural hinterland of Hong Kong.

2

The New Territory

Above the dry windblown grass, the humped summits of surrounding hills and grey lichen-covered rocks, a yellow biplane droned against towering clouds and sky. A weighted pennant fluttered to the ground, a message to say 'You have been posted to the New Territories as District Officer'.

When this news came we were staying in a lonely stone hut, one of a number of scattered holiday homes for missionaries high on Hong Kong's largest island, Lantau. A friend, flying in a Tiger Moth biplane, had spotted us and thrown down his exciting news. We read the scribbled note as the yellow wings grew small in the sky and looked around the wide horizon, a world of secret islands and ridge upon mysterious blue ridge of mountains reaching across the New Territories into China. District Officer in Hong Kong's New Territories would be different from District Officer among the kampongs, rice, rubber, and jungle of Malacca from where we had come two years before. It would mean learning a new dialect, Cantonese, after having already spent two years, not entirely wasted, learning to speak Hokkien, the language of the next province northwards along the coast from Hong Kong.

District Officers were eccentric specialists, occasionally seen but not much to be heard; an unwelcome reminder, perhaps, that Hong Kong was still a colony. We were to join these exclusives and to begin twenty years' work on the other side of the dividing harbour and beyond the mountains. Hong Kong's swelling population was growing by a million every ten years, and factories were working night and day to supply cloth, garments, plastic flowers, wristwatches, pots and pans and simple electrical ware to the world, and to provide employment for impoverished millions. It was a time of great change and challenge. New towns had to be built and infrastructure provided. To do this, land had to be found. Squatters swept from the hillsides of the city had to be resettled. Terraces were scraped from the hills and the earth dumped to cover centuries-old fields and to push the foreshore out into the sea. In twenty years these were to become cities of half a million people, wiping out farms and villages and thrusting over land and among lives which had not changed much for centuries.

The District Officer was in the midst of this: a creature of Imperial Britain found wherever red appeared on the globe. There were District Officers in Africa, South-East Asia, on remote islands, in the West Indies and in India; faintly eccentric figures in their white shorts and long socks, wearing a solar topi, or on parade grounds in easily crumpled, plain, white, buttoned-up uniforms and trailing sword, and later in dark grey worsted suits and trilby hat. At the height of their powers they were police officers, magistrates and Land Officers, variously known by the Chinese, casually but without disrespect, together with the rest of the expatriate community, as 'red-haired', 'foreign devils' or 'big noses'!

There were Land Officers, Collectors and District Officers throughout the Empire – titles which understated the lightly borne but heavy responsibility which reached into the heart of the traditions of society wherever they were to work. They adjudicated on boundary disputes among the bunds dividing one field of rice from another, or of plantations of coconut palms, decided on inheritance and pronounced on the resolution of quarrels involving customs which were not their own. They collected rent, sold land and acquired it for public purposes, and certified all private transactions between the people in their jurisdiction. They were the eyes and ears of colonial government, political officers, and the 'father and mother' of the people..

The New Territories were literally new territory added to Hong Kong at the end of the nineteenth century. At that time, the Germans, French and Russians were each taking advantage of a debilitated government in China to secure substantial land holdings. In that distasteful phrase, China was 'up for grabs'. The Americans, too, as a sideshow to the Spanish-American War, were assembling a fleet in the deep shelter of Mirs Bay in Hong Kong waters as a prelude to intervening in the Philippines.

The island of Hong Kong together with the end of the Kowloon Peninsula gave no room to manoeuvre, no *cordon sanitaire* between Hong Kong and China. A muddy tidal river over the mountains well to the north of Kowloon was thought to be a better boundary. It would create a buffer of rural land between Hong Kong and the villages of China and a hinterland for the growing city, and it would provide room for the city to breathe and expand and for the troops to exercise. Inclusion of the surrounding sea up to the high water mark on the Chinese shore, and a twenty square mile boundary embracing a straggling necklace of islands, provided a welcome safe stretch of territorial water for Her Britannic Majesty's ships and for the yachts of the taipans to sail unmolested. However, at the end of the nineteenth century there was a growing conscience in Westminster at the propriety of appropriating outright the territory of other nations, and so, with some huffing and puffing in Britain's parliament and the slow arrival of hesitant telegrams, the land was leased for 99 years until 1997 rather than being summarily annexed like the rest of Hong Kong.

Claiming this new acquisition provided moments of anxiety and tension when British troops advanced across the territory and were attacked by villagers, and even farce when the relieving forces setting off from Kowloon in a gunboat in thick fog hit rocks and had to proceed with dented pride and bow. There were later moments of humour when deciding on the line of the boundary: the map produced from the long boot of the Chinese intermediary had so little detail that it had to be set aside for one surveyed by the British. Later, troops, undeterred by the shallow muddy stream which was to be the border, kept on going, and meeting no resistance, marched northwards through rice paddies and unconcerned villages, eventually to be ordered to retreat, protesting, to the river line.

In Hong Kong, despite petitions and protests from the captains of commerce, a walled village (the so-called Kowloon Walled City) where the visiting Chinese magistrate had his tax-collection office was excluded from the lease. Within a short while the sensitivity of including a bit of the Qing government apparatus within the controlled area was brushed aside as posing an unacceptable security threat. The magistrate was obliged to vacate his *yamen*. But more of that later.

By 1899 all had been settled and the rights of the inhabitants set out by proclamation, and headmen, to act as intermediaries — committee men — had been appointed. The attractive gates, curiously made of iron rings, at the entrance to one of the small walled villages where resistance was the strongest, were taken as booty in retribution for its vigorous opposition, and removed to Ireland to the home of the Governor, Sir Henry Blake. They were brought back, ceremonially, a quarter of a century later.

Land and property run as a continuous, important thread in the life of Hong Kong. The very first Governor received a royal reprimand for privately parcelling out the prime sites of land on the barren foreshore, some leased for 999 years to the most influential of the merchant houses. Such favouritism was brought quickly to an end. Land thereafter, by peremptory order from the Queen in Balmoral, was to be sold at public auction to the highest bidder. A hundred and fifty years have passed and this remains a guiding principle. Land was a scarce and valuable resource, and the sale of land by the government was from the earliest beginnings a principal source of revenue. Even today, property and construction account for half of the Hong Kong economy.

Instead of the few inhabitants who greeted the first boat in 1841 as it beached on the narrow foreshore of the steep slope of Hong Kong Island, there were, in the newly leased territory, thousands of acres of privately owned fertile farmland. There were owners of property who, through their carefully kept genealogies, could trace their land titles back many hundreds of years.

It made no difference that the land was in China. The first thing to be done, in 1899, was to follow routines developed in India and South-East Asia, to measure, map and record ownership of all land and property and then to lease it back to the owners. Order was then restored. So anxious was the administration to complete this task that land surveyors were brought in from India, and their faint pencillings in Urdu in the Land Registers can still be seen beside the Chinese names. Now the people were anchored to their land holdings and the Land Offices became the centre of rural life.

Memorials recording buying and selling, mortgaging, inheritance and the settlement of disputes were all registered in the Land Office, and the District Officer — the Land Officer — was the arbiter of it all, his final signature settling the legality of all transactions. Much later, the factual and accepted accuracy of these musty records going back to the beginning of the century was of paramount importance when the expansion of development into this rural hinterland began.

After the end of the Pacific War cheap imported rice replaced rice won by back-breaking toil in the paddy fields of the New Territories. The sons of the soil, the villagers, left the land, many of them to migrate to Britain and later to continental Europe. Poorer immigrant farmers from Chaozhou flooded in and began to supply vegetables to the markets of Kowloon and Hong Kong. Battery chicken farmers and large-scale pig farmers rented other land, and then small-scale factories spread from the city as the needs of goods for export grew. Abandoned cars and construction machinery, worn-out bulldozers and cranes were dumped on the land, and empty container boxes from the container shipping revolution were piled high above the villages. The smiling rural plains, golden twice a year with ripening grain, were no more.

Sir Henry Blake, Governor when the new territory was 'acquired' in 1898, made a point of reassuring the people that their ancient rights would be respected and that Chinese law and custom would be followed. 'Land required for public offices, fortifications, or the like official purposes would be bought at a fair price.' The 'official purposes' were at first limited to the building of roads, public offices and reservoirs, and, generally speaking, the payment of a 'fair price' settled the matter. The owners of property in the New Territories are inclined to take a wholly pragmatic view of things. If there is a more comfortable living environment to be had than the lightless, waterless, drainless, centuries-old ancestral home, they have little compunction about knocking it down, unrestrained by sentiment for things old. If their land, too, can yield a more profitable return than farming they will not be hindered by having to turn their backs on a traditional way of life. This attitude was an important factor when it came to the building of the new towns and the acquisition of ancestral land.

To sidestep contravention of these earlier promises and the certain objections which would follow, a way had to be found in which the owners of agricultural land could profit from development without themselves having to be involved in building and development. Examination of the plan for the new town provided the answer. It was estimated that three-fifths of the land acquired would be needed for infrastructure and 'official purposes' and two-fifths would be available for private development. Landowners were able to surrender their agricultural land and receive this ratio of building land in exchange, paying the difference in value between the two. This simple 5:2 formula not only paved the way for eventual urbanisation, but with the sharp rise in land prices, enabled the landowners to sell their rights to building land and to become rich beyond belief.

One of my first jobs as a District Officer was to acquire land for the widening of the road through Tsuen Wan and to start to remove a village which had been there for many dynasties. The formula of land exchange and a generous grant of land for the building of new village houses which were more spacious and comfortable than the dark, ancient, village houses provided a quick and simple solution; and with this same formula came widespread development as Hong Kong expanded.

3

Tsuen Wan and the Islands, 1959–1961

Tsuen Wan

Tsuen Wan was over the hills and along the coast west of Kowloon. White-walled villages were hidden in valleys; huts and factories straggled up the hillsides; families lived on tiny sampans at anchor in the bay, and vegetables were grown anywhere not immediately wanted for living and working. From 1959 we lived in Tsuen Wan for just under a year, while the incumbent District Officer, Hal Miller (later Sir Hal Miller, a Member of Parliament and Chairman of the Conservative Party), returned to England.

The resettlement of urban squatters from Kowloon into seven-storey grey barracks of concrete had begun. These blocks were cramped and uncomfortable, but families were away, at last, from leaky roofs and safe from fire and typhoon winds. Silk-weaving factories from Shanghai, with their tall wooden looms for weaving fine patterned brocades, were housed in a special block with high ceilings. Industrialists, with their money, machines and men brought from Shanghai, were busy spinning, weaving and dyeing cloth for export to the West in such quantities that Britain, to protect the Lancashire industry, retaliated with import quota restrictions. Tin beaters, knitting machines, pressing machines making bright plastic flowers where no flowers grew, any activity that would make a living, were crammed into seven-storey factory blocks similar to those which housed the people.

In a nearby inlet from the sea, the pale grey hulks of aircraft carriers, relics of the Korean War, were being broken for scrap to be rolled into reinforcing rods for the building boom to come, and across the water a monstrous, rotting midden of rubbish was slowly filling part of the bay. In another corner of the growing town, night soil, collected in 'honey-buckets' from tenements without lavatories, was stored in tanks to 'mature', later to be pumped into tankers and distributed to vegetable farms. Cinemas were built and banks opened, and churches and clinics found space among the many shops.

The old villages, which were slowly being encircled, elected their representative leaders and, collectively, formed a so-called 'rural committee'. The committee spoke for everyone and everything that was taking place: custom and tradition, typhoon damage, the increasing encroachment on the lives and possessions of people, school shortages and medical facilities.

There was no town council, no Development Board, no focus for this swirl of activity. I was supported by a staff of Chinese, old hands who told me what they thought I ought to know, how to placate, cajole, find imaginative solutions to emerging problems, and at informal meetings harness the energies of the leaders and the wealthy to do the things that the government, with its practical plans and barely sufficient policies and money, was unable to do. There was no recognised slaughterhouse, no market for the butchers — the sale of meat took place on stalls beside the footpaths — no playground for the release of energy, no outlet for philanthropy. Even the District Office was housed in a wooden shed, despite its precious collection of land deeds and records from the last half-century.

We were a mixed bunch: a young British banker, the courteous, determined, shrewd owner of a dyeing factory, a portly and breathless former Shanghai cinema clerk who now owned a string of banks and cinemas, a politically astute, lean, village elder with sunken cheeks and slicked-back hair, and the benign, evasive chairman of the rural council of the entire New Territories. These were the principal leaders of this growing town. These were the people who found the money and drummed up support to build schools and to help the missionary clinic and who organised basketball games on land reclaimed from the sea. It was they, after a short discussion with me, who were the founders of what became one of Hong Kong's leading and respected charity hospitals.

Tsuen Wan is ringed by mountains which slope steeply up behind the town to a thousand-metre summit, often shrouded in mist. Its many villages were hidden in narrow valleys or on the shelf of land bordering the sea. Each village was a private society, the houses built row on row in a small compressed rectangle with narrow lanes between, reached on foot along winding paths between small fields of rice and vegetables. They were grey-tiled with lime-washed, windowless walls, each with a small courtyard. Through the main arched entrance to the village, a central and wider path led to the great, faded crimson doors of the ancestral hall, and on the wall behind the altar, a bank of narrow shelves held the small slips of wood recording the names of family forebears from the time of the founding of the village. Behind each village, if space permitted, was a thicket of dark and evergreen banyans with fat and twisted trunks, trailing their air roots to the ground. One of these villages has been spared from demolition and survives among the tower blocks, highways, walkways and the railway, as a visible reminder of times past.

Half hidden in the trees backing on to the mountain and looking out to the sea and islands were temples and monasteries, their quiet precincts in sombre reds and yellows, grey tiles, courtyards and cloisters home to solitary monks and old, stooped nuns in grey habits, in sharp contrast to the feverish activity of the town below.

Tsuen Wan had been a small country town, a collection of shophouses serving the needs of many villages in the surrounding countryside as well as families living on fishing boats and sampans in the bay. When we lived there the scrub-covered slopes which stretched like tongues from the surrounding hills were being terraced for yet more housing blocks, and streams of dump trucks were filling in the bay, squashing the sampans into a corner until their families, too, had to move ashore into housing. Forty years later Tsuen Wan has grown into a great conurbation of an unbelievable 700,000 people, with marble-entranced shopping malls, an underground railway terminus, and multi-storey buildings with factories lodged on each floor instead of apartments; and the bay, where in the fifties the grey-hulled ships of war were lying to be broken up, has become by a strange twist of fate the largest container port in the world.

The acceptance of removal and resettlement, and continual displacement of people on an epic scale, has all taken place without major disorder, going almost unnoticed by the rest of Hong Kong, and has been a recurring feature for the past half century as a million people have been added every ten years to Hong Kong's population. Now the increase has slowed, and prosperity and later marriages have brought with them a decline in family size, but to balance this, people are living longer and life expectancy in Hong Kong is one of the highest in the world. In addition, every day, mainly to reunite families, one hundred and fifty men, women and children cross the line dividing Hong Kong from the rest of China and settle in Hong Kong. Small though the daily count is, in ten years it means homes and social services will be needed for an extra half million. Many others come not only from China but from around the world to serve the needs of an expanding and changing economy. Some forty years ago, a British Colonial Secretary spoke of Hong Kong's 'problem of people'. He was not wrong, but the solution lay in cleverly devised public housing programmes and an expanding economy. Hong Kong will not stop growing until some time in the twenty-first century a balance can be found between the pressure of population from within China and the capacity of Hong Kong to absorb more people.

We were to live among this community in Tsuen Wan, to get to know its people and to watch it grow. We lived in a small, flat-roofed house built by the Parsee owners of the local brewery, with a pillared door and a curious circle of interconnecting rooms. It had a spectacular view looking out over humped islands and a constant passage of boats thrusting against the current or careering wildly with it. Sailing junks with their high sterns, swinging umber sails, and nonchalant deckhands beat their way past the house taking a short cut through Hong Kong waters to ports further along the coast. Sometimes at night the sampans of 'bright light' fishermen would scull beneath the cliff and toss in their fish bombs, scooping up the unconscious fish and scattering only when, with a shout and a hurled brick, I caused a rival, unsuspected explosion. It was as though we were in the lounge of a liner; hours could pass watching the sea. Now the house has been smartened up with a car park and viewing platform for tourists to photograph the great new bridges which span gaps between the islands and lead to the city and the airport.

While still in Tsuen Wan, I was to receive villagers resettled from the site of the floor of Hong Kong's latest reservoir, Shek Pik. I went in the company of my fellow District Officer to the schoolhouse of a village on Lantau Island. Already the bulldozers were at work scouring the valley floor for the reservoir. I rang the school bell to tell the villagers to leave their houses and watched as they said goodbye to their village for the last time and walked with their few possessions, without looking back, to the pier, to a landing craft which was to take them to their new homes in urban Tsuen Wan. By the evening nothing was left. With quiet acceptance born of centuries of hardship, the deal for their removal had been struck, and from then on they got on with their new urban lives, far away from their ancestral home

After almost a year I had been involved in clearing land, setting out the terms for the removal of villages, finding land for a community centre, persuading the meat merchants to take their pigs to a slaughterhouse, building a temporary market for the butchers, agreeing with the architect that the Shanghai silk merchants needed a special building for their looms, fixing the boundaries of a Taoist Institute, convening the first meetings of a Hospital Board, helping to settle a protracted dispute with the owner of an ironworks, reaching agreement with the shipbreakers to tow their hulks to another bay, finding another bay for a log pond for the wood merchants, resettling ship repair yards on an island opposite the town, dealing with the aftermath of a typhoon whose drenching rain had broken a catchwater and washed away half the main road, and a fire among squatter huts which had left several hundred homeless. Of course work on this omnium gatherum of subjects could not be concluded in one year, but work had begun. We then moved to another life among the scores of islands which, more by luck than judgement, had been enclosed in the new squared-off boundary with China in 1898.

The Islands

Leaving Tsuen Wan, I was to relieve the District Officer of the islands, Dr James Hayes, for most of 1961 while he returned to England for 'home leave'. After three or even four years in Hong Kong, home leave meant two months' travel by ship and then at least six months' holiday.

We had to move from our house overlooking the sea to the busy streets of Kowloon to be near the pier and the *Sir Cecil Clementi*, the launch which carried officials to the villages and settlements of the islands. We discovered from a relative of the Clementis who lived down the lane from my wife's home in Berkshire that Lady Clementi was alive and well. Sir Cecil had retired in 1926 as one of Hong Kong's most distinguished and remembered Governors. He was a member of a great family of soldiers and public servants whose name is found on memorials throughout the East, a Chinese scholar whose calligraphy still marks the entrance to the archway of a monastery in the western New Territories. We sent a photograph of the launch and began a brief correspondence with Lady Clementi. I can see Lady Clementi's confident handwriting to this day as her relief nib sputtered across the page — 'Cecil was a great walker, one of his most memorable journeys was from Turkestan to Kowloon'! The Clementis were married in Hong Kong's St John's Cathedral at the turn of the century and spent their honeymoon in tents in the eastern New Territories high above the sea looking out past a cluster of islands to the broad waters of the Pacific Ocean. Incidentally it was Sir Cecil who, as he was retiring, recommended that the question and extension of the New Territories lease should be negotiated. The Chinese government was in disarray and in his view there would never be a better time. His proposal was not pursued.

The *Sir Cecil Clementi*, with her pale blue hull and cream funnel, was a familiar sight for many years, chugging with dignity on her errands, but was gradually outmatched by fast ferries, jetfoils and catamarans. To justify herself to the auditors, she was designed to carry, in a tiny hold, building materials, cement for village paths and pipes for water supplies. Making space for a hold meant that there was little room for a cabin; a night out to reach distant villages meant a night asleep on deck for those who were hardy enough to brave the certain possibility of an early morning shower. On the inside of the saloon door was a photograph of a distinguished Sir Cecil in full dress uniform, hand on sword, and for those who knew, if you slipped the catch behind the photo, there was a mirror for the ladies to straighten their hats, *de rigueur* before going ashore! For the entertainment of village elders, the launch had a tiny galley and a cook famous for his single dish of chicken curry. Around the cramped, hospitable table many problems were ventilated and solved. I can still hear the country dialect of a village elder with toothless face and clawlike hand, twisted by the premature explosion of a fish bomb, explaining the difficulty of living in his village on a shore miles from anywhere. The *Sir Cecil Clementi* was much loved. Like so much of old Hong Kong she has gone to the breakers.

Not much had changed in the islands where time began many thousands of years ago, as is witnessed by shards of pottery, post holes for houses, and the remains of meals of aboriginal people, the Yue, who have links to the people of Vietnam and even further afield to Burma and south-west India. Hong Kong, as it says blandly in Hong Kong's Basic Law, has been part of China since ancient times, and if proof is needed it is there in a solitary domed Han tomb among the crowded housing estates of Kowloon. On the islands were typical grey villages with their tightly packed rows of houses, secure from marauders, backed by trees and hills, their paddy and vegetable fields sloping down to the sea. One by one I visited them, spending long days tramping over hills and along foreshores, sitting with village elders talking about their lives and families and the problems of remoteness from the bright lights of the city. The old men, some still with their seaman's caps, as young men had gone to sea. Now bent and weather-beaten, they would talk about the great ports of the world, London, Liverpool, Swansea, while quietly living out their lives at home once more among the rice fields, the rhythm of the seasons and their timeless villages.

Not all the islands were sparsely populated. Cheung Chau, shaped like a dumbbell and over an hour's ferry ride from Hong Kong, was a small market town for the fishing fleet which crowded at anchor in its sheltering western arms. Ships' chandlers, rice shops, restaurants, medicine shops with their dried herbs, strange things in bottles and row upon row of labelled drawers of the Chinese pharmacopeia, and grocers with strings of pungent salted fish lined the crowded alleyways. It was a privilege to step ashore into this other world and, in case there were any lurking evil spirits, to be greeted first by a burst of firecrackers on the pier and then the leaders of the island community wearing long blue gowns in honour of their official visitor; a privilege to be warmly welcomed into an almost independent land, as if untouched by colonial rule.

A stream of supplicants throughout the day visited the island temple to the God of the North. There were no prayer books or Sunday services; the temple was there and no one would think of an enterprise, the birth of a child, failure or success in business, marriage, setting sail or returning safely to harbour, without a visit to the temple to kneel before the altar to find out what the gods had in store by shaking out one of the numbered sticks from a bamboo cylinder or by clattering down the wooden oracle 'beans'. It was a dignified building reached by stone steps between grey granite guardian lion dogs, a drift of incense smoke making the air blue, the temple keeper in a worn vest stooped over his books of horoscopes, indifferent to the hopes and fears and prayers that filled the air.

Each year, in the courtyard fronting the temple, three high cones of bamboo poles were built and dressed with a close-packed coat of white steamed buns. To one side, under a canopy, huge, frightening, painted paper statues of the guardian gods on a frame of bamboo slivers provided an auxiliary altar. On a day appointed by geomancers, after consulting the phases of the moon and the signs of the zodiac, a procession was held around the narrow alleyways of the island, past a gaily decorated reviewing stand where the island elders in their long gowns welcomed the District Officer and other officials and guests. Preceded by gongs and plaintive, reedy pipes, clashing cymbals and the deafening beat of the huge drum of the island musicians, lions and unicorns pranced along. Children under the age of five, colourfully dressed either as legendary figures or to depict contemporary scenes, performed magical balancing acts, one child balancing on another's tiny outstretched palm or on a fan, without revealing the hidden rigid iron frame to which they were strapped. They were borne on the shoulders of elderly women to provide entertainment for the gods and, of course, for the thronging islanders and their guests from a less traditional world.

After nightfall, at a given signal and with a great 'Haroosh!', the young men of the island scrambled up the towers of buns, grasping as many as they could to give to family and friends. Sometimes the towers keeled over under the strain, sometimes there were fights to seize the greatest number of buns. Finally the paper gods were burnt and life returned to bustling normality. Nowadays a regulated distribution of buns takes place, and the old excitement is no more. The soggy buns are said to bring good luck and health to the recipients and the whole festival is said to be a thanksgiving for delivery from pestilence. Although the island claims it for its own, I have seen similar versions of this festival in other parts of China, and suspect it has a far more ancient, long-forgotten history.

Beneath the everyday activities of these market towns and villages were rivalries and factions. A District Commissioner of eccentric habit, reputed to have greeted his guests while hanging by his toes from a doorway, introduced a set of election rules — the Barrow Rules — so as to bring some legitimacy and real representative status to local leaders. Young District Officers after the war, many of whom had served in the Forces, or in one instance in the Friends Ambulance Unit during the Civil War in China, were swept along with the democratic spirit of those post-war years, and using the Barrow Rules introduced and held one-man-one-vote village elections. Villages were grouped together to form rural committees, and provided with a written constitution which, as time went on, was made more comprehensive and detailed. Their role was advisory, but because of the strength of rural opinion, their advice could not lightly be ignored. While no one would pretend that there was full-blown democracy in the New Territories, already by the 1960s, as distinct from urban Hong Kong and Kowloon, there were the beginnings of a representative system on which in later years it was possible to build.

Men dominated rural life. Daughters left their village to be married and entered the village of their husbands; sons brought their brides back to live in the village of their ancestors. This frequently resulted in villages where a single surname prevailed and dominated village life. Land and property were inherited by men, and, reflecting this, only men had the vote. Following the example of my predecessors I introduced a new constitution for Cheung Chau, paving the way for the registration of voters and supervised elections for the island's representatives. All Cheung Chau residents were registered, including merchants and those with special interests, fishermen living in houseboats on the water, and members of the powerful Chamber of Commerce. The island electorate ran into several thousands, and at the time more people voted and elections were harder fought than those for the urban council for the whole of Hong Kong. The attempt to pass the new constitution gave rise to a bitter struggle: vested interests were defeated, face was lost, apple carts were overturned, but after a meeting which lasted into the night, when the secret ballot was counted the new constitution had won the day.

In the first tier were the village representatives. The second tier, which grouped villages together in rural committees, collectively formed a rural council or Heung Yee Kuk. The origins of the Heung Yee Kuk, however, belonged to an earlier era. It harked back to the 1920s, a time of great turbulence and shifting fortunes in mainland China, of power struggles, warlords, the growth of political movements such as the Chinese Communist Party and the Guomindang, and of differing ideologies. It would have been superficial to suppose that Hong Kong's citizens would not be affected and would remain impartial observers of these great events.

Emotions came to a head in 1925. A group of textile workers were locked out of a Japanese mill in Shanghai, and an angry protest followed, which led to a worker being shot. Thousands then marched on the police station in Shanghai's Nanking Road. The police fired on the massed protestors and eleven were killed. This was followed by a lengthy strike in Hong Kong, a boycott of British goods and a walk-out of thousands of workers who returned to their native villages. In June of that year, a similar protest march in Canton was fired on by British troops from Shameen, the foreign concession. Fifty-two Chinese were killed and a hundred wounded. It was a time of great anxiety, of rising nationalism and the mobilisation of political forces, particularly rural and peasant movements. The Heung Yee Kuk was born as a grouping of rural, commercial and industrial interests as a local reflection of this general mood and was eventually given recognition by the government as the Rural Council for the New Territories. It remains so to this day, with an even more elevated status, a mention in the Basic Law and representation in the Legislative Council.

Then, as now, most of its representations and confrontations with the government were about land. When Sir Henry Blake had issued his proclamation to the people of this newly acquired and leased territory, he had, after all, said that their customs would be respected. To the landowners this meant that they would have the same freedom to do what they wished with their land as they had enjoyed from time immemorial, and nearer to the present, during the Qing dynasty. In the 1920s this difference of opinion centred on the attempt by government to extract a payment for the right to build on their land. Despite Sir Henry's declaration, soon after the New Territories were leased the Governor of Hong Kong had persuaded the British government that, for the sake of good governance and the maintenance of law and order, the laws of Hong Kong should be extended to the new territory. Queen Victoria, in Balmoral, Scotland, gave her hand to this fiat by an Order in Council in 1899. Never mind what Sir Henry had said, disputes had to be settled thereafter according to the laws of Hong Kong as a whole.

In the late 1950s electoral fraud and vote rigging in forming the thirteenth term of the rural council led the government to intervene and to bring into being a representative structure with statutory backing. Rural committee chairmen and vice chairmen, Justices of the Peace and a handful of elected special representatives formed the new Heung Yee Kuk Rural Council, whose statutory responsibility it now was to advise the government on all matters affecting the New Territories. The new committee on Cheung Chau, together with twenty-six other rural committees, sent its representatives to this council.

Hong Kong Island and Kowloon had no similar institution. There was an urban council consisting of some members appointed by the Governor and others elected on a limited franchise. Its remit principally included the cleaning and hygiene of urban Hong Kong, and public housing and recreation. With this limited franchise and responsibility, political parties, the Civic Association and the Reform Club struggled to excite a largely indifferent electorate. Their annual debates tended to stray outside these statutory boundaries but they scarcely caused a ripple on the surface of the political life of Hong Kong. There was nothing resembling the man-to-man plain speaking and sometimes hard-fought debates which characterised life in the New Territories. District Officers, accustomed to the system of consultation and public battles which characterised life in the country, carried this spirit with them when they were promoted to positions in the centre of government, and in the course of time it was they who became the proponents among their peers for a more open government for the whole of Hong Kong.

Cheung Chau was separated by a narrow channel from Hong Kong's largest island, Lantau. In 1840, after weeks of bickering over the surrender of British seamen accused of murdering a Chinese, Liu Wei-hsi, during a brawl in Tsim-Sha-Tsui at the tip of the Kowloon peninsula, the Emperor's commissioner in Canton, Lin Zexu, expelled the British from Macao. The British were armed with the results of a prophetic marine survey made in 1794 by the frigate *Jackall*, one of the fleet of ships which accompanied Lord Macartney's fruitless embassy to China to set up a permanent diplomatic mission. *Jackall* sailed past Lantau, because of its unsheltered soft-mud anchorage, to get to the deep water and narrow channel separating Hong Kong Island from Kowloon. After that, Lantau was left in lonely grandeur until 1898. It is an island of considerable beauty, rising via an undulating stretch of sharply ridged peaks to a height of nearly a thousand metres. Small villages grew up where centuries of erosion and tidal retreat had left patches of arable land fanning out along the shoreline. In 1960 the construction of the Shek Pik reservoir was to turn the attention of Hong Kong's planners to the island for almost the first time. A motorable road was needed from the nearest sheltered ferry pier to the reservoir, houses were needed for engineers, and then, because of its remoteness and because there was land for which there was no other use, prisons were built to house an overflow of offenders from urban Hong Kong.

Bordering an ancient path of great granite slabs leading steeply upwards from the fishing port and salt pans of Tai O were monasteries and nunneries among shading banyan trees, providing a few precious remaining years of quiet retirement and prayer for elderly amahs, some still keeping the long black queue of their single status, who had thriftily saved during their long years of work.

Po Lin, the largest of these monasteries, a Buddhist foundation, lay on the small plateau beneath the peak. After it had been renovated in the 1970s, the abbot came to see me, as Secretary for the New Territories, about building a great bronze Buddha on a conical mound facing the monastery. The Hong Kong government's secular policies gave no official encouragement to religion, but people everywhere flock to temples and seek the comfort of prayer. Although doubting that the huge sum of money to achieve it would ever be raised, I gave the project my blessing and recorded my agreement in a letter. This put a stamp of authority and respectability to the fundraising. The letter became a treasured possession of the monastery, and for obvious reasons was on public view in a glass case for many years. With the opening up of China in 1978 the monks and their supporters were able to draw on China's resources to design and cast, in an armaments factory, the huge segments of bronze to make up the statue. The great Buddha was built and stands today, an arm raised in benediction, looking over the broad waters of the Pearl River estuary, and visited by thousands. In recognition of my contribution I was asked to participate with the then representative of the Chinese government in Hong Kong, Director Xu Jiatun, head of the New China News Agency, in lowering the last bronze panel into the crown of Buddha's head: a colonial civil servant and a Party member in strange communion!

Governor Sir Cecil Clementi, before he left Hong Kong in 1926, granted a favour to a devoted woman servant who herself wanted a piece of land in that quiet valley leading to the peak on which to build her own small retirement nunnery. Fifty years later I received a request to permit renovation and expansion of this nunnery on to the adjoining empty hillside. Again it seemed to me that nothing but good could come of providing, at no expense to government, for devotions which bring solace and peace to so many. Now there stands a faithfully designed and crafted Temple of a Thousand Buddhas, with cloisters and refectory, on the site granted by Governor Clementi to his amah.

The mountains of Lantau rise steeply, green and blue, from the sea, the northern shoreline stony and grey and the south bathed by clear ocean waters lapping silver-sanded beaches and hidden coves. A small fort, a few hundred years old and in which a handful of Manchu troops had been stationed, guarded the seas to the south. It stood on a small steep promontory looking over the Pearl River estuary, neglected and forgotten. The colonel of a battalion from the Royal Warwickshire Regiment, temporarily serving in Hong Kong, asked me for a place to camp and to undertake a community project. I suggested they camp on the foreshore behind a crescent of golden sand and clear and map the fort. They pitched their tents and enjoyed a week away from routine. On the last night I visited them on *Clementi* for a mess dinner beneath canvas, in full kit, the regimental silver on the table. Wine and port flowed freely and the completion of a successful project climaxed suitably by the officers escorting my dinghy back to the boat, marching, fully clad, into the warm waters of the South China Sea.

Following the building of the Shek Pik reservoir at the beginning of the 1960s, other development followed slowly. The citizens of Hong Kong discovered Lantau and its treasured environment almost for the first time. A few years before the return of Hong Kong to China, an island on the north shore of Lantau was chosen as the site for an airport to replace Kai Tak, into which the planes still roared, almost incessantly, over the roofs of urban Kowloon. Building the airport on North Lantau involved the construction of three bridges to cross the gaps between the islands which fronted our old house in Tsuen Wan, and the building of highways and a rail line from downtown Hong Kong. Now the airport stands hugely grey, with scalloped roof, on the far horizon and the great hanging bridges glow at night with strings of lights and pink and purple floodlit piers. And in the valley below the peak, adjoining the airport, shine a thousand lights of a new town to house workers for the airport and daily commuters to Hong Kong. As though it were a symbol of further changes in store, that Lantau is destined to play an even greater part in the development of Hong Kong, the great new airport stands near to the walls of a crumbling Qing dynasty fort.

As for us, four years and more had passed since leaving England. This was more than the normal tour of duty before returning to our 'country of origin' for the regulation several months' leave — long enough, if you carelessly overstayed the six months the tax collectors allowed, to be liable to pay British income tax! We were to be away for more than six months, so, to avoid the tax collector, towards the end of our leave we had to leave the Berkshire countryside and with our two children spend some extra weeks among the snow in Switzerland. From there we embarked at Genoa to return again to the farmland, market towns and villages of the New Territories, to Yuen Long, a district which covered the whole of the north-west.

4

Yuen Long, 1962–1967

Yuen Long was known for its proud and independent spirit and had fought with determination, but with hopelessly inadequate weapons, as the British troops advanced westwards across the territory in 1899. It was a district of many villages, a central market town, rice fields, fishponds of grey mullet, oyster beds along the coast, and a fairy-tale history which linked the oldest group of villages to a Sung princess.

Hong Kong was always short of water, but there was plenty to be had north of the border in the rivers which stretched for hundreds of miles inland from the Pearl River estuary. In 1957 the Chinese government offered to build a reservoir near the border to supply Hong Kong with water for which Hong Kong would pay what it charged the Hong Kong consumer. It was a good deal, and Hong Kong agreed. An earth dam was built just across the border from Hong Kong in six months, by thousands of workers carrying baskets and wheeling barrows of soil, and from the dam a huge black pipe was to snake its way across the paddy fields to feed into the Tai Lam reservoir in Yuen Long. The villagers objected noisily. It meant acquiring farmland, interfering with the geomantic environs of villages and causing a lot of disturbance. The villagers were determined to exact their pound of flesh. A former Assistant Commissioner of Police, a no-nonsense Scot called Norman Fraser, was hastily summoned back from retirement, and he found the right degree of compensation to quieten their discontent. In 1962 I was appointed to succeed him.

Shortly after our arrival in Yuen Long, the continual trickle of illegal immigrants who made their way by land and sea into Hong Kong from neighbouring Guangdong turned into a flood. There has been no satisfactory explanation for this sudden exodus. Some say it was because of the distress and food shortages being felt in villages after the 1957 Great Leap Forward, when the energies of the whole nation were diverted from food production and concentrated on attempts to make steel in backyard furnaces. Others say that rumours had circulated that the border was open. It was an extraordinary event. I went with Norman Fraser to the border, and standing on a small grassy hill we watched, in the summer sun, the long lines of people winding down the steep mountain paths like an epic being played out against the great wide screen of China. Men, women and children rested, hands hooked on the wire, with quiet anxious faces pressed against the rickety fence used to mark the boundary on the British side. When night fell a hundred arms pulled down the fence and the watchers and waiters walked across the fallen wire into Hong Kong.

Over a hundred thousand people came into Hong Kong during those months. Some were rounded up and sent back across the border where the railway line from China crosses into Hong Kong. People from the city rushed to the border looking for their relatives. There was pushing and shoving and some attempt in sympathetic villages to prevent this forced repatriation, and then, as though a tap had been turned off in China, the flood of people ceased.

Hong Kong, 'a barren island with hardly a house upon it', has always been host to immigrants from the rest of China, to those who seek to make their fortune or merely to change their lives, and are attracted to Hong Kong's promise of rags to riches or good fortune. There are attempts to stop them, but the journey to Hong Kong, with its long, indented coastline, inaccessible over long stretches, and the constant passage of thousands of river vessels, is worth a try. Until the end of the seventies there was no agreement with the authorities in Guangdong over the return of illegal immigrants, and up until then if they reached home ground and 'touched base', to cover what was really a serious situation with a lighthearted sporting phrase, they were able to register and obtain an identity card and security.

As I write now, in 2003, immigration from China continues to be a subject of daily concern. In those days thirty years ago, in the districts of the New Territories which reached up to the border of the Shenzhen River, illegal immigration from China was part of the backdrop to our work.

In 1958, while the rest of Hong Kong was sleeping, a catastrophe unfolded over the hills of the north-west New Territories. The heavens opened, and in a brief period deluged Yuen Long with several inches of rain. Yuen Long, situated on a plain not many feet above sea level, was flooded, people were drowned, crops and livestock destroyed. This led to a great scheme of flood control which involved driving the embracing arms of wide concrete ditches through fields, fishponds, villages and even the town itself. To put a brave face on it, and as a palliative to this great upheaval, a plan was prepared for this quiet market town, and development began which has continued ever since. From being a small country town, Yuen Long is now a city of several hundred thousand people.

Yuen Long, reached along a narrow road twenty-five miles from downtown Kowloon, had been largely left alone by the mandarins, taipans and dwellers on the Peak. Indeed, there was not much to show in the 1960s for more half a century of colonial rule. There was a narrow road, and at the approach from the south-east two small, wooded hills, on one, the district office, on the other, the police station. These were little more than cottages with verandahs and tiled roofs tarred black against torrential summer rains. Half a mile down the road a straggle of shophouses lined the main street.

With the construction of the flood control drains — 'nullahs', as they were called, a Hindi loan word brought by Indian surveyors — Yuen Long began its march into the twenty-first century. The road to the town was widened, which meant cutting its way through a village. This called for the ordained ceremony to propitiate the gods, presided over by a Taoist priest in full canonicals of red and yellow with a stiff, black beretta. The names of the village men were inscribed on paper slips to be solemnly burnt; a cockerel had its throat cut and its blood, mixed with wine, was sprinkled on the ground. The villagers and the priest, murmuring his mystic Taoist incantations to the tinkling of a small bell, walked the boundaries of the village in solemn procession. The gods satisfied and the villagers compensated, demolition commenced.

This was a scene to be repeated time and again during the next few years as bulldozers and dump trucks destroyed the rural surroundings of the town to make way for tower blocks, offices and housing estates and to provide Yuen Long with the amenities which had not been dispensed in the first sixty years of colonial rule. There had been no complaint from Yuen Long that it had been left to its own devices and way of life; equally there was now a calm acceptance of the changes that were to take place. No doubt many would live more comfortably, but a way of life was to disappear and with it an attractive pastoral scene.

The only market had been built, not by the government, but by a Hop Yick 'shared interest' company. The citizens and leaders of Yuen Long had in the past provided for the needs of the community. Local charity had built a small hospital dispensing traditional medicine and was just beginning to provide people with a western alternative. Firefighting was done by the villagers themselves with copper sleeve pumps, which now gathered dust and verdigris behind the altars in ancestral halls. Villages had their own security guards, and where the long arm of the government's tax collectors did not reach there was even a local system of taxation, the Weighing Scale Commission. The commission was put out to tender and a levy paid on every transaction in the market certified against the weighing scale. The weighing scales themselves, used by stallholders in the market, were suspended from a horizontal pole along which a gradated scale was marked by brass nails; the goods to be weighed were placed at one end, the weights at the other, and the merchant suspended the pole from a chain in the middle. The money collected from the Weighing Scale Commission was used for good works, providing subsidies to schools and helping the poor and needy.

There were three markets in the northern New Territories, close to the border with mainland China: at Tuen Mun, Yuen Long and Tai Po, and each had a Weighing Scale. Tsuen Wan, formerly a collection of scattered villages, had never reached the status of having a regular market, but the other three towns held their markets by mutual consent on separate days throughout the year, three days for each in each half month according to the lunar calendar.

Yuen Long boasted a small cinema and an amusement park of doubtful reputation, but the main entertainment took place in the early morning when the men of the town gathered in the restaurants for their breakfast of rice porridge, steamed dumplings, bean curd and crisp, fried, golden brown flour sticks, there to discuss the ebb and flow of rural life, feuds and rivalries, the rise and fall of personalities and the strange workings of officialdom.

They had much to talk about in 1963. This was the year when Typhoon Wanda, gathering strength over the South China Sea as it neared the estuary of the Pearl River, raged for many hours over Hong Kong, with the roar and howl of a jet plane. At the warning of a typhoon essential staff stayed in the District Office in order to venture out, as soon as the winds abated, to report flooded huts and villages and roads blocked by fallen trees, and to summon help if needed from the nearby military camp. The frightening wind howled and roared for hours. Yuen Long was in the west and suffered its usual flooding, blown-off roofs and fallen trees, but that year the hurricane winds pushed the sea before it at high tide and flooded the towns and villages along the eastern coast. Many were drowned. Ships broke their moorings, and, drifting before the gale, ended up like stranded whales on the islands to the west. Fishing boats which had not found shelter capsized or were smashed against the rocks. Old men like myself tell tales of Typhoon Wanda which, until another like it comes along, is still, nearly forty years later, the benchmark for all subsequent storms.

It was as though the gods wished to destroy us by sending us mad. The year of typhoons was followed by drought. The sun shone like India before the monsoon, the fields were parched, and despite help from the reservoir in China our reservoirs began to dry. With increasing severity, household water rationing was tightened to four hours' supply every fourth day. Those living on the hillsides and in squatter settlements formed long queues patiently waiting for a turn at standpipes, and carried away their precious buckets and cans to last four days until the standpipe tap was turned on again. Tanker ships were chartered to sail up the Pearl River towards Canton to a point where the sea water was sufficiently diluted by fresh water from distant mountains. There they filled their holds with water pumped from the river to sail back to Hong Kong where, from a rapidly constructed pier at Sham Tseng, a pipeline allowed it to discharge into the drying Tai Lam reservoir.

We were fortunate because Dunrose, the District Officer's house, had its own supply of water from a stream far up in the hills. This dried to a trickle in the great drought, but did not dry up completely. We suddenly became very popular with our friends from town who enjoyed coming out for the uninhibited pleasure of a shower and to fill their cans to take back to town.

The elders of Yuen Long played their part, and after a day of abstinence from meat they dressed in white long gowns and accompanied by me — for the presence of a high official was required attendance when there was serious business to perform — wound their way up into the hills to the source of the perennial stream which fed the plain. There, beneath a huge leaning granite boulder, we offered up thin sticks of incense three times and made three bows to the gods at a small shrine in the gloom beneath the rock. Our duty done, leaving the incense smouldering, we wound our way back across the fields. Sure enough it rained, but sadly not enough to break the drought.

The headquarters of 48 Brigade, the military units of the British Forces stationed in the New Territories, was situated east of Yuen Long town in a broad plain of villages and paddy fields surrounded by mountains. Gurkha infantry battalions of the brigade were stationed in outlying camps nearer the border. There were Churchill tanks, artillery and helicopters, and on a small airstrip, even an occasional visit by fighter planes. It was an impressive organisation whose brigade commanders were invariably strong personalities. No one questioned how much use the brigade would have been in the event of a shooting war with the several-million-strong People's Liberation Army, but they were a reassurance, and as it transpired, they were to play an important role during the years of the Cultural Revolution. All units were anxious to help in whatever way they could. The birthday of Tin Hau, a local deity of great importance in the community of farmers and fishermen, provided an opportunity.

Every year on the birthday of Tin Hau, a patron goddess of fishermen and farmers, a procession took place from each village to a temple which was now land-locked but which hundred of years before had been built within easy reach of the sea. This was no ordinary procession. Villages tried to outvie each other in the magnificence of their towering tableaux of brightly coloured paper on a frame of slivers of bamboo, covered with pink flowers, images of servants to please the goddess and other elaborate scenes. From each temple the ageless small images from local shrines were carried on the poles of a personal sedan in their gilded tabernacles, followed by a straggle of families, young and old. Cymbals clanged out their staccato message punctuating the wailing and parmping of small brass trumpets, and crackers cleared the devils from their path. There was huge excitement among the crowds lining the route. The extensive Chaozhou community of merchants and vegetable farmers, who had no village and temples of their own, had the most highly trained band of rhythmic, clashing cymbals and a troupe of dancers, with painted bodies and faces in the style of the performers of the Peking Opera, who weaved from side to side in imitation of the padded snake image held by the leading dancer. There were prancing lion and unicorn dances and long coiling dragons with their attendant clashing of cymbals and thumping of huge drums wheeled on a special barrow. As they reached the temple at the end of their pilgrimage there was a rough and tumble to capture lucky numbers which were fired from a crude bamboo mortar and floated down; and then the roast pigs, which had been carried on crimson wooden trays as offerings to the altar, were slit from head to tail and the meat divided among the throng. Tired, elated, the villagers straggled back to their homes and the gods were returned to their temples for another year.

The Tin Hau festival was an opportunity to invite the brigadier of our local forces to conduct a review of a different kind. A carpeted stand on bamboo scaffolding was built in the main street and there stood Brigadier Taggart with local dignitaries to review the passing Tin Hau parade of village gods, dragons, lions and unicorns, with its accompaniment of drums, cymbals and trumpets. This parade, which replaced the former higgledy-piggledy wandering procession to the temple, was a great success. Thousands now flock to see it and it is a regular date in the Yuen Long calendar.

After the procession we went off to lunch on honey-basted roast pig, monster oysters from the bay fried in deep batter, and heavy grey mullet from local fish ponds steamed with pickled lemon. This took place in the villa of Chiu Lut Sau, Justice of the Peace, a genial, rotund, wealthy rice merchant. Subsequently Chiu Lut Sau invited us to become 'godparents' to his eldest grandson. A solemn small boy was brought in and he knelt before us, offered us tea and a pair of chopsticks and bowed three times; we in turn presented him with a rice bowl. Ours was now a serious relationship and we have been close personal friends to him and his family for forty years. Our 'kai tsai' is now a successful accountant and stockbroker and himself father of three boys, two of whom have just entered university in England.

The Festival Review was the beginning of lasting friendships and of many projects in which the officers and men of 48 Brigade helped the local community, building paths and roads to outlying villages as training for their bulldozer drivers, and bringing out their rubber boats to rescue flooded villages. The troops were not a token force. The tanks regularly rumbled and screeched their way through the town to fire their guns along a range of hills and occasionally conducted field training across the dried stubble of paddy fields. The artillery, too, had a number of special points around the district from which they were able to fire their big guns, lobbing their shells over the surrounding villages and frightening passing motorists out of their wits. On the Queen's Birthday the troops left the New Territories for a grand parade through the streets of Kowloon with bands and pipers, tanks and guns, and smart marching battalions of Gurkhas. This was Hong Kong in the 1960s until military parades went out of fashion.

Norman Fraser, my predecessor, had been determined that Yuen Long should enter the First Division of Hong Kong's 'amateur' football league. (All the players were in fact recompensed for their services and the quality of the team depended on the funds available.) Led by the portly, red-faced chairman of the Meat Merchants Association, local leaders provided the resources, players were enrolled and, moving up through the divisions, Yuen Long became the champions when I arrived in 1962. In due course there was a triumphal procession through the town accompanied by the rapid fire of strings of firecrackers, followed by celebration dinners. As District Officer I was president of the local Sports Association and as a result I became a member of the general committee of the Hong Kong Football Association and subsequently its European vice president, later its vice patron. (Ten years later this was to lead me to become one of the very few members of the government to visit China.) The team was dubbed the 'Farmers' and continued to play in the first division until expense, uncertainty of success and dwindling support led it to withdraw. By that time, following urging from a spirited and energetic member of the Portuguese community, the Hon. A. de O. Sales, who was chairman of the Amateur Sports Federation and Olympic Committee, I helped the president of the association rewrite the constitution to introduce professional football, and to end the days of the 'shamateur'.

There was no football ground in Yuen Long, but the government's distinguished, austere and inspiring authority, the Financial Secretary, Sir John Cowperthwaite, was willing to help people who were willing to help themselves, so he agreed to acquire the land, provided the people built the ground. Our house became the meeting place for subscription dinners, the community rallied round, the money was raised and the ground was laid out. On it the government subsequently built a modern stadium. The villages of China have no football or sports grounds, and this, of course, was true of the New Territories: land is for using, not for playing. Yuen

Long among all the towns and villages of the New Territories, after so many years, was the first to have a football pitch!

This spirit of self-help is part of the Chinese ethos and there can be no place with more charitable organisations than Hong Kong. Hong Kong's first hospital for Chinese was provided by Chinese philanthropists and schools were either provided by churches or by Chinese organisations. Yuen Long was no exception to this philosophy of self-help. The first hospital which prescribed Chinese herbal medicines was founded by local philanthropy, so too were the first schools. Years later, the government gradually began to help with subventions and subsidies, but even so, generally the management of hospitals, schools and so forth was left to the people. This was particularly true of the New Territories. It was not until the fifties and sixties that the District Offices were provided with a simple plan for village primary schools which could be built in modules by local contractors with funds provided by the government.

The family's responsibility for looking after elderly parents, too, persists without persuasion while our near neighbour, Singapore, has had to legislate to provide for this Confucian rubric. And parents go to extraordinary lengths to scrimp and scrape to provide their children with the best education they can afford — and the children respond obediently with outstanding results. This urge to improve, and not to wait for a benevolent government to provide, has contributed immeasurably to a continuous upward movement of Hong Kong society. There are countless stories similar to that of the lift attendant who sent his sons to Oxford, and parents in a tiny resettlement flat whose family of children qualified in Canada as doctors, lawyers and accountants.

Each year has its festivals and remembrances. Some are unobtrusive, when worship is a private matter, such as the burning of joss sticks at the door or at the wayside scene of a traffic accident. Others are great public occasions, when long narrow boats with dragon heads and tails, propelled with as many as sixty paddlers, surge forward to the steps of a temple bordering on the sea so that the bulging carved eyes of the dragon head may be brought to life by a daub of red antimony; always, too, before a dragon, lion or unicorn dance, there is the same bringing to life and the murmured prayer, 'May fair winds blow, gentle rain follow and the nation and people be at peace'.

True to these traditions, every ten years in Yuen Long and in many other towns and villages, there is a week-long propitiation ceremony to clear the evil spirits away from the years ahead and, by nights and days of fasting and ritual, to bring prosperity to the town and its people. A huge 'opera house', an elaborate cathedral-like edifice of bamboo and tin sheets, is built within a few days, and in it audiences of a thousand or more can watch folk opera written around the legends of China's history. The players, with brightly painted faces to exaggerate and distinguish their roles, richly embroidered robes, peacock and pheasant feathers, high-pitched nasal voices and elegant gestures, are loved by country audiences. Monstrous statues of the gods made of coloured paper on a framework of bamboo slivers occupy a pavilion in another corner of the festival ground, with an altar for incense and offerings. It is a week of rigorous fasting and prayer for the elders of the town, while the rest of the community comes together to unite in prayer for a good future. The village elders take their responsibilities very seriously. One year, a young, strong and healthy doctoral research student from Britain was permitted to join these rituals of fasting and praying and waking at unusual hours, and was completely and utterly exhausted by it. At the end of the week, in a dramatic fire, the paper gods are consumed in a tower of flame and topple to their end. The scaffolding comes down and the players depart as swiftly as they came.

These were the regular festivals, but there was nothing to focus year-round general interest in the arts. I called the head teachers of the district schools together one summer afternoon and timorously suggested to this formidable assembly the formation of an Arts Committee. There was instant acclamation and agreement. It was a committee waiting to happen. An opera was held to raise funds for a year of exhibitions of paintings and photographs and to buy Chinese instruments for an orchestra. Self-financing ballet classes were arranged and became immensely popular with, quite extraordinarily for this isolated Chinese market town, a French ballet instructor. A void had been filled. Years later these activities are continuing and have served as a model which spread to the eighteen districts of Hong Kong.

Those were years of hard work and enjoyment. At weekends the accumulated work of the week, away from the interruptions and decisions in the office, waited to be done. Urban development gathered pace, and with it grew the demand for land. For more complicated land dealings the office had help, at first with a call from a chartered surveyor once or twice a week, and then, as development increased, full-time help. The clearance of squatters for development for which no resettlement buildings were available required inexhaustible patience to persuade them to accept a meagre disturbance payment and cash to buy cement and materials to build themselves another flimsy hut. Buying, selling, mortgaging, inheriting, resuming, disputing, every type of land dealing created by an economically active community ended up and was recorded in the Land Registry of the District Office. An extremely complex rural society looked to the independent, fair and impartial leadership of an official to galvanise it, to intervene and solve its disputes and to make proposals for activities which simply needed a word from a non-partisan voice from outside the community as a catalyst for action.

The government had a scale for the provision of community centres but Yuen Long, with its vigorous community, but a population of only about a hundred thousand in and around the town, was too small to qualify. We were a thriving, vigorous community without a centre, without a Town Hall. The government accepted the challenge: 'Give us the centre and we will look after it.' It was built and, surmounting protest from some officials in the central government who thought it far too grand a title, it became the Yuen Long Town Hall. A local management committee was formed, and Yuen Long now had a place of its own for the Arts Committee to hold its exhibitions, for ballet classes and the orchestra to practise, for the registration of marriages and for a kindergarten.

As I have mentioned, Yuen Long was twenty-five miles along a narrow and winding road from Kowloon, and although many years later the road was widened to become a highway, at the time of which I write after leaving Yuen Long for a few miles the road passed through a corridor of paddy fields and flooded fields of water chestnut and lilies, with here and there small grey brick village houses huddled together. Near the villages a straggle of open-fronted shops lined the road and spilled their goods on to the footpaths, while behind the fields and villages the hills rose higher as the road neared the sea at Tuen Mun (the name means something like 'fortress gate' in Chinese, but it was known only as Castle Peak by the English speakers).

The shelter of Castle Peak bay was a forest of leaning masts, brown, folded sails and the rounded fat sterns of fishing boats rearing high above the water; other smaller junks with flat sterns kept in a huddle by themselves, and slow, sculling sampans enlivened the scene. On a bluff in a bend in the road was a temple to the three religions of Confucius, Lao Tse and Buddha, which overlooked the tin shacks of predatory fish merchants, loan agents to the fishing fleet who sold their catch on to the market. There were provision stores and ships' chandlers, and just off the shore a decorated two-decked barge for celebrations, weddings and feasts.

From there the road followed the foreshore for ten miles or so, winding in and out of small sandy coves and rocky headlands, and passing through the growing town of Tsuen Wan before entering the crowded streets of Kowloon. I have perhaps given the impression that once there we never left Yuen Long, but several times a week we made the twenty-five mile journey to Kowloon, and if we needed go further then crossing the harbour meant waiting in patient lines for the vehicle ferry or catching one of Hong Kong's major tourist attractions, the Star Ferry.

It was on one of these journeys that I went to tea with Trevor Clark, a tall, rather gaunt, senior member of the government who had previously served in Nigeria. We met in the coffee shop of the Hilton Hotel, together with Captain Olaf Work, manager of Holts Wharf on the tip of the Kowloon peninsula and home of the Blue Funnel line. We all three knew of the Outward Bound organisation: Trevor from the school in Nigeria, Olaf from the Holt Shipping Company which was one of the founders of

Outward Bound, and myself from my term at Gordonstoun where we had met Dr Kurt Hahn whose idea Outward Bound was. It had been devised in response to a request from the British government to see what might be done to reduce the sometimes needless loss of life at sea in wartime. Jane and I had spent a few days at Aberdovey, the home of the first Outward Bound school, and we had helped in founding a school in Malaysia.

Courses at the world-wide Outward Bound organisation aim to develop confidence, principally in young people of all shapes, sizes and backgrounds, that they are capable of overcoming some of the seemingly impossible challenges they will encounter in their daily lives. Now we three gathered over tea in the Hilton Hotel and agreed that the Outward Bound experience was one which would bring enormous benefit to Hong Kong's young people, who had little opportunity in their crowded city environment to gauge their potential and experience the challenge and pleasure of hiking, climbing, camping, sailing and canoeing beneath the rugged cliffs along the remote eastern seaboard. With the support of leading companies familiar with the aims of the movement, and in due course with generous help from the Jockey Club, Hong Kong joined the movement. Since then tens of thousands of young men and women have experienced the release of energy, developed the new attitudes to the outdoors and found the confidence that come from participating in Outward Bound, and this has added immeasurably to Hong Kong life.

We had been in Hong Kong for nine years and in Yuen Long for more than four. During this time we had been 'home' to England once. Service in the colonies, even in a developed city like Hong Kong, meant long years away from family and friends in the United Kingdom. Our life in the New Territories meant that we had been even more cut off than usual from a circle of Hong Kong friends. When we returned to England, after a brief enquiry after our health and journey, no one was the slightest bit interested in what we had been doing while away for so long on the coast of China! But for us, those four years in Yuen Long changed our lives, for not only had we become remote from England, we had also been somewhat isolated from the normal life of expatriates in Hong Kong. Now, after forty years have passed, we old friends from Yuen Long still meet to celebrate birthdays and wedding anniversaries and sometimes just to gossip.

5

Seeds of Reform

A dministrative officers in the colonial service were formerly
known, diminutively, as Cadets, and before leaving for Hong
Kong, or after a few years there, were sent on a specially
designed course at Cambridge University. I had missed this,
but it was agreed that it would be good for my soul to get
away for a bit. Because of the years already spent in district work I asked
to go to Oxford to make a special study of local government under the
supervision of Professor Bryan Keith-Lucas, an authority on comparative
local government who had been greatly involved in advising on
constitutions for newly independent territories. We found that the
professor had recently moved from Oxford to the new University of Kent
at Canterbury, so, in September 1966, we rented an ancient cottage at
Boughton Aluph and for the next two terms I worked under his
supervision.

I read widely about the way other great cities had tackled their
problems of governance — New York, Montreal, London. I compared
continental systems with the British and reflected on the likely influence
of China's domestic politics on our affairs. I thought that Hong Kong was
not big enough to be split into a number of small councils following the
British model. Our ideal way forward, if we were starting from scratch, I
concluded, was to have a Greater Hong Kong Council, but it was not
practical to introduce an elected lower tier of government with far-reaching
powers without changing the Legislative Council whose members were

appointed by the Governor. A Greater Hong Kong Council would soon challenge the existence of the more important Legislative and Executive Councils. Moreover, far-reaching change in the sixties and seventies could not realistically be introduced without discussion between the governments of Britain and China, and would undoubtedly lead to an unpredictable reaction and raise prematurely the question of the very future of Hong Kong, for which no one was prepared.

'One Country, Two Systems', 'Hong Kong People Ruling Hong Kong'. These words used by Deng Xiaoping have been repeated time and time again in the past fifteen years. 'One Country, Two Systems' describes the situation which had always been the case since the founding of the colony in 1841. Hong Kong was administered and its political, social and economic systems developed in a vastly different way from that of the rest of China. There were always two systems, China and Hong Kong. On the other hand, 'Hong Kong People Ruling Hong Kong', as an objective under the British, had so far failed to make much headway. The inclusion of people's representatives in the councils of government was rehearsed, with different emphases and at different times, almost from the very beginning of the settlement in 1841. It was not something which the British overlooked or failed to proceed with in a deliberate attempt to hang on to the reins of power. It was looked at time and again and then set aside as inappropriate or untimely.

Gladstone, in March 1848, summed up Britain's objectives in occupying Hong Kong, and his words resonate until the year of the final transfer of sovereignty in 1997. 'It [the occupation of Hong Kong] was decided,' he said, 'solely and exclusively with a view to commercial interests and for those engaged in trade with China. As a Naval and Military station, except for the security of commercial interests, Hong Kong is unnecessary.' These words set the tone.

Hong Kong's Governors persistently tried to prise open the door. Governor Bonham, as early as 1849, recommended the appointment of representatives of commerce to the Executive and Legislative Councils so as 'to afford opportunities at all times of enabling the public generally to make their wishes and desires known to the local government'. In 1856 Governor Bowring writes: 'My principal objective is to introduce the popular element into its government so as to make that element subservient to its prosperity, as I have reason to believe its introduction would be acceptable to public opinion.' Bowring went further to propose representation of the foreign and Chinese community. It was the middle of the nineteenth century, and officials and politicians in Great Britain were totally ignorant of circumstances in Hong Kong. Both these recommendations were rejected by London because it was thought that they were premature.

Nevertheless, Governors kept on trying, and in 1880, in response to a recommendation from the young and impulsive Governor, Pope-Hennessy, the first Chinese voice was heard in the Legislative Council when Ng Choy was appointed. But even this single appointment was objected to by the merchants, lawyers and professionals of the expatriate community. In 1892 they made representations to the House of Commons over the head of the Governor and the Secretary of State that they, and only they, should elect members to the Legislative Council, and that the franchise should not extend to the Chinese because their sympathies, their family interests and their traditions 'lay with the neighbouring Empire', meaning, of course, China. This proposal by the expatriates would have meant, in Governor Robinson's words, 'a small alien minority should rule the indigenous majority'. 'The mercantile community', Robinson said, 'do not settle here and their only concern is to make a decent competency and then to leave.' Their proposals, to Robinson's way of thinking and that of the Secretary of State, were outrageous and had to be rejected outright. Hong Kong should remain a Crown Colony in the firm control of its officials.

In 1896 a second Chinese member was appointed to the Legislative Council, and once again similar arguments were deployed by the expatriates. Chinese merchants and their families and workers, it was said, wished only to get on with their business and employment, and regarded themselves as still living in a part of China. For these reasons, the colonial power did not believe it was necessary to take any measures to hand over power to the indigenous community, and in any case, they had made no demand or agitation to participate in government.

These voices have to be heard against the nineteenth-century background of Britain's imperial ambitions, of notions of racial superiority reinforced by strongly held religious beliefs. They have to be seen against the unfolding drama of the encroachments of foreign traders and the cultural invasion of China, the determination to win the trade war and to open up China to western commerce and Christianity, and repeated calls for China to open up its markets (a drama whose last act has been played out a hundred years later with China's application to join the World Trade Organisation). Neither can what might have been best for Hong Kong be considered in isolation. Minds were made up in Hong Kong and Britain at the end of the nineteenth century by what was happening in the rest of China — the gradual decline and fall of the Qing dynasty, the horrifying and drawn-out terror of the Taiping Rebellion, the Boxer Rebellion and the siege of the Embassies, the rise of nationalism and the overthrow of Manchu rule. They were troubled times.

We move to when Governor Stubbs, after his arrival in 1919, gave his view of the situation. Talking of the Legislative Council, he said:

'The case of this Colony differs from those of such places as Malta and Ceylon in that there is no permanent population except to some extent the Chinese, of whom the vast majority have never taken the slightest interest in the administration of the Government. The Europeans are a migratory body . . . [T]he result of establishing an unofficial majority [i.e. in the Legislative Council] would be to substitute Government by a body of amateurs, whose interests are necessarily those of the moment rather than the future, for Government by trained professionals.'

In China the years before the beginning of the Second World War were full of uncertainty and turbulence. Against this background Hong Kong had its own particular troubles. There were anti-foreign strikes by mechanics and by Chinese seamen. Workers downed tools and withdrew their labour. Many left Hong Kong and returned to their villages in

Guangdong, confirming the assessment of previous Governors that the broad loyalty and sentiment of the working population was toward their own home towns and villages.

'The gradual decline of European dominance of Hong Kong can be traced from this pivotal movement. Chinese participation in every avenue of Hong Kong was now an established fact, and a new generation of Chinese was growing, influenced by ideals from the Mainland yet determined to assert themselves in their home of Hong Kong.' (*The Quest of Noel Croucher*, by Vaudine England, Hong Kong University Press 1998)

It was not until after the Second World War and the middle of the twentieth century that serious attention was once again given to the issue of local representation. The end of the war marked the crossing of a watershed and the determination on the part of the elected Labour Government in Britain to bring the curtains down on the Empire. The stated objective of the British Government to its colonies became the granting of self-government leading to independence. Hong Kong was not left out but needed a different approach. It could not have moved towards independence because of the certain intervention and probable occupation by Chinese forces. The chosen path, once again, was to try to make the government more representative. Sir Mark Young, the Governor, put forward ill-thought-out proposals for giving the people of Hong Kong a greater say in their affairs based upon the creation of a colony-wide municipal council. The idea was not new but when previously put forward it had been alleged, with some justification, that a municipal council whose boundaries were co-extensive with the boundaries of the colony would threaten the very existence and power of the Legislative Council; as indeed it would. Despite this, Sir Mark pressed on and announced his proposal, setting aside his misgivings secretly expressed to the Colonial Office as to the popular enthusiasm for these reforms.

Refugees from the mainland flooded in to escape the closing stages of the civil war in China. Arguments against the municipal council proposals were raised by the appointed members of Executive and Legislative Councils, while other, more popular nationalist voices were raised in their support by many Chinese organisations. Sir Mark,who seems already to have had '1997' at the back of his mind, nevertheless reported to London that his proposals were greeted with considerable apathy by the Chinese community, and he ascribed this to the fear that the council would become a battleground for political forces — Guomindang and Communist. He went on to say, with great intuition, that in any case, many Chinese foresaw the return of Hong Kong to China and did not wish to involve themselves in something which could be judged to be unpatriotic.

Sir Mark Young's term of office came to an end in 1947, and he was succeeded by Sir Alexander Grantham. The volume of refugees from disturbances in China grew at an alarming rate. Legislative Council was strengthened by the appointment of a few more members, and the proposal to create an elected municipal council with powers which would have threatened its existence was dropped.

Hitherto no attempt had been made to recruit Chinese officers into the higher, exclusively British expatriate ranks of the senior civil service, the Cadets. Although this would not have been as politically sensitive as moving towards a more representative government, it came far too late and slowly, and contrasted poorly with other colonies reaching independence where localisation was an early established policy. It seemed as though Hong Kong had all the time in the world

From then on, for a period of almost twenty years, Hong Kong was preoccupied with developing the economy and housing the homeless. The repercussions of the Korean War and the chilling atmosphere of the Cold War which seemed to hold the whole world in suspense spilled over into Hong Kong; the lingering political antagonisms following the defeat of the Guomintang army erupted into mob violence in 1956; there was tension across the Taiwan Straits and the shelling of Quemoy. In the sixties there was the sudden influx of over a hundred thousand illegal immigrants who poured over the border from neighbouring Guangdong. There was drought and long queues at standpipes. The worst typhoon in living memory had swept across Hong Kong, leaving a trail of death and destruction. In 1966 and 1967, there were more riots. It is an understatement to say that Hong Kong had more than enough to do. The situation was unstable, the community restless, living from hand to mouth in appalling conditions and not having put down its roots.

It was an atmosphere not conducive to elevated thoughts about democracy and political reform. As the author and astringent commentator Dick Wilson said, 'It would have been like trying to organise elections on a railway station'.

Despite this stormy background, at the end of the sixties Governor Sir David Trench decided that something had to be done to make government more representative. He appointed a civil servant to write a report on what should or could be done, particularly in view of the growing population and development of new towns. The Urban Council looked after urban Hong Kong and the Kowloon Peninsula, but not the New Territories where new towns of half a million each were already being built. A handful of members of the Urban Council were elected on a narrow franchise, but the public attitude to this opportunity to exercise their civic rights was one of positive uninterest and very few of the limited electorate bothered to vote.

The Dickinson Report on Local Administration duly appeared in 1966. It was, I suppose, inevitable that it would recommend a British model of local government and overlook the fact that in Britain that model was being challenged, with much debate about the usefulness of some of the lower tiers of government. Britain was thinking of regions when Dickinson was proposing smaller councils, ignoring the fact that in a place the size of Hong Kong there was economy and efficiency to be found in a single authority. Some members of Dickinson's working party disagreed with his proposals and instead recommended as a first step that district offices should be set up in the urban area similar to those in the New Territories, so as to bring government closer to the people.

This second attempt to map out a more representative system of government at a local level was due to receive another rude shock. The first attempt after the war had been overtaken by the end of the civil war in China and an influx of refugees. This second attempt was also to fail.

In 1966 simmering discontent in the densely packed and comfortless housing estates of Kowloon boiled over onto the streets. People were tired of years of hard work with little improvement in their lives. Unrest, agitation and discontent found a focus around a minor increase in cross-harbour ferry fares. A young man began a hunger strike at the ferry and before the situation was taken seriously by the government, riots broke out in Kowloon. The police responded with tear gas and baton charges. A curfew was imposed, which caught me and my wife enjoying an evening out with friends. Tear gas began to seep into the restaurant, so we broke the chain which, not unusually, barred the rear exit and hurried for home along the now empty streets, leaving our car to the mercy of the mob, who with some delicacy later broke the parking meter but left the car unscathed.

The government was taken by surprise. What had suddenly gone wrong? The Chief Justice, Sir Michael Hogan, held an inquiry which, after hearing blame and recrimination, concluded lamely that the government was out of touch with the people, that there was a communication gap.

But there were tidings of a more serious nature. Hong Kong was anxiously watching events in the mainland, where mobs had taken to the streets to attack 'rightists' and any who had bourgeois connections or who had strayed from the path of Mao's thoughts, or who was associated in any way with or polluted by western ideas and culture, even attacking and destroying China's precious heritage. It was the beginning of a time of turmoil which was to last for twelve years. Dickinson's ideas for local councils in Hong Kong were quietly forgotten and disappeared into oblivion, and in due course District Offices were introduced into the crowded city streets.

It is a curious overlap that despite the outrages of the Cultural Revolution, which are well documented, the admission of China into the United Nations actually took place in October 1971 in the midst of this turmoil and the exile to distant farms of some of China's foremost leaders and most distinguished intellects; and that in February of the following year, the visit of President Nixon and Secretary of State Henry Kissinger took place, which led to the communiqué issued in Shanghai at the end of their visit. In this important cornerstone of all subsequent policy, the United States and China stated their views on world affairs, in particular the question of Taiwan, where the United States acknowledged that all Chinese on either side of the Taiwan Strait maintain that there is only one China and that Taiwan is part of China, and that the United States Government did not challenge that position.

China had come in from the cold, and shortly afterwards the Chinese Ambassador to the United Nations declared that the question of Hong Kong was not a matter for the United Nations to decide and deliberate but was a matter for China to decide when the time was ripe. A firm marker had been put down twenty-six years before the ending of the New Territories lease, a warning to Britain not to try any clever tricks, any unilateral political adventures. In any case, with China in the throes of the Cultural Revolution it was inconceivable that Hong Kong could have begun a sensible dialogue on political development. China's words in the United Nations were a warning to other countries not to meddle, and for the British it pointed the way to approach the question of the future when the time was ripe.

The Hong Kong government moved cautiously to open its ears to the views and advice of the public. Boards and committees, which were advising the government on all aspects of policy and activity, were strengthened by bringing in fresh, younger blood. These several hundred committees, involving several thousand of Hong Kong's citizens, survive to this day. Professor Ambrose King of the Chinese University termed this the 'administrative absorption of politics'. It was not Machiavellian, but no doubt inviting leaders of public opinion to sit down to discuss policy and plans with government officials stopped people taking to the streets. Moreover, it seemed at the time that there was no other choice. The challenge to the critics who say so frequently and repetitively, 'But yes, democracy should have been introduced earlier', is to ask 'But when would you have done it?' Looking back at those years of mass immigration from China and the struggle in the sixties against all manner of outrageous fortune is to say 'Well, what about the seventies?' China was in the grip of the Gang of Four, the Cultural Revolution was at its height, China was in unimaginable turmoil, the British Embassy in Beijing had been sacked and burned, schools and universities were closed, libraries, temples and much of China's heritage destroyed, and intellectuals and China's leaders denounced and set to cleaning pigstyes and wearing dunce's hats. The so-called windows of opportunity revealed a storm-tossed world, shaking fists, patient squatters queuing for water, housewives and businessmen demanding their money from bankrupt banks. Should Hong Kong have pushed on regardless of China? The answer lies in the short shrift given to proposals introduced in 1995, without China's acquiescence, by the last Governor of Hong Kong.

6

The Cultural Revolution

I n 1967 the years of the Cultural Revolution began traumatically. We watched the British Consul in Macao being made to stand in the burning sun to endure the vilification of the masses He was then withdrawn from Macao to Hong Kong, never to return. Corpses with their hands bound floated down the Pearl River, and the strikes and riots of the Cultural Revolution spread to Hong Kong. There were marches to Government House, vehement denunciations of the British and attempts to force the government to capitulate. Mobs surged out of crowded resettlement estates followed by tear gas volleys and baton charges, and rioting surged back and forth along the streets. There were savage attacks on people, and there were exploding bombs. A courageous Chinese journalist was burned to death in his car. Helicopters landed on the roofs of buildings to flush out cells of rioters. The Bank of China, draped in banners bearing revolutionary slogans, had barbed wire on its roof to prevent this while, typically, across the road on the cricket ground, white, flannelled cricketers continued their games against the backdrop of slogans, banners and revolutionary songs.

For a few months I went back to Yuen Long as District Officer, there to meet old friends and to urge them to remain calm. I walked about the town and visited the market in an eerie atmosphere of suspense. We had a field telephone wired from the Gurkha barracks next to our house to our bedroom, which sometimes in the middle of the night would emit a frog-like croak followed by a Gurkha voice saying 'Testing, testing'.

After a few weeks I was appointed Deputy District Commissioner, and my days as a District Officer came to an end. Kenneth Kinghorn, the District Commissioner of the New Territories, was a stocky figure with a chuckling sense of humour who had a rumoured reputation for locking difficult files behind the combination of his safe and who liked to sit in his office, when everyone else had long gone home, with a bottle of beer, puffing a cigar while quietly reading his papers.

There were threats to the lives of leaders who had responded to a call to express their support for the government. Small but dangerous bombs were exploded at some of their offices, and real bombs and fake bombs wrapped in red paper, sometimes with the warning 'Compatriots keep away', were left in the roads, causing a great deal of nuisance. In each New Territories town, public security organisations were formed and, following threats on their lives, members of the executive of the Heung Yee Kuk, the New Territories Rural Council, were allowed to carry revolvers, which they did in bulging trouser pockets.

When the northern boundary of the new territory had been drawn in 1898 it sliced off part of China where it projected, like a headland, into the South China Sea, leaving a bay on each side. From the head of the bay in the west, and going eastwards, the border followed the course of a short river which, while broad at the mouth, quickly narrowed to a small stream as it rose into the mountains. From there the border passed through a narrow gap and then dropped down to another bay in the east where there was a small market town. Here the border had been drawn down the middle of the street of a small village and fishing port, Sha Tau Kok, with, literally, China on one side of the street and Hong Kong's New Territories on the other, with no barrier in the middle.

Hong Kong police were stationed in small 'Beau Geste' forts at various points along the border to keep a watchful eye mainly for illegal immigration from across the way. Northwards, the border looked on to a typical rural scene of farmland, grey brick villages and farmers quietly working in the commune fields against a backdrop of steep, grass-covered mountains. In 1967 the atmosphere changed as the fever and agitation of the Cultural Revolution spread to the communes north of the border. On one fateful day, militia advanced across the boundary at Sha Tau Kok and opened fire, killing police in the small police post. The police were not equipped to deal with armed incursions, and Gurkha troops were despatched to relieve them. From then on, for more than twenty years, soldiers maintained security and dealt with illegal immigration all along the border, until near the time of the return of Hong Kong to China.

Farmers from the north had always had the right to cross over to tend to their crops in their ancestral fields south of the river. In 1967 this peaceful *modus vivendi* came to a rude halt. The farmers who crossed into Hong Kong brought with them bright red banners, the excitement of revolution and a detestation of the foreigners who occupied their country and of the police who served them. We were variously and insultingly called 'white-skinned pigs' and the police 'yellow running dogs'. The main crossing point of the river at the border consisted of a temporary bridge of steel girders with a small police post at its end. This was the point at which lorries assembled to pick up vegetables and livestock destined for Hong Kong markets. In 1967 the farmers crossing daily, morning and evening, within a few feet of the Hong Kong police could not refrain, in their state of high emotion and revolutionary zeal, from taunting and confronting their yellow running dog compatriots, just as their fellow revolutionaries were doing in the streets of Hong Kong and Kowloon.

On one occasion down by the bridge, a District Officer, Trevor Bedford, and a Battalion Commander, MacAlister, were encircled and threatened with axes and mattocks. Shortly afterwards an extraordinary thing happened. Two off-duty police, mistaking the way, rode on a motor bike across the border and disappeared from sight. Police Inspector Frank Knight, who went to investigate, was hustled by angry peasants across the border bridge and likewise disappeared. A barricade was thrown across the bridge and movement across the border came to a halt. It was easy to close the border but clearly it could not remain closed; there was a need to restore the flow of produce and to let the farmers get on with looking after their fields. Negotiations, which began with three readings taken from Chairman Mao's red book of writings, were held just across the border between a delegation from Hong Kong, consisting of the District Commissioner Kenneth Kinghorn, the Assistant Political Adviser to the Hong Kong government, and myself, together with local officials from China. These were strange and anxious times to face the criticisms and demands of Chinese officials in their sombre, rankless uniforms, then to return, as the sun was setting, to a waiting helicopter to be whisked back to Hong Kong to report the day's discussion.

After many such long discussions, publicly reported agreement was reached to pay compensation for crops which had died for lack of water, to remove stretches of barbed wire from fields, to exchange certain personnel being held by Hong Kong, and for the return of the two wandering policemen. Police Inspector Knight, despite his considerable girth, had earlier managed to climb out of the building in which he was being held, and in the darkness had made his way across the fields, crossed the stream and wriggled up under the border fence to return to Hong Kong.

To the west of the territory, oyster beds fringed the shallow waters of Deep Bay. Rocks encrusted with large oysters were laid out in lines stretching from the shore across the oozing tidal mud into deeper water. International protocols meant nothing in these muddy waters; the villagers from Shek Ha, on the Chinese side, lived on whichever side of the border convenience and profit dictated. One morning in October 1966 a great fleet of junks, red banners streaming in the wind, surged across the bay and surrounded an oyster bed reaching out from the Hong Kong shore. Officials sent to investigate were abused and intimidated and reminded that Mao Tse-tung would prevail and live for ever, that they, and not the errant villagers who had opted for an easy life in the fleshpots of Yuen Long on the Hong Kong side, were the rightful owners, and moreover they had documents issued by the Hong Kong British authorities, which had expired many years before, to prove it. Valour was sensibly the loser and discretion the winner. Behind the scenes negotiations between villagers settled the issue. Those on the Hong Kong side understood better how to farm that particular oyster bed, but they had to recognise the paramount authority of the revolutionary committee of the commune. Agreement was reached and tension relaxed .

Sometimes the situation bordered on the absurd; for example, when the cattle coming across the border in railway wagons had revolutionary and offensive slogans painted on their sides. Workers in the slaughterhouses of Hong Kong went on strike until the queue of many thousand pigs a day needed for Hong Kong's markets backed up into the interior of China. Common sense eventually prevailed and slaughterhouse operations started up again. On another occasion, at the end of a day fraught with tension, the Gurkha company buglers at one of the posts matched their skills with those of the Border Defence Unit on the other side.

Long months with daily incidents along the border required a calm and sensitive approach to prevent escalation into an even more dangerous situation. In counselling a calm approach the Governor once mused to me, 'Sometimes I wonder which side you're on.' But we were close to the action and better judges of reaction and were able to coordinate the daily level of response to whatever provocation there had been. A committee was formed under the aegis of the Commander 48 Brigade, Brigadier Peter de C. Martin, with membership drawn from the Police, Army and New Territories Administration (PAGENT), which met daily to analyse and decide how to respond to these potentially dangerous situations. After these excitements were over, the committee continued and was extraordinarily useful subsequently in countering surges of illegal immigration, deciding how to strengthen our border fence, causing a road to be built along the length of the border and working out how to replace the old bridge at Man Kam To.

The rioting, the bombs, the burnings and the killings came to an end and in 1968 Hong Kong returned to a nervous and shaken normality. Individuals and organisations had rallied to the side of the authorities, but many were so frightened that they had turned tail and headed for Canada, the United Kingdom and the USA. In China, however, the 'ten years of turmoil' were just beginning, and for the next decade Hong Kong anxiously watched the twists and turns of cultural revolution in the life of the people of China.

The government did not concern itself solely with the suppression of riots but mounted skilful campaigns to win over hearts and minds and sustain confidence. The communication gap, identified by the Chief Justice as a factor contributing to the Star Ferry riots of the previous year, was brought into sharp relief by the events of 1967. It was quickly closed by adopting those ideas of members who had openly disagreed with the findings of the Dickinson Report on local administration in 1966, Hong Kong and Kowloon were divided into city districts. Shop fronts for District Offices were set up into which people could walk from the street to take their troubles or to ask for information and advice. The invisible walls between the bureaucrats in one department and another were broken down, and where useful their work was coordinated by a District Officer. Mutual Aid Committees were formed in public housing estates, each of which housed tens of thousands of people, as well as in private high-rise apartment blocks, to bring people together to share a common interest in the security and upkeep of their buildings.

7

Principal Assistant Colonial Secretary (Lands)

With the gradual return of confidence after the stress and tension of 1967, Hong Kong property prices began to rise. My masters judged it was time to move me away from rural politics and development and crises on the border to Hong Kong Island, away from people to paper, to files, minutes, memoranda and the preparation of a stream of papers for the weekly meeting of the Governor's Executive Council — Hong Kong's Cabinet. It was before the Colonial Secretary, sensitive to the changing mood, changed his title to the more politically correct Chief Secretary, and senior officials, who had long since discarded their white drill uniforms for business suits, ceased to be addressed as Cadets and became simply Administrative Officers. Government was lean, and as Principal Assistant Colonial Secretary I was responsible, together with three assistants, for Land Policy, Public Works, Rent Control, Housing and Rating. Property and construction account for nearly half of the economy, the stock exchange index is influenced by it, banks are heavily dependent on it, and it is a major topic of conversation. Restricted circulation (blue) and confidential (chrome yellow) papers flowed from our office in a never-ending stream, and more than half the time of the Governor's advisers on Executive Council was taken up with land, property and development.

Rent control of pre-war tenements was introduced immediately after the war when a tide of refugees flowed into Hong Kong and the fierce demand for accommodation had caused rents to skyrocket. Grey and crumbling pre-war buildings with open floors and a kitchen and washroom at the back were subdivided, a family in each cubicle, sharing common facilities. A principal tenant on each floor collected rent from the hapless families on behalf of the owners. Laws now prevented the landlord from increasing rent, and inevitably, having had his income from the property forcibly reduced, he did nothing to maintain his buildings which fell into increasing disrepair.

With the easing of the housing situation and the consequent easing of the pressure on rents, and with the growing number of public housing estates, legislation was introduced gradually to remove rent control in keeping with Hong Kong's philosophy to let the market decide. This revived some interest in redevelopment; but even today, in this glittering modern city and despite the intense effort to build sufficient housing, the legacy of divided tenements and cubicle life lingers on. Sub-tenants still pay an exorbitant rent for the privilege of living with their children in a small windowless space, with nowhere to hang their washing, sharing lavatories and kitchens with other families.

A major confrontation occurred in 1972. Hundreds of leases on land in Kowloon were due to expire in 1973, when they would be renewed to bring them into line with New Territories leases which had an automatic right of renewal until three days before 30 June 1997, when the lease of the New Territories itself expired. The Kowloon leases, when they were written, optimistically entitled the Crown to charge a premium on renewal, which in the government's view should be based on market value. After all, so the argument went, the owners were getting back title to land for a further period and should pay what it was worth. This was logical and legal but not practical. It touched a raw nerve of Chinese sensitivity. This was, after all, part of China and the concept was alien. There were protests and petitions, meetings with the Governor, and debates in the Legislative Council. The government relented and agreed to charge a new and low rent based on the rateable value. Another storm had passed, and incidentally in its passing a way had been found to manage the renewal of title to land in the leased New Territories, whose leases were also due to expire in June 1997.

The building of Hong Kong never seems finished; reclamation follows reclamation and the harbour narrows, buildings are torn down and replaced with something higher. The deafening banging of pile drivers is taken for granted, and tunnels pierce the mountains and burrow under the harbour. Architecture has changed from the dull and practical to multi-coloured glass-walled buildings adorned with cathedral-like towers and globes. When we arrived, the harbour was crowded with cargo ships, and wharves and warehouses lined the shore. Shipping changes in the early seventies meant that wharves with warehouses were no longer needed. Companies were formed to build a container port which has grown to be the largest in the world. Now as you look across at Kowloon from Victoria, the central part of Hong Kong, you see the cliff-like walls of hotels and offices. Gone are the immense funnels and the great strong ships of the Blue Funnel Line which docked at Holt's wharf next to the Star Ferry at the tip of the Kowloon Peninsula; now hotels, shopping malls and offices stand in its place. I asked the property company which demolished the warehouses to construct a promenade deck around the end of the peninsula from which people could enjoy the harbour view of Hong Kong and watch the ships go by. Disappointingly, there are few other places on the city's long waterfront where it is possible to walk along the side of the harbour. However, all is not lost, and as I write, plans are being implemented to reintroduce and extend this obvious attraction. At the end of the promenade, all that is left of the railway station, where one could once buy a ticket to London crossing China and Siberia, is the clock tower standing in inexplicable solitude.

If you look west from Hong Kong beyond the harbour, the steep ridges of more green islands rise from the sea, and in the distance the blue of Lantau Island beckons, an island which is bigger than Hong Kong itself. There is so much more to Hong Kong than the crowded streets of the central city which gives it so much of its international reputation. In the hills above the eastern shore of Lantau, the bell tower and chapel of a small Trappist monastery hides in the trees and supplied fresh milk from monster, heavy-uddered Friesians to our hotel guests.

Next to the monastery is Discovery Bay, where small villages nestled between the steeply rising mountain and the wide sandy arc of the bay. Behind the villages there was a large tract of scrub-covered hillside, some grass plantations and a small farm in a hidden valley owned by the Lantau Development Company. There was a small pier and sheds for an abattoir built especially to provide for the importation of cattle from the Northern Territory of Australia, to prevent the Australian ships from becoming contaminated through contact with diseases from livestock from China and South-East Asia. No cattle were ever imported and there are few who even remember this strange proposal. Later in the sixties it was suggested that the shallow waters of the bay might be filled in in a wide reclamation for a town of half a million. This plan, too, died a death among the files.

Some years later a proposal was put to the government for the building of a self-sufficient modern residential suburb at Discovery Bay. It would have a green environment, no motor vehicles, and would run its own ferry service to the city. The owner of all the land, Edwin Wong, was persuasive; his models of the scheme were convincing and seemed to epitomise the entrepreneurial spirit which had made Hong Kong. He refined his proposals and indicated that the public requirements would all be met: the police and fire stations, the water supply, the roads and drains. At that point financial disaster overwhelmed ambition; the mortgagor threatened that unless someone could be found to take his place, the bank holding the mortgage (as it happened, the Moscow Narodny Bank) would foreclose, and by implication, Russia would become the extraordinary owners of a large tract of Hong Kong hillside. A Hong Kong citizen renowned for his quiet business acumen stepped in and took over. Gradually over the next few years, the principles of the scheme were established and building began. Now the town is a success story and has a character of its own; the atmosphere which inspired its initiator has been maintained and the peace and quiet is jealously guarded by its many thousand residents. It fell to me to explain this scheme and other large ideas for developing land to the new Governor, Sir Murray MacLehose, who arrived in 1971.

Sir Murray (later Lord MacLehose) was a tall, thin, no-nonsense man from the Diplomatic Service who had a vision for Hong Kong and a clear perception of what we ought to be doing to put our house in order. There were many things under our noses which were not being done which we officials should have seen for ourselves — but had not! The appointment of Sir Murray broke with the custom of appointing Governors who were familiar with colonial administration, having served in other colonies, and knew how the system worked. Although Sir Murray came from the Diplomatic Service, he had previously been in Hong Kong as Governor Sir Robert Black's Political Adviser. During that time he must have made up his mind that Hong Kong was ready for a shake-up. Whether Whitehall had thought through the consequences of bringing in a Governor from outside the Overseas Civil Service twenty-six years before the change of sovereignty, it certainly turned out to be an inspired decision, and the establishment of a closer link with the Foreign Office meant that forbidden topics relating to 1997 were more easily mentioned. Of course it led to disappointment among those reaching the end of their careers that the pinnacle of the Colonial Service career had been removed, that they could no longer climb to the top and that promotion now stopped at the level of Chief Secretary.

It would have been simple for Hong Kong to have gone on muddling along, tinkering with things and making adjustments here and there. We needed a refit. It was time to clean up Hong Kong in more ways than one. The foundations of the great city which was to return to China in 1997 owe much to Sir Murray's attack on the debilitating acceptance of poor housing and rubbish strewn streets, crime and corruption and to replace negligence with the sense of pride and belonging which his leadership fostered.

Not long after his arrival, management consultants McKinsey and Company were appointed to look at the way Hong Kong was administered. This led to a reorganisation and redistribution of responsibility, the creation of policy branches and policy secretaries, and the separation of the formulation of policy from its execution. The object of these reforms was to create a more dynamic and decisive government as a necessary preparation for the tasks which lay ahead.

Why was Hong Kong so dirty compared with Singapore? Why was crime on the increase? Why were there persistent reports and suspicions of corruption in our police force when there was a specially assigned anti-corruption unit within it? Sir Murray initiated and in his shirt sleeves personally led Keep Hong Kong Clean and chaired Fight Crime campaign meetings, and transferred responsibility for the fight against corruption from the police to an independent body. And in what was a seminal speech, he said that the shortage of decent housing was the greatest source of unhappiness in Hong Kong. He followed this up by asking me, as Principal Colonial Secretary (Lands) to let him know, as soon as possible, how many housing units would have to be built to solve the housing problem within ten years. I called a small group of officials together, each with knowledge of a bit of the answer — overcrowding in private tenements, the number of squatters, the natural growth in population, immigration, and so forth. Using the back of an envelope, we came up with the answer that we needed to build housing for 1.5 million people to meet urban demand. Another group, led by the New Territories District Commissioner, Denis Bray, estimated that there were another 300,000 needing permanent accommodation in rural areas. These figures became the target for a ten-year housing and development programme: new towns were to be built, interconnecting highways constructed, harbours reclaimed and villages and farmland cleared and compensated. The building and expansion into modern Hong Kong had begun.

In the early seventies a Hong Kong textile industrialist initiated a proposal to build an oil refinery in Hong Kong to bypass the refinery in Singapore. Here was an opportunity to join the industrial big league and to break out from textiles, toys, watches, plastic flowers and electrical goods, which shared the bulk of Hong Kong's industry. Lamma Island just to the south of Hong Kong was the chosen site, and detailed investigation began. I went with colleagues to Japan in order to be persuaded that oil refineries were not really bad after all! The visit provided a brief opportunity to see serene temples and gardens as well as throbbing machinery, nests of pipes, tanks, chimneys and drifting steam. But much as we tried to overcome the environmental impact by putting oil tanks in rock caverns, measuring decibels, and siting the chimneys among mountains, the serenity of the view to the south of Hong Kong would have gone for ever, of islands stretching to the horizon floating in a calm sea. And then, quite suddenly, the price of oil shifted and investors' interest in building a refinery evaporated. No more was heard, and Hong Kong was spared this first of its many future ecological challenges.

Three years quickly passed in producing paper after paper for the weekly meetings of Executive Council involving everything to do with land administration, building and development; in formulating policies to meet new challenges; in writing persuasive memoranda on grants of land for worthwhile causes, on land for international schools, on a policy for urban renewal. There were memoranda on land for container terminals and universities, an Arts Centre, land for special industries, an agreement with the China Light and Power Company and the oil terminal companies to build a bridge to their island installations, and policies to approve the change of land use from shipyards, sugar refineries and warehouses which lined the waterfront in the nineteenth century so that the great housing estates of today could be built.

My colleagues and assistants in the Lands Branch and all who were involved in land and development shared the excitement of contributing to that great swirl of activity which hits the Hong Kong visitor as he walks along its downtown pavements. For me it was endlessly exciting, as I lay awake at night writing in my mind the phrases for the papers which would bring about the successful completion of these great undertakings.

The *Mulbera* was the twin sister of the *Mantola* which I joined in Hull in January 1945. She was 'a solid straight up and down 9,000 tons.' (See p. 2)

District Office, Alor Gajah, 1966.
'There were paddy fields at the end of the lawn.' (See p. 7)

Going the rounds, District Officer Yuen Long 1962. (See p. 35)

Yuen Long in the sixties. (See p. 37)

The Elders of Yuen Long prepare to pray for rain. (See p. 40)

Ten-year propitiation ceremony in Yuen Long: "Clearing the evil spirits away from the years ahead". (See p. 45)

Daoist priests at a Da Chiu, ten-year propitiation ceremony. (See p. 45)

As Chief Secretary participating in a Da Chiu. (See p. 45)

The kick-off of the inaugural match between Hong Kong and Guangzhou in the early seventies. (See p. 127)

Island House, 'a narrow driveway linked the house to
Tai Po and the outside world.' (See p. 92)

Man Kam To 1976 'the rusty bridge was too weak to carry trucks.'
(Hong Kong at the bottom, Shenzhen across the Bridge) (See p. 99)

'Sir Edward Youde arrived on a fine windy day in 1982.' (See p. 134)

Sir Edward Youde in Kat O, with Chairman Lau Yam Man of the Rural
Committee, 'entering the world of unchanged China.' (See p. 136)

Her Majesty the Queen visits Tsuen Wan new town, 1975.

Victoria House, Barker Road, home of the Chief Secretary. (See p. 160)

8

A Visit to China in 1973: FIFA

A desire to know more and to understand better the complexity of Hong Kong's swirling, extraordinary life had led me to follow an opportunity to become involved in the intricacies of the world of soccer, its players, officials and local and international politics. Study of the language had also led me into history and a growing desire to delve more deeply, to discover China at first hand, to know more about the great country to our north. I never felt that we had 'gone native' as the whispered word has it, but perhaps that's how we looked to those who had not had the opportunities for the deep immersion which work in the New Territories involved

We shared this curiosity to learn more, in a very small way, and of course much later, with those impulses which led Mildred Cable and Francesca French across the Gobi Desert, and Isabella Bird, the widow of a country parson, to travel alone in 1894 on a five-plank *wu ban* through the 'Yangtze Valley and Beyond'. In 1973 there occurred an unusual and unexpected opportunity for us to visit the virtually closed world of China.

The Hong Kong Football Association had four vice presidents: two Chinese, one European, and as a legacy of the time when the Forces played a prominent role in the sporting life of the colony, a representative of the Armed Services. I was elected European vice president and, in 1973, was asked by the president, Henry Fok Ying-tung, who was later to become a Deputy to the National People's Congress, whether we would like to visit China. Since the end of the civil war in 1949 and the creation of the

People's Republic, it was unheard of for anyone from the Hong Kong government to visit China. China was a closed world. This was a unique opportunity. The invitation was discussed with Sir Murray MacLehose who, rather to my surprise, gave us permission provided we flew from London. To cross the border from Hong Kong would have given rise to unwelcome speculation about the reasons for our visit.

The fever and pitched battles of the Cultural Revolution had entered a less violent stage. In 1971 China was admitted and Taiwan expelled from the United Nations. A team of ping-pong players from the USA had played their historic games in Beijing and in 1972 President Nixon and Secretary of State Kissinger had visited China and signed the Shanghai communiqué restoring their fractured relations. Some world sports organisations had already recognised China and relegated Taiwan to the status of China Taiwan or Chinese Taipei. But the Federation of International Football Associations, FIFA, to which the Hong Kong association belonged, had expelled the representative of the People's Republic in the 1950s and ever since had maintained the membership of the former 'Republic of China' representative from Taiwan. It was absurd that the national teams of China — at that time representing a quarter of mankind — more than twenty years after the founding of the People's Republic could not play soccer outside China. It was against this background that I was invited to Beijing.

On a cold, wintry day in 1973 Jane and I went nervously to the Chinese Embassy in Portland Place, London. We were nervous because Hong Kong had not long before been through the traumatic experiences of 1967. No one in the Hong Kong government had been permitted to venture into China and there was no communication between Hong Kong senior government officials and their counterparts. China had been a closed world for over twenty years, and we were now about to talk to Chinese officials and to visit China when only a few years before, in an attempt to humble the British administration, riots had rocked Hong Kong. Our reception at the Embassy to apply for visas was impersonal, but in a week or two, we were given visas to arrive in China on 13 February 1973.

We went by a strange route, flying from Paris to Cairo, then Rangoon, and on to Shanghai. We were alone and about to enter an unfamiliar world, made fearful, too, by the dire pronouncements on the customs declaration forms on the penalties for not being able to give an exact account of money spent in China or for not ensuring that we left China with everything with which we had entered. Jewellery had to be itemised on the declaration form earring by earring.

The plane from Rangoon to Shanghai was almost empty; nobody spoke to us. We were leaving one world for another. Arriving in Shanghai, we queued for immigration in the dimly lit hall among men swathed against the cold in grey, blue and green padded overcoats and soft caps. Swiftly we were ushered out of the line of waiting passengers and our worries were over. 'No need to fill in forms, you are our guests!' There were a few hours to wait, spent talking idly with the help of an interpreter speaking the common language of mainland China, Putonghua, rather than Cantonese, to a representative of the All China Sports Federation and the head of Shanghai football. Then we walked across the tarmac in light rain to the four-engined propellor plane to Beijing, filled with men in blue and green rankless uniforms, flat caps or fur caps with ear flaps, and friendly faces. Two hours later, as we approached Beijing, they pointed out to us in the dusk the patches of snow and wintry farmland. At the foot of the steps we were greeted by a smiling Secretary General Sung Zhong and other officials of the All China Sports Federation, among them Mr Da in cloth cap and huge padded coat and young, thin Mr Liu, who were to be our companions for the next two weeks.

We drank glasses of tea and chatted in the dim light of the VIP room and were quickly driven off in black limousines with smoked glass windows along darkened streets and past patches of piled snow, bare branches, ghostly figures on lightless bicycles and a few cars. The Peking Hotel, with its huge banqueting halls, high-ceilinged rooms and empty corridors, was old, comfortable and warm. We had a suite of rooms, and scarcely had time to wash after our long journey before dinner with an official. He asked us what we wanted to do while in China. I said I left it to him, and he replied, with an old-fashioned look, that he knew what we wanted and then reeled off the things we would do and the places we would visit on our thirteen-day journey. These were the cities which have become so familiar to the millions who now visit China, but during those wintry days we were strangers from another world among the crowds of local Chinese.

We drove to the former Imperial Palace, the Forbidden City. Frozen snow lay in the shadows, and the courtyards thronged with people in blue padded winter coats, grey and green uniforms, fur caps, red stars, and ruddy pink faces. This was a pattern we were to see everywhere in China. Whatever the time and no matter what the weather and day of the week, there would be crowds of sightseers looking at pagodas, museums, gardens, and temples, and filling the markets. Here already was a different China from that created by the media. It was a strange paradox. On the one hand a people, unregimented, walking freely about, warmly clothed, enjoying their leisure time, and on the other, a people in the throes of one of the great upheavals in modern times, involving a nation of nearly a billion — the Cultural Revolution.

We were standing at last in the impressive centre of a great country, the scene of so many confrontations between the Middle Kingdom and the West. We stood spellbound at the vastness of the square in front of the towering crimson walls of Tiananmen, its great doors closing the tunnel leading to the palace. We walked slowly through and entered the spacious courtyards leading from one palace hall to another, their yellow tiled roofs all clothed in a wintry haze. We were silent before majestic raised halls, blue, red and gold, with their carved balustrades and white marble dragon-carved panels leading up to each new platform, and with their bronze lion dogs, phoenix incense burners, red pillars and decorated ceilings; we marvelled at treasures of jade, gold and ivory, among them a recently discovered burial suit of small jade tiles.

For two days we visited stadia and training facilities. We saw young athletes strengthening their muscles by dragging their feet through sand, and supple child gymnasts spinning strings of somersaults. We also watched a ping-pong tournament between Cuba and China, and joined the Cubans to watch the film *The Red Detachment of Women*. We visited a craft factory producing ivory objects, cloisonné, stone carvings, and rice-paste figures, and where they carried out eggshell painting and painting the inside of snuff bottles. We watched an elderly man carving a jade bowl, who carefully unwrapped the bindings around the handles for us to see the full beauty of his workmanship. There were dinners and speeches, sweet rose wine and thimbles of strong white spirit. 'Friendship first and competition second' — an unlikely thought which always brought a disbelieving smile to faces round the table — was the saying then in vogue, and it provided a useful toast as China pursued her way to back into the world of international competition.

On Friday, 16 February 1973 we woke early for a visit to Tsing Hua University. I had earlier asked to visit a university during this revolutionary period in order to catch a glimpse of another side of China's life. Parties of workers were shovelling up snow on the street as we drove along the bumpy roads to the almost deserted great buildings of the broad campus. We were met, in their blue, buttoned-up jackets, by members of the Revolutionary Committee of the University and some teachers. A professor explained that there had been ten thousand students who had all graduated during the early part of the Cultural Revolution, but then the university had closed. It had now opened again with a planned student enrolment of four thousand. They were trying to evolve a new approach, a combination of work and study, and to absorb students who had been selected from all over the country by revolutionary committees for both their revolutionary zeal and their academic prowess. It was hard to tell, but on our walks around the classrooms there seemed little evidence that this approach was working. The library was poorly supplied with books, but there were other important hopeful auguries: in one room packing cases marked the first delivery of a gift of computers! We drove away, waving to our forlorn hosts on the steps, saddened by the wasted interruption of the Cultural Revolution.

The Summer Palace was shadowy in a cold, grey, winter mist, with lingering snow piled around the roots of ancient gnarled cypresses and the tall temple roofs lost in cloud. Thick ice covered Kunming Lake and embraced the charming necklace of hooped bridges linking the islands. Weather made no difference to the hundreds of visitors who were taking photos, laughing and leaning against the bronze dragon and phoenix, sliding or taking a short cut across the frost-covered ice, and the soldiers from the People's Liberation Army, in their bright olive-green uniforms and red star caps, enjoying a day's leave.

It was here that the Empress Dowager, with her retinue, enjoyed her summers in rooms of intricately carved furniture, cupboards with dragon doors, and porcelain and jade ornaments, and looked out at courtyards, pavilions, and ornately painted, meandering verandahs. And facing her across the lake was her insolent whim, constructed using money intended for the Navy, a white marble copy of a Mississippi paddle steamer!

There was serious talk at dinner in the evening when officials from the All China Sports Federation set out China's position on the question of China's membership of FIFA. It was suggested that Sir Stanley Rous, the then chairman, need not consider himself bound by decisions taken many years previously. I said I thought China's membership should be put to the vote at FIFA's annual meeting; and so it was, time and again, but only after several years of debate and obstructive politicking was China able to resume her place in the world body.

In the night the wind had blown the clouds away and the huge red flags on Tiananmen swirled against an intensely blue sky. We were taken through the vast spaces of the Great Hall of the People where the architect lived on site in 1958 and completed the building in less than a year. The meeting hall holds seven thousand people, with no pillars to obstruct the view of the stage. Banquets for over a thousand are held there, and meetings take place in palatial provincial rooms where Hong Kong, after its return to China, was to have its own place. This great building was a dramatic reminder of the immensity of China and its huge population.

There was no time to linger. We were quickly driven away in our grey saloon through streets lined with the dusty low roofs of the *hutung* courtyard houses, villages within the city whose ancient wall was being demolished and history disregarded to make a convenient route for a ring road. We drove on through winter farmland, past vineyards and fields of winter wheat and on up a narrow road winding through rocky hills to the Great Wall. A biting wind blew from the bleak, desolate land and snow-rimmed mountains to the north. On the wall soldiers, sailors and families, their faces raw with cold as they struggled up the slopes, were as pleased as we were to realise an ambition shared by all Chinese — to stand at last upon the Great Wall, guarded through centuries of bitter weather by garrisons driven by the unimaginable terror of tribes to the north. Of a visit to the wall, Dr Johnson had reputedly said: 'You would do what would be of importance in raising your children to eminence. There would be a lustre reflected on them for your spirit and curiosity. They would at all times be regarded as the children of a man who had gone to see the Great Wall of China. I am serious, Sir.'

We returned to the plain to the tombs where, secure in a valley below the protecting wall and at the end of a broad avenue, great marble statues of elephants, camels, mythical beasts, courtiers and warriors lined the route of the solemn cortege as it passed to the last resting place of the emperors of Ming. There, set among cypresses and surrounded by mountains, the emperor was buried in a great hall deep in the earth down flights of steep steps. The white marble slabs of the barrel roof fitted smoothly without a chink between, and a marble throne with a dragon carved lazily along its back stood behind the great doors across which the last servant to enter had dropped the bar, closing the tomb as the burning incense slowly extinguished and the candles flickered out to their long night. We returned to the sunlight from this secret place and were shown the gold vessels, head-dress and other ornaments which were meant to accompany the emperor through eternity.

We had enjoyed our few days in Beijing and were sad to leave the long, hazy corridors of the Peking Hotel for the train ride to the south. Secretary General Sung Zhong and his colleagues were waiting in the gloom on the cold platform with a moving farewell and an invitation to come again. Little did we know how often in the years ahead we would find ourselves once more in Beijing, watching it develop from quiet, dark streets and sombre uniforms to the bright lights and mammoth buildings of the end of the century.

That evening, before we climbed into our bunks on the train, we passed a delightful hour introducing Liu, our interpreter, to the pleasures of Scrabble. We slept, woken briefly by the long whistle of passing trains, and in the morning we were moving through flat farmland. Drooping willows bordered irrigation streams and even the railway embankment was planted with cabbages; every inch was cultivated around the villages of mud brick roofed with rice straw. Peasants across the vast expanse of this agricultural plain were levelling, weeding and ditching, or pulling rubber-tyred carts, working untiring and silent. We steamed on for hours without change, until approaching Nanjing we rose on to the great viaduct leading to the bridge across the broad, brown waters of the Yangtze.

Plane trees line the streets of most Chinese cities. In summer they create a tunnel of green shade; in winter in Nanjing, their bare branches were latticed together over our heads along streets of shops and workshops. So conditioned were we by pictures of a regimented communist society that we had not expected to see shoppers and such busy streets.

We were lodged in what seemed to be a former missionary's compound with spacious houses scattered among magnolias and drooping pines. We drove in slanting rain to Zhong Shan Ling, the tomb of Dr Sun Yat Sen. High in quiet woods, reached along a broad sloping avenue broken by stepped terraces and lined by prayerful deodars, stood the great mausoleum. Its dark blue tiles were outlined against the grey sky; above were wheeling hawks, below, bright yellow oilskin umbrellas and cheeks reddened by rain driven on the wind.

Early next morning we drove again to the bridge and past the sentry with his drawn, thin-bladed, shining bayonet who guarded this vital link between north and south China. Far below, steamers, barge trains and square-sailed junks moved on the brown flood, and above us towered the steel girders of the great bridge. We stood in the raw, biting wind as a train belching smoke and steam thundered ponderously past.

When the Russians had withdrawn their support from China in 1952 they left the bridge barely begun, unkindly taking their plans with them. There were problems of finding the right steel and then building the bridge 35 metres deep into the water of the fast-flowing river. We were told that at the peak fifty thousand workers and volunteer students had come from the districts around Nanjing to work on the bridge, using the masses when there were no machines to do the work. Below, in the entrance hall of the bridge tower, there was a great white statue of Chairman Mao Tse-tung, his hand lifted in salute, against a background of rich red glass.

Driving past towering, colourful posters of the Cultural Revolution, of workers of all nations striding into the rising sun, their determined fists clenched, we arrived at a grimy vehicle works which had started life in the far north as an armaments factory but which now, removed to the south, painstakingly produced a minuscule thousand lorries a year. Workers' wages were no more than 100 RMB (renminbei or 'people's currency'), but food and lodging were cheap, and although cotton cloth was rationed, there were ample supplies of woollen and synthetic materials. As living proof of this, bundled up against the cold, Comrade Da, our constant companion, was wearing no less than four layers on his legs — two pairs of inner pants, one white and one grey, a blue knitted pair and thick woollen trousers — while beneath his padded long coat there seemed to be no less than five more layers of jackets, pullovers and vests. Various layers eventually had to be shed on the journey south to Guangzhou, to be stuffed temporarily into a travel bag, as the climate became, for Mr Da, a northerner, uncomfortably warm.

Our onward journey took us to Wuxi in an unheated diesel train which hooted its way through the plain bordering the river, its sturdy, white-walled village houses set in fields of winter wheat. A crowd of bystanders watched curiously as we loaded ourselves into the grey 'Red Flag' saloons and then drove beeping our way through the narrow streets, lined with the blotched grey trunks of plane trees. The streets, almost empty of cars, were crowded with people walking, cycling, pushing laden carts and packed into buses.

The pattern of the next few days at Suzhou and Hangzhou was the same: streets, parks, monuments and ornamental gardens, all filled with people. Busy farmland and tea plantations and temples which had survived the first fierce onslaught of the Cultural Revolution were once again filled with curious visitors. Everywhere we were met by officials from the All China Sports Federation, everywhere we were banqueted. There was much to learn. We watched great bags of silk cocoons tipped into hot water to loosen the glue binding the threads together and saw the careful unwinding of the thin filaments. We saw young girls carving sandalwood fans and making exquisite small, painted figures from black clay. At the Suzhou Embroidery Institute we looked in awe as the girls stitched gossamer threads of coloured silk to bring to life exquisite pictures on fine gauze which could be viewed equally well from either side.

In Guangzhou, nearer to home, the people were less relaxed, less content, aware of the contrast between their lives and the lives of their kinsmen in Hong Kong. We said farewell to Da, left our Scrabble behind for young Liu and boarded the train for the border. It was a strange feeling to approach Hong Kong from the other side, north of the border, and to pass the small office in which in 1967 I had spent so many anxious hours. We were at the end of a journey which had taken us out of one world into another, a world behind the Bamboo Curtain about which so much had been written and spoken. We had seen the crowded cities, the parks and the countryside, not arranged for our benefit and different from the picture painted by the media of a dour, surly and regimented people. But we could not forget the other, different, picture of those who were spending wasted years in bitter conditions and harsh toil, exiled far from home by the turmoil of the Cultural Revolution.

All travellers to strange and exciting places have shared the experience of returning home to a casual enquiry, and before you can get the words out of your mouth, the conversation switches to familiar topics and, disappointed with the lack of interest, you are left with your memories. The memory of that first journey in China is with us still. It removed our apprehensions of this strange and generally unfamiliar world. Although the reason for the visit had been China's ambition to regain her place in the world governing body of football, FIFA (and I had now a better understanding of her position), we had had an opportunity to see China at first hand, many years before her decision to modernise and open up to winds from around the world. The knowledge we gained stood us in good stead in the years ahead, when China was mentioned by those who had not set foot in it. As for football, it was the first of many visits around the world to find a solution to China's entry. I have included an account of this long-drawn-out affair for it reveals a little-known aspect of China's growing relations with the wider world and the international community. My own view on the question of the claim of the People's Republic to represent China on the world body of football was no different from that of the United Nations which had voted China in in 1971. On this issue in the years that followed, sometimes as a delegate to FIFA and to the Asian Football Confederation, I naturally gave my support to China.

In every way it had been an extraordinary visit. The United Kingdom had been one of the first countries to recognise the new regime in China following the defeat of the KMT forces and their retreat to Taiwan in 1949. The famous games of ping-pong had been played, and it was amusing to read that the news bulletins distributed to hotel guests reported our visit to Beijing in the same breath as they noted the visit of Henry Kissinger to Hong Kong.

Alone among my colleagues in the government, and because of this involvement in the mysteries of the world of football, I had been able to visit Beijing and talk with the Chinese Minister for Sport. It would be another five years before the Governor himself would visit Beijing. My visit marked another phase in the moulding of my approach to matters involving China and their resolution. It was another step in the long journey which had first brought me to the Far East, to learn Chinese and to read extensively about China's history, particularly its last two hundred years. In 1967 I had also come face to face with the fierce rhetoric of the Cultural Revolution, and all who worked in the New Territories were exposed every day to discussion with their parishioners and often had to fight their corner and sometimes to explain a different point of view from higher authority. These experiences, cultural and administrative, were gradually shaping me for the more momentous decisions which were to follow.

9

China and FIFA: The End of Waiting

In the seventies, soccer was still the principal spectator sport in Hong Kong and key matches would attract many thousands on their days off. When there was time I joined the crowds in the stands on Boundary Street. It gave me an opportunity to learn about another part of Hong Kong life. This link with football had led to my visit to China, and in my role as vice president of the Hong Kong Football Association I became a delegate to the Congress of the Federation of International Football Associations, FIFA, where the question of China's entry was voted upon.

In June 1974 the Congress was held in the fairgrounds of Frankfurt, a vast complex of buildings where Frankfurt has been staging fairs for hundreds of years. There were about four hundred delegates of whom 122 were voting members. There was little excitement until the motion proposing the admission of China was introduced; then delegate after delegate, speaking with great emotion and rhetoric, supported China's admission. Kuwait proposed the motion and Iran, Pakistan, Jamaica, Ethiopia, and Saudi Arabia supported it. The Swiss delegate then spoke solemnly and effectively, reminding the voters that if they voted to admit China by a simple majority, contrary to the constitution of FIFA, they would be guilty of misconduct.

After all the polemics and the passion there was a wrangle as to whether the vote required a three-quarters or simple majority. The result turned on this constitutional issue. In such a large assembly it was almost impossible to secure the necessary three-quarters majority and the People's Republic of China lost by about ten votes.

There was then a vote for the presidency and Sir Stanley Rous, who my notes record had alienated the Soviet bloc by his support for Chile, and the pro-China group by his inflexibility on the China issue, was defeated by the Argentine candidate Raoul Havelange, who then began a reign which was to last for more than twenty years.

Later that year the issue was debated at the Asian Football Confederation in Teheran. I was one of two delegates to the meeting from Hong Kong, and because of the interest then current in the Sallang Tunnel which was being constructed by Russia through the Pamirs, we decided to travel via Delhi and Afghanistan before flying on to Teheran. We looked with awe at the jagged mountains surrounding Kabul, before motoring down to the narrowing defile of the Khyber Pass, scene of one of Britain's major military defeats, and up the narrow winding road to the newly opened tunnel which was to play such an important role in the later invasion by Russia. Now as I write, after the destruction of the World Trade Centre in New York and the need to deliver Afghanistan from the grip of the Taliban and Al Qaeda, I remember those jagged mountains and hostile country, the poor villages of stone and mud, the turbans and loose cloths, the donkeys and bicycles and the thronged bazaar. Afghanistan, with its long history of invasion and conquest, a melting pot of races and religions, is once again emerging from turmoil.

At the meeting in Teheran, China's entry to the Asian Confederation was not on the agenda, but by a simple majority vote it was decided to add it as an emergency item. The majority of Asian delegates then voted to admit the People's Republic to membership of the Asian Football Confederation, to take the place of Taiwan. Asia had defied the international body, and this then resulted in a stand-off, with FIFA threatening to expel Asia from the world body. The Asian Football Federation stood firm, and for the international federation it proved too big a step to expel the whole of Asia from the world body so the stalemate lasted for several years. The FIFA Congress met in Montreal at the start of the Montreal Olympics with no resolution, and again in Buenos Aires before the World Cup in 1978.

In Buenos Aires a different approach was employed. A resolution was proposed that it was more appropriate for the People's Republic to represent China in accordance with the FIFA statute of one country, one association. But that was too simple. The meeting began early, and there were nineteen speeches on the China question. Finally the amended resolution was put to the vote and passed. The Chairman, to everyone's astonishment, then said it should be put to a later Congress to decide. There was uproar, cries of 'No', and consternation from the floor. An adjournment was called lasting an hour. The officers returned to the platform to announce that the Executive would consider the situation and call an Extraordinary Congress in a year or two to decide!

Four years had passed since the question had been raised in Frankfurt. Asia, controversially, had shown the way. Gradually the climate of opinion changed, some diehards departed the scene and more countries came to see that whatever the legal arguments for denying China membership, it was illogical and absurd to keep China out of the international body. Finally a way had been found based on the one country, one association principle.

After our meeting in Buenos Aires we were driven to the stadium for the opening of the World Cup through a parkland of wintry trees lined with statues. After the obligatory rhythmic display, the flags, stars, balloons and bands, the fine words of sport and friendship, and the grand occasion, the opening match between West Germany and Poland was a wretched affair, the players leaving the pitch to jeers from the packed stadium.

We left Argentina by way of Bolivia and Peru. Descending by plane between snow peaks we landed, light-headed, at La Paz high in the Andes, and entered a world of people with mahogany complexions and aquiline noses, the women with layer on layer of skirts, bowler hats and shawls. At dawn, we drove along a stony road through the russet sunrise, half way to heaven, to the shore of Lake Titicaca and then across the lake, stopping by a sparkling stream amidst mud-walled villages, tiny patches of golden barley on the hill slopes and browsing donkeys, alpaca and llama. On the lake, unperturbed flocks of flamingo, bittern, waders and herons searched among the reeds. A boat from antiquity, woven of reeds, paddled slowly past and country people with weather-beaten faces and voluminous skirts added a touch of blue and red to the golden land.

Our train from Puno climbed slowly away from the lake through a valley of yellow tufty grass, dry stubble and occasional fields of late, eared barley. Range upon range of hills reached into the sky, some so high they were dusted with snow. At 14,000 feet, we reached the pass of the highest railway in the world. Then we coasted long hours down to Cuzco, the golden grass giving way to willows, eucalypts and poplars backed by steep black, red and gold hills and patches of golden barley.

From Cuzco in the cool morning a toy train switched back and forward until, having worked its way to the top of the basin, we looked down on the tiny brown tiled roofs of the town nestling in the hills and beyond them to the mountain snow. The valley narrowed to a gorge into whose cliffs ancient narrow trails were cut. Everywhere were orchids, begonias, yellow daisies and bromeliads.

From the station at Machu Picchu the bus followed hairpin bends up to the lost city in the skies on the crest of a precipice. We wandered among old terraces of cultivation and the great grey, perfectly fitting stone blocks of temples, meeting places, prisons, sacrificial stones, and sundials, while all around us were the jagged purple and blue ranges of forested mountains. The spirits of an ancient people filled the air speaking their strange tongue. We were awestruck by their dedicated years of work, prayer and sacrifice and transported by the magic of Machu Picchu.

It was an uplifting end to a long journey and a disappointing meeting in Buenos Aires, but ultimately the way had been found for China to take her place in the world of international football. These accumulated efforts in the world of sport, over many years, finally culminated in the decision of the International Olympic Committee to grant the 2008 games to China, and the admission of the Chinese Football team to the World Cup competition in Japan and South Korea in 2002; and now there is even a representative from Hong Kong, Timothy Fok Chun-ting, on the Olympic Committee.

10

Back to the Land

A hundred years ago the markets and villages of the New Territories were linked by tracks, the more important flagged with great slabs of granite, climbing over the mountains, through the paddy fields and along the shoreline. There were no carriages, wagons or carts — no vehicles — and therefore nothing which could turn a cart track or a bridle path into a road. To make the New Territories more accessible, more governable, roads had to be pushed out along the coast to the west and, most important, to the north over a pass in the hills to Tai Po, which in April 1899 had resisted the occupation of ancestral lands by the invading British troops taking over their new possession. Reports describe a force of a thousand armed men entrenched in positions on the hills, whose muskets failed to inflict injury on the British, who fired their cannons in reply. Bombs had exploded. There had been angry riots at the Tai Po temple and a fusillade of bricks had descended on negotiators, who scattered into the hills, where from their hiding place in the scratchy undergrowth they watched a hundred or so men burn their flimsy police post of bamboo mats. The arrival of troop reinforcements quelled the opposition who, it was suspected, had been reinforced by Triads and hoodlums from across the new border at Shenzhen.

Tai Po market stood at the end of a long inlet from the sea whose narrow mouth broadened into wide, calm water flanked steeply on both sides by the grass slopes of rugged mountains, vivid green in summer and sunburned brown in winter, interrupted here and there along the watercourses by the vestigial trees of primordial forests, home of wild boar, barking deer, pangolin, snakes and civet cats. When the road reached Tai Po, engineers, looking for a source of material to create an embankment across the mud flats, sliced the top off a small island that stood at the entrance to the town. This created a delightful and breezy place to build a house and a home for the first District Officer of the new territory, with a breathtaking view down the channel to the sea. This house, Island House, was our home from 1973 for the next twelve years.

Tai Po at that time was a small country town. It had recently grown in size when rows of apartments had been built along the main street to resettle villagers removed from the site of a new reservoir which was needed to keep pace with Hong Kong's continuing search for water. This reservoir was built by damming gaps between islands and then pumping out the seawater, but it had left land-locked villages, backed by steep mountains, without access to the open sea. The evacuees were country people, but they fitted into the measured pace of life in the market town, and from then on Tai Po began to grow.

The water at the Tai Po end of the inlet was shallow, and at low tide shining mud flats lay behind our house, from which we looked down on the fishing boat anchorage. The house stood four square, whitewashed, verandahed, with a tiled black tarred roof. Behind the house was a tree-lined stretch of lawn and a great granite sugar-loaf boulder. In the corner of the house, a light tower provided a not very serious attempt to guide ships down the channel. Huge trees covered the slopes: rosewood, camphor, lychee and shimmering, silver, thick-barked eucalypts. Around us on three sides were the peaks and slopes of high hills, and to the east the silver sea. A narrow driveway linked the house to Tai Po and the outside world.

I went to Tai Po at the start of the MacLehose ten-year housing programme, first as District Commissioner, but within a few weeks the appointment was changed to that of Secretary for the New Territories. The appointment as Secretary was anomalous and frowned on by the purists. It did not fit into the McKinsey pattern which separated the formulation of policy from its execution, because strictly speaking the Secretary for the New Territories had both a policy input and a managerial and executive role. The job required a new authority, a Secretary, and the target to build housing for so many in such a short time required a more dynamic approach. Until then housing had been fitted into other priorities; now there was to be an intensive ten-year all-out effort to solve the question of poor housing once and for all. Tenements were to be relieved of overcrowding, squatters were to be removed from hillsides, people who had lived for years in cramped, stifling, wooden huts, because they had not lived in Hong Kong for long enough to qualify for a permanent home, were to be cleared, and houses, huts, factories, and anything getting in the way of development removed and the owners resettled. The government set aside a separate budget, created a new engineering department and appointed project managers. I had the job of overall coordination and had to ensure that all was kept in balance and that, in the furious pace of development, human factors were not forgotten.

Our team was left to get on with its work without interference. There were occasional visits from the Governor but, for the most part, other high officials stayed away. We seemed to have more visits from amazed members of the British Parliament than from our own government.

On the way to Tai Po, land in the Shatin valley fringed the shores of a broad inlet. It lay hidden from Kowloon behind a barrier of thickly wooded mountains whose arms stretched out in sharp peaks and outcrops of grey granite, among which stood a group of strangely balanced rocks in the form of a peasant woman holding a child, known as Amah Rock. In the blue distance to the north, the Pat Sin (Eight Immortals) range of eight peaks closed the view. A few centuries-old villages were dotted around the valley. In one corner were white flowering tung oil trees and on the valley floor grew a type of rice with short hard grains formerly sent as tribute to the emperor; and where the paddy fields ended, before reaching the sea, were fishponds fattening grey mullet and carp.

In the early days of the century, winding down the valley along the edge of the water, the Kowloon to Canton railway had been pushed through the mountains and opened the valley to the city. Around the railway station a small hamlet of shops and roast pigeon restaurants had gathered. By their side was a small disused airstrip. It was here on 18 March 1911 that Charles Van den Born, having patiently waited for the wind to drop, first took Hong Kong into the age of air travel in his contraption of wood, wire and doped linen. Crowds, led by the Governor, had collected and special trains packed with spectators waited on the tracks, but after a long wait in the cold afternoon, all departed. They were too impatient, for the wind dropped and, watched by the remaining faithful enthusiasts, the aeroplane puttered its way into the air and circled the airstrip. (A replica of this Farnam biplane now hangs in the new air terminal at Chek Lap Kok, opened in July 1997.)

We began building the new town at Shatin in 1974. Now, at the end of the century, its population has long since passed the half million mark and each new extension seems to point to opportunities for further expansion to meet a never satisfied demand. Bulldozers stepped the lower slopes of the hills into broad platforms, and a constant stream of orange dump trucks wound down the hillsides and carried the spoil to fill in the sea, avoiding the villages but reclaiming the vegetable fields, the paddy and the fishponds. The new town literally rose out of the water — housing blocks twenty to thirty storeys high, markets, schools, police and fire stations, playgrounds and parks. There was even space, by filling in the sea, to build a new racecourse, a big brother to the racecourse in Happy Valley on the island of Hong Kong, with stands for seventy thousand, and in the centre of the track was created a landscaped park.

In the mid-seventies the increase in oil prices caused a dip in the economy and threatened to slow down work of reclamation. To meet the challenge the sea itself was sold to developers to fill in and build their own small town. The railway was electrified and the right to build in the air over the sidings and the stations was sold, to become soaring residential blocks to help pay for the railway. After weeks of negotiation the old huddle of tin-shed shops at the centre of the settlement was demolished.

In its place a concert hall and a new shopping centre were built looking out over the park and the river channel. Some years later, while acting Governor, it was a great delight to me to plant a banyan tree and to open the hall for its first concert with Sir Neville Mariner and the orchestra of St Martin in the Fields. All this had been done in less than ten years; where the only music then heard was the clash of cymbals and the urgent drumbeat of a lion dance, now was the sophistication of an orchestral concert.

This pattern was followed at six new towns. Each had its engineering and planning team, and each had its District Officer to safeguard the public interest and to negotiate the safe removal and clearance of tens of thousands of people, mostly from flimsy shacks into a safe haven of concrete and a home high in the air. It never ceases to astonish how different experience in Hong Kong has been from cities of the West. Families from the villages and farmlands of the mainland, who had settled in huts on the land and hillsides of Hong Kong, moved into multi-storeyland with none of the fuss and failure of high rise homes elsewhere. Having failed as a social experiment, high rise blocks are being demolished elsewhere, while Hong Kong builds higher and higher. Part of the reason for this different attitude lies in Hong Kong's much criticised high density. Our high homes are not surrounded by vacant parkland. Out of the window other housewives can be seen going to market, children going to school and elderly residents watching the fish in water gardens. There is always something to see.

Our plan at first was to build towns which had both homes and factories so that residents did not have to spend hours on crowded buses getting to work in another town. Our careful plans were frustrated at the end of the seventies as China's economic reforms caused the migration of industry to China where labour costs were cheaper. Hong Kong's economy changed to serve the finance, investment, hotel and tourist industries and as employment shifted away from the new towns to downtown Hong Kong and Kowloon, priorities shifted to the building of roads and railways for commuters.

At the end of twelve exciting and dramatic years we had reached our target. We had built homes for 1.5 million people, but sadly we had not solved the housing problem. Illegal immigration from the swelling population of southern China and natural growth had caused Hong Kong's population to run ahead of our aspirations. So it seems that at the end of every ten years there is a new beginning, new promises and a new effort to solve the housing shortage, new targets to be set and the pursuit of the will o' the wisp when everyone in Hong Kong will be happily housed.

11

Breaking Down the Fences

*T*he river selected by the Colonial Secretary, Stewart Lockhart, in
1898 to mark the limit of Britain's 'new territory' intrusion into
China starts as a stream in the mountains at the eastern end of the
boundary. In 1976 its upper stony course meandered down past an
abandoned lead mine and through paddy fields and quiet grey-brick
villages until it reached the sea in the west. It passed under the rusting
iron girders of a Bailey bridge, so called after its inventor, designed to be
thrown quickly across rivers for advancing armies, but now over which
barrows of vegetables were daily wheeled and pigs and cattle transferred
on their journey from the distant interior of China to the markets of Hong
Kong.

It was over this crossing at Man Kam To that a Public Works
Department steamroller must have found its way into China during the
occupation by the Japanese. In my office was a file containing one sheet
of paper recounting how a team went to bring back the steamroller at the
end of the war. It recorded a solemn discussion about the return of this
renegade roller, which took place over cups of tea, seated under a tree in
one of the villages in neighbouring China. How I wish that all our problems
could be solved in such a gentlemanly fashion!

At the Bailey bridge crossing, the water slowed to where the tide
from the bay to the west twice daily pushed back its muddy brown waters.
Downstream the river widened, twisted, and turned between the high
banks of fishponds fashioned out of the flood plain, and then crept slowly

over wide flats of glistening mud which at low tide lined Deep Bay, so called because it marked a deep indentation in the coast of China.

Oyster beds line both sides of the bay, for which leases had been issued by the Hong Kong government, and farmers traditionally crossed from villages on the mainland side to tend the beds. The leases had expired and in the troubled times of the Cultural Revolution the ownership of the beds was a source of friction and dispute as to the legality of incursions by mainland workers into Hong Kong waters. The beds yield a plump monster oyster too risky, because of pollution, to be eaten raw but succulent fried in batter or threaded on a string to be dried, like washing hanging on a line, for later consumption. Oyster farmers fasten a wooden handlebar to a plank and use this to thrust themselves to their oyster-encrusted rocks over the squelchy mud. On the mudflats, water birds flock in their thousands to feast on fiddler crabs, mud skippers and shrimps stranded by the receding tide.

Lining the shore, tall green mangrove thickets conceal a fringe of tidal fishponds. A daily deposit of mud over centuries has left inland the original shore which, as the sea retreated, was then fringed by paddy fields growing a strain of rice which would grow in brackish water once a year when the rains came. Beyond the paddy fields are fishponds where grey mullet fry gathered from the bay are fattened on a diet of droppings from the pigs and ducks kept in sheds built over the ponds. Finally, between the fishponds and the forest of evergreen mangroves which line the bay there are tidal ponds whose sluice gates are opened to let in the flooding tide with its cargo of unsuspecting crabs and prawns who swim and fatten in the pond. They are netted in the mouth of the sluice gate as the pond is emptied on a falling tide. This fecund wetland ecology was given to the World Wide Fund for Nature (of which I became the chairman) to manage, and is now protected by the international Ramsar Convention.

There, particularly during the winter migrations, great flocks of water birds feed and fatten on the mudflats. Some have flown immense distances, many from Lake Baikal in Russia, while cranes come to escape the snows of North China, and a few hundred of the sole remaining blackfaced spoonbills in the world come to scoop up a wintry harvest. Other tiny birds are recorded as having flown to Japan and to Western Australia. Now there are extensive boardwalks through the mangroves and hides from which visitors and groups of schoolchildren can watch this magic display.

The Treaty of Nanking, leasing the New Territories to Great Britain, drew the boundaries of the new territory at the high water mark on the north bank of the border river and at high water on the coastline of the bays to the east and the west. Fifty years later there was an unwritten understanding that, since the establishment of the People's Republic, Hong Kong vessels did not exercise the right to approach or land on the shore of either bay. Similarly avoiding friction on the land border, the fence followed the south, or Hong Kong, bank of the river. These were practical and sensible arrangements which kept the security forces of both sides from becoming entangled. But the high water mark boundary led to a curious situation when it came to removing the rusting Bailey bridge, which had been put in place by the army after 1945 and which was the only vehicle crossing of the border.

In the years before 1976, and after the excitements of 1967, tension had gradually lessened on the border. Farmers were once again crossing to Hong Kong to cultivate their land and there was talk of opening a through train service to Guangzhou (Canton). The rusty bridge at Man Kam To was too weak to carry trucks to pick up vegetables and livestock. I led a small group of Hong Kong officials to discuss with officials from China the construction of a permanent concrete bridge. We met in the railway station across the border from the Hong Kong station at Lowu, and in a friendly meeting reached agreement on the basic principles: the type of bridge to be built and who would be responsible for building it. We also agreed to follow the terms of the treaty demarcating administrative responsibility, that the bridge pier to be built on the high water mark on the Chinese side would be built by Chinese engineers. Hong Kong would build the rest. Our bridge was a practical, no-nonsense design. Our colleagues from China suggested more attention to aesthetics. We agreed, and so the bridge was built with key pattern rails and more elegant lamp standards!

But before work could start, the rusting bridge had to be moved to one side. Both sides worked as a team. Since it was a military bridge, I watched the Gurkha engineers pull back the bridge onto the Hong Kong side and launch a temporary bridge across to the side of the old one. Later the beams for the concrete bridge were also pushed across in the same way. On 3 June 1976 I went to the bridge and stood, while rain bucketed down, to watch the removal of the Bailey bridge. In a simple way, literally building bridges after many eventful years, the basis for future cross-border cooperation was established. Now there is, in addition, a second wide bridge crossing in the west complete with immigration and customs controls, where fleets of container trucks, buses and cars queue every day to cross the border.

The border fence was a poor barrier to determined illegal immigrants. Until you have seen with your own eyes it is not possible to believe that strong will and muscles in a few seconds could carry you over a sixteen-foot-high fence topped with barbed wire. On the Hong Kong side this barrier wound its way up into the mountains, into thick undergrowth and across stream courses, making observation of the length of the fence impossible. At the end of the seventies the tide of immigrants swelled until sometimes several hundred made the crossing in a day. The unwritten rule had always been that if you were caught coming in you were pushed back but, if you evaded capture, often with the complicity of villagers and van drivers, and reached the sanctuary of Hong Kong you had touched base and were not sent back. Indeed, until the bridge was built there was no convenient way of returning illegal immigrants to the mainland.

Once again we met officials across the border in the railway station, and agreed a method, using a closed and windowless truck, for returning illegal immigrants found in Hong Kong without identity cards across our new permanent bridge at Man Kam To, back to their homes in China. Every resident of Hong Kong was issued with an identity card, and carrying it was made compulsory: to go to school or hospital, to get a job, to open a bank account, all needed an identity document. When the cards were issued, those immigrants already in Hong Kong were registered and given a card and thereafter anyone caught without a card, anywhere in Hong Kong, was rounded up, taken to the border and carried in a truck across it. From there they were returned to their villages. We knew from persistent crossers who were caught time and time again that the punishment for crossing to Hong Kong was not severe. Gradually the fence was strengthened, sensors were attached to it, and a motorable track was built behind it, and with the help of the bridge the flood of illegal immigrants dried to a determined trickle.

Following the opening of China in 1978, in an atmosphere of *détente*, it was not long before fast catamaran ferries from Hong Kong began to travel to towns along the rivers which criss-cross the Pearl River delta and planes began direct flights to China, and instead of trudging across the bridge at the border you could board a train in Kowloon and travel non-stop to Guangzhou. These changes, unexciting in themselves, signified the beginning of transformation in the life of Hong Kong.

The quiet land of villages, paddy fields and fishponds north of the border was also to change dramatically. Somewhere in the offices of the central government in Beijing, without Hong Kong knowing, a decision had been taken to develop a city across the river from Hong Kong. It was to become a Special Economic Zone. I accompanied the Governor, Sir Murray MacLehose, at the end of 1981, together with his Political Advisor, David Wilson (who became Governor in 1987 and Sir David), to meet the mayor and the planners and to winkle out what we could of their plans. We were shown a minuscule plan of a development zone stretching from east to west, blanketing the whole of the region between the mountains to the north and our river line. Workers' lines were already being constructed, and everywhere there was demolition, earthmoving, construction and most of all, confident determination. We came away convinced by what we had seen and heard that Hong Kong would have to respond to this challenge, that Hong Kong people would have to shake off their disdain bordering on contempt for what was happening in China and establish both formal and friendly channels of communication. Crowds of press and cameras from Hong Kong followed us on our visit. 'Look to the north,' the Governor said on his return, but years of isolation and looking outward to the rest of the world had become ingrained in many Hong Kong minds and even now, more than twenty years later, there are a stubborn few who have little interest in seeing the changes for themselves. It is astonishing to reflect that a city and its suburbs reaching seven million people could be built in twenty years along our northern boundary and that a quarter of a million people a day would cross the bridges from Hong Kong into China for work, shopping, eating and entertainment.

The Shenzhen University was among the first buildings to be built in this new city to the north. I remember standing on the roof inspecting the campus with, once again, that strange feeling of looking back from the other side of the fence at the waters of Deep Bay and the mountains of Hong Kong. The Vice President, white-haired, spoke slow but excellent English. I asked him where he had learned it, and he replied that he had been one of the Boxer Indemnity scholars and had studied in the 1930s at Imperial College, London. The Boxer Protocol, signed after the Boxer rebellion at the turn of the century, awarded an indemnity of about $333 million to the foreign powers to be paid over a period of years. The British and the Americans did not simply put it into the Treasury, but in an enlightened way, used the money to create an education fund for Chinese to receive higher education in their countries. The Vice President I was chatting with was one of these scholars. His English had survived the long years of isolation and the harsh penalties of the Cultural Revolution. He remembered his stay in England with great affection. Others of these Boxer Indemnity scholars were highly distinguished, and at least one became a Nobel Prize winner. This outcome of the Boxer rebellion and the siege of Peking is a fascinating sidelight on international relations.

In place of the silence of the previous twenty years, the visits to Shenzhen, the agreements we reached and the officials we met paved the way, at that time, for greater informal contact between the Hong Kong government and officials of the New China News Agency which represented the Chinese government in Hong Kong. We were able to follow up our visits with the director of the agency, Xu Jiatun, over dinner at Government House, where he and Sir Murray talked about ways further to improve cross-border communication.

The long years of isolation which had begun in 1949, when the People's Liberation Army halted its advance against the retreating army of the Guomindang at the boundary fence, were over. There was no more dramatic indication of this than the changes at the border, or Boundary as it is now correctly called.

12

The Expiring Lease

evelopment, get up and go, has been an abiding theme in the life of Hong Kong from the moment on a cold winter morning of 26 January 1841 when Captain Elliot took possession. There was nowhere to live, but within a matter of months the first houses and offices had been built along the foreshore. Behind them, steep, treeless hillsides strewn with huge granite boulders reached up to the skyline ridge of the island. A trace, following a track along the foreshore, was laid out for the Queen's Road whose winding route, now far from the waters of the harbour, remains even today a crowded principal transport artery.

Beyond the harbour in which the merchant and naval ships lay at anchor was the enticing land of the Kowloon Peninsula. It was not long after 1841 that unsanctioned expansion of the colony began to take place there and a kind of squatter colony grew up, and during typhoons ships made use of the safer anchorage in the western arm of Kowloon Bay rather than the exposed waters of the central harbour. Despite all this unofficial activity, a surprisingly long nineteen years passed before the enterprising Harry Parkes, the British Consul in Canton, exchanged a paper with the Governor General of Canton leasing the southern end of the peninsula for 500 taels of silver. This act of unofficial imperialism was frowned on by the powers that be, but was not repudiated. Later the commander of the Hong Kong garrison, Major General von Straubenzee, lent support to the acquisition and pointed out that the burgeoning city of Victoria fell easily within the range of Chinese guns situated on the peninsula. Thereafter events in a wider arena provided an opportunity to regularise matters. Taking advantage of the seizure of the lorcha *Arrow* (a lorcha is a small sailing vessel with a Western hull and Chinese rigging) by the Chinese, hostilities were commenced by the British, an incident known as the *Arrow* War. Hostilities were ended by the 1860 Treaty of Tientsin, which further opened China to entry by the Western powers. Harry Parkes, not missing a trick, managed to tack onto the treaty the cession of the southern part of the Kowloon Peninsula to the British.

Kowloon at that time was simply a part of rural China, a busy place of farmland, villages, temples and markets, and it was not until the end of the century with the leasing of the New Territories in 1898 that the rest of the peninsula north of Boundary Street up to the Lion Rock range of hills and beyond to the Shenzhen river came under British administration and subsequent development.

Land in this new territory was usually divided into small lots for paddy farming, and land holdings were small, irregular, inaccessible and incapable themselves of making a contribution to our housing target. But in a few cases there were families who owned much larger holdings, big fishponds, orchards and extensive areas where the sea had been impounded behind a bund, and these larger tracts could be developed by their owners into housing estates.

In the north-west of the New Territories, in 1912, the government had sold to a family trust the right to enclose several hundred acres of marshland from the sea to be used for brackish-water paddy and fish farming. A bund with sluice gates was built along the seaward end and the wild marshland brought into productive use. But from then on there was continual friction between the owners of the former marsh and the inhabitants of ancestral villages whose drainage channels had been interrupted by these interlopers. Things came to a head each year when, during the heavy rains of summer, the area flooded and the men controlling the sluices would not let the water flow away so they could catch the fish which had escaped from their overflowing ponds and were swimming freely about in the floods backed up behind the bund. There were angry protests from the villagers and scenes of wild excitement as the village children plunged into the water to catch the fish.

Later, in the sixties, in the desperate search to increase Hong Kong's water supply, it was proposed that the 'marsh' should be used to hold water pumped from the flood plain of Yuen Long. But as agreement was reached to pipe more water to Hong Kong in huge pipes reaching across the country from the East River far away in China, this other plan was filed away and is now forgotten.

During the seventies the remaining 'trustee' sold the area, Tin Shui Wai, to a property developer who put forward an astonishing plan to build a town for half a million people. The government administration was at a loss as to how to respond. Could it, should it, be taken seriously? Could one company be allowed to embark on such an extravagant proposition? We were in the throes of our own plans to build on a scale of millions and there were those who could not readily accept the diversion of government effort and resources to deal with this application. Others were deeply sceptical that a private developer could accumulate the capital resources to build on such an ambitious scale. There was subconscious annoyance that a single developer should have possession of so large a parcel of land, which would have taken the government years to acquire and scrape together and finance. The government was accused of dragging its heels and not sticking to its side of the bargain to provide the linking road system, but by the time the proposals had flowed backwards and forwards, committees met and dissolved, and owners, officials, consultants, lawyers, planners, architects and engineers come and gone, a fresh question had arisen as to what would happen when the New Territories lease expired. To develop such a large area would extend beyond the expiry, in 1997, of the lease.

Other developers, unfazed by this question and with sufficient resources, could see the potential and took up the challenge. There was a division of the spoils; the government took one share and the private developer his. Sand was pumped from the sea bed of Deep Bay to fill up the fish ponds and reclaim the area. It is with a wry smile, now, remembering the earlier saga and protracted arguments, that I see, as I pass on that way to Yuen Long, the soaring tower blocks of Tin Shui Wai puncturing the skyline, a light railway, shopping malls, schools, social centres and a new town of tens of thousands of people.

There were three aspects of these private initiatives which weighed heavily on the mind of government. Firstly, it was important not to be seen to be granting a particular developer a favour which was not available to others and thus raise the spectre of corruption and croneyism; secondly, the schemes should fit in with the government's general policies and plans for providing housing; and thirdly, there should not be a significant diversion of government effort to provide supporting infrastructure. I dare say, too, that subconsciously there was a reluctance among some officials to acknowledge that sometimes the private sector could come up with something which had not been thought of in the corridors of power. Nevertheless, some of these schemes went ahead, provided they were self-supporting. All of them introduced an element of precious variety into a property market which was in the doldrums. Apartments in Hong Kong compared with elsewhere are small, and very few have the luxury of gardens, green and recreational space. Some of these developments provided houses with gardens instead of flats in high-rise apartment blocks and, for a lucky few, fulfilled a suppressed need for room to move, fresh air, and the chance to grow a few flowers.

By the end of the seventies the expiry of the ninety-nine-year lease of the New Territories on 1 July 1997 was getting too close to enable property developers to go to the banks for money for plans which would take many years to come to fruition. While they were left with the shortening end of their lease in Hong Kong, some were already going north of the border to build factories where they could acquire the right to use land for twenty-five years, with a promise of renewal. For those that had ears to hear, this was a clear and early indication that a solution would be found to the Hong Kong dilemma; for if Hong Kong investors could acquire rights to use land in Shenzhen for twenty-five years just across our border in China, why should they not have the same privilege in Hong Kong when Hong Kong returned to China? There was, of course, no answer to this and for most it was too good to be true to believe that in 1997 leases would simply be renewed. The future of property development became more and more a topic of conversation and wagging of chins. It was something which could not be left to sort itself out; almost all the land needed for future expansion was in the New Territories, which would return to China in 1997. Quite apart from urban expansion, land was needed for projects which were vital to the economy such as extending the container port, constructing power stations costing billions, building a new airport in the longer term, and much more besides. Hong Kong simply had to know the answer.

The years of Hong Kong's isolation were over, China was opening to the world, and Hong Kong people were travelling freely into China. There was a new and pragmatic leadership in Beijing. Surely the unmentionable could now be mentioned against a background of real problems rather than as an academic exercise in foreign relations? It was time for the Governor of Hong Kong to pay a second visit to China, the last one having been as long ago as the 1950s, so little communication did Hong Kong have with China. While visits by British Ministers were planned as part of the general thaw in Sino-British relations, if the Governor went, Hong Kong people would expect the subject of the lease, which was uppermost in their minds, to be raised.

It was against this background that the visit by Sir Murray MacLehose took place in March 1979. There is a first-hand account of this visit, the first for more than twenty years, by Sir Percy Cradock, British Ambassador to China at the time, in his book, *Experiences of China*. Contrary to the custom whereby the details of the subsequent discussion were first dealt with by lesser officials, Chairman Deng Xiaoping decided that he would be the first to see the Governor. In the vast spaces of the Great Hall of the People Deng started by saying, in essence, that sovereignty over Hong Kong lay with China whatever the political future was for Hong Kong, but it would remain capitalist; and he used a Chinese expression to say that investors were not to worry, rather sentimentally translated as 'put their hearts at ease'. He refused to be drawn on the limited suggestion by the Governor that land leases could simply be extended beyond 1997 while leaving the more sensitive questions of the governance of Hong Kong on one side. Deng repeated that investors were not to worry and that other matters could be left till later. It was a rebuff which did nothing to solve the question of the expiring lease, and was a very tame message to relay to the Hong Kong business community. The media were not satisfied and kept the pressure up for many years, itching to know what more had been said.

In the follow-up to this visit there were straws in the wind indicating that China would recover sovereignty in 1997, but disappointingly, the question of what to do about the expiring leases in the New Territories was to drag on for a further four years.

In 1981, to make plain an order of priority, China published her nine-point proposals for Taiwan. These were that after reunification into the body of China, Taiwan could continue to enjoy a high degree of autonomy as a special administration. Broad hints were then given out indicating that these proposals could apply equally to Hong Kong. It was even suggested during a visit to Beijing in January 1982 to the British Lord Privy Seal, Humphrey Atkins, who as a junior Foreign Office Minister was responsible for Hong Kong, and more substantially to Sir Edward Heath three months later, that Hong Kong should study the proposals for Taiwan. Deng Xiaoping, as Sir Percy Cradock records in his book, put the question directly to Heath as to whether a solution on the lines of the nine-point plan for Taiwan could be agreed, in which sovereignty would pass to China while Hong Kong would remain a free port and an international investment centre. It would be run by Hong Kong people and would become a Special Administrative Region. These hints and nudges were not pursued by the British government.

Apart from high-powered encounters, at another level, after thirty years of not speaking to one another, Hong Kong community leaders found that they could travel to Beijing and could meet the leaders of

China face to face and talk about the future of the place they had made their home. This was an extraordinary change in their lives and had a profound psychological effect. Hong Kong was again being treated as part of China. The veneer of colonial Hong Kong, had it been realised, was already beginning to be worn away.

It is hard for anyone to come away from the country's capital city and such meetings unmoved by the impression of its size and greatness. All were told the same message, and most came away warmed by their encounters and conversations with the leaders of the nation. For those visitors from Hong Kong, the meetings carried with them, in addition to their swelling emotion and pride in their country's long history, if only subconsciously memories of the humiliation of the Manchu invasion and domination, of violent and shaming encounters with the West, of the injustices meted out by the Versailles Treaty which allocated the former German colonial possessions in China to Japan, of invasion by and war with Japan, and of the ending of the civil war. After a miserable two hundred years, as Mao said in Beijing in 1949, 'China had stood up'.

Hong Kong's community leaders, the Vice Chancellor of Hong Kong University, organisations representing industry and commerce, charitable associations, the Hong Kong Observers (a group of young and enthusiastic commentators on the political scene), the Heung Yee Kuk, the elected representatives of the indigenous people of the New Territories, all these and many individuals travelled to Beijing for an audience with China's leaders. The same message was repeated many times and then repeated by the media in Hong Kong to a wider audience. Sovereignty would be resumed.

No mention was made of continuing British administration. Hong Kong people, not the British, would be ruling Hong Kong. Sir Percy Cradock writes that on only two occasions did a delegation speak in support of continuing British administration and they were met with a sharp rejoinder. Whatever their private thoughts and worries might have been, others listened to the message that the rule they had known for so long, and under which so many had prospered, was coming to an end. In

Britain the government was preoccupied with the Falklands imbroglio and unable to interpret and digest the strong and unpalatable messages that were coming from China. The reality had to wait until the Prime Minister herself visited Beijing in September 1982.

Meanwhile, land in the New Territories, where the bulk of development was taking place, continued to be sold on a lease expiring three days before the end of June 1997, the end of the lease of the New Territories from China. Hong Kong had to wait another two years to be reassured by the conclusion of the agreement with China that these leases would be renewed on expiry in 1997 for a further term of fifty years until 2047, and new leases would carry a term of fifty years reaching even beyond 2047.

13

'Hong Kong People Ruling Hong Kong'

Before deciding with the support of his Executive Council to embark upon his visionary programme to build homes for one and a half million people in ten years, Sir Murray MacLehose had remarked that the shortage of decent housing was the biggest single source of unhappiness in Hong Kong. Now this source of unhappiness was to be removed. But it was not simply a question of housing; schools, police and fire stations, clinics, shopping centres and markets, parks and playgrounds, all these had to be provided if the people were to be persuaded to leave the familiar environment of Hong Kong and Kowloon and move to the unknown New Territories.

Work began simultaneously at six small towns and almost overnight the inhabitants of these peaceful sites found themselves living next to a great construction effort. Each was a world of trenches, cranes, diggers, steel rods, hammering pile drivers, trucks and concrete, and swarming workers. Fields were buried beneath a deep layer of orange dirt from the hills, and where land was reclaimed from the sea, no sooner had it been filled than piles were driven deep down through it, sometimes sixty metres or more, until they reached bedrock. A little more than three years later, families were moving into their new but small apartments, excited at their new environment and their escape from being crowded together in bunk beds with toilets doubling as kitchens. The new arrivals to the old market towns were so content with their new homes and living environment that the thought never seemed to enter their heads that they had no one to represent them. What representation there was, was by a committee elected by the villagers who had been surrounded and swamped by the high-rise buildings.

Tsuen Wan, which in 1958 had received the first thrust of urban expansion, by 1978 had grown to the size of a city. Multi-storey apartments had climbed over the hills and into the next valley, and bridges had linked it to its neighbouring island. It was a quaint anachronism that a population of several hundred thousand was still represented by a rural committee elected by a few hundreds. Sir Murray asked me what I thought. My interim solution was to create an advisory board whose members would be chosen and appointed by the Governor. Without displacing the existing power centre, this body would bring together the various stakeholders in the town's affairs and would include the chairman of the rural committee around whose villages the town had been built. The members would give advice to the District Officer, who managed the town, its people and their affairs. The concept was put to the Governor's Executive Council, which supported it. The board was given no executive responsibility but was empowered to discuss anything affecting the well-being of the residents and was not precluded from stepping outside purely local concerns. Nothing was ruled out. When their lives were affected they could discuss the shortcomings of the central government, and even, when the time came, the future of Hong Kong. The experiment was successful, and we had taken the first step towards creating a system of representative government. It was infectious. Other advisory boards followed in all eighteen districts of Hong Kong.

In June 1980 the government published proposals entitled 'A Pattern of District Administration in Hong Kong'. This Green Paper noted the introduction of compulsory secondary education, demographic changes and the shift of population to the new towns, and the need for participation in their management.

Until then, Hong Kong had been centrally directed. It was time to 'give closer attention to monitoring the effects and coordination of government programmes at the district level'. A small group of officials, myself included, had met privately with the Chief Secretary, Sir Jack Cater, and recommended adding elected representatives to the boards. This recommendation, too, was accepted by the Governor and Executive Council. For the elections, voters needed only to be resident in Hong Kong for three years and to be over the age of 21. For the time being, 'within the imperative of stability which the special circumstances of Hong Kong require the other arms of government, the Executive and Legislative Councils, would continue to evolve as required by their own particular circumstances'. A journey of a thousand miles begins with the first step.

It was decided, first of all, to elect one-third of the members of the boards in each of the districts of Hong Kong, and when their terms of office expired after three years, to increase this proportion to two-thirds. The remainder of the boards consisted of members appointed by the Governor. These members were drawn from among people in each district who could bring particular knowledge and experience to the work of the boards but were unlikely to participate in public, and possibly political, elections. Although the appointed members were removed as a result of the changes introduced during the governorship of the Rt. Hon. Christopher Patten, their membership was restored by the government of the Special Administrative Region after 1997 and continues to this day. The inclusion of appointed members is generally supported by both the elected members and by community leaders in the districts. It is criticised and condemned by democrats on ideological grounds, but the appointed members bring special knowledge and experience to the work of the boards, which is what counts at the district level. It is a measure of their contribution that some appointed members are even elected to be chairmen of their councils.

While these developments were taking place, younger people representing different sectors of the community were introduced into the Legislative and Executive Councils, but this amounted to nothing more than a stopgap measure. No thought had been given to a situation which would not involve British administration, and hitherto the approach to developing a more representative system had been conducted at a measured, some would say leisurely, pace in keeping with this view of the future.

Changing the system of representation during the course of any discussion with China about the future could only be carried out within the limits of what might be acceptable to China, otherwise discussion would have come to a halt. We were treading on eggshells. I was involved in writing plans for change which could be implemented and explained without dire consequences for the negotiations. Writing them meant writing them alone, because the issues involved against the background of the discussion were so sensitive.

In April 1984 I helped to draft a booklet for public consultation – a Green Paper – on the 'Further Development of Representative Government', which was to be published in 1984, just two months before the agreement with China was signed. In it Hong Kong was to develop a system of government to represent authoritatively the views of, and be accountable to, the people. Hong Kong was to preserve and build on existing institutions and to maintain government by consensus. It would allow for further development. The words used to spell out the government approach to this described the Hong Kong system as follows: 'it operates on the basis of consultation and consensus. It is not a system based on parties, factions and adversarial politics.' It is said that the system had grown up around two separate approaches as to how the people should be represented: first, based on where they lived; second, based on what they did. These were described separately as geographical and functional constituencies. The Green Paper rejected suggestions that direct elections to the central government should be introduced there and then, in the following words: 'direct elections have emerged or been introduced as a standard feature of the governmental system in many countries where they have proved well suited to the society they serve.' It went on, in sublime understatement, 'they have not, however, been universally successful as a means of ensuring stable representative government'. In Hong Kong the preservation of stability and harmony were of paramount importance: 'Direct elections would run the risk of a swift introduction of adversarial politics and would introduce an element of instability at a crucial time.' Direct elections had to wait; these cautious rationalisations also hid the reality of China looking over our shoulder.

Functional constituency members were to be elected to represent organisations and associations whose members – engineers, accountants, doctors, etc. – could contribute their expertise to the work of the Legislative Council. This was a development – an extension – of the policy which the Governor had been following in making appointments to the Legislative Council from among these functional sectors. The system has been attacked and criticised again for its lack of democracy, but it served a useful purpose during a period of change when stability was a major concern. Much of the legislative programme involves technical and financial matters and it is arguable that the presence of these experts is useful when these subjects are being debated.

In order to introduce members representing the place where people lived, it was also proposed that members of the District Boards become an Electoral College to elect members to the Legislative Council, so as to avoid the 'introduction of adversarial politics' at a crucial time.

The Green Paper proposals setting out this approach were generally well received. They filled a communication gap and the majority accepted the need for this gradual approach: 'the need to ensure that the prosperity and stability of Hong Kong are not put at risk by introducing too many constitutional changes too rapidly was widely recognised.' But it ruffled China's feathers. China suspected that there was a hidden meaning hinting at an independent Hong Kong behind the words that had crept into the final version, that the system would be 'firmly rooted in Hong Kong'. This was no more and no less a reflection of the words 'Hong Kong people ruling Hong Kong', and looked at another way, it was a way of saying that there was to be no lingering or hidden control. But were the British up to their tricks again?

There were more mundane matters of public administration to be decided. History had left Hong Kong with unbalanced urban administration and management. Urban growth had centred on the site of the original settlement in 1841 and its extension in 1860 to the Kowloon Peninsula. Until the end of the nineteenth century, rural China surrounded Hong Kong with paddy fields and ancient villages and ringed it about with sparsely populated Chinese islands. The European business and residential districts were well planned and laid out, but the surging population of the Chinese settlement which grew up around the central district was overcrowded, without sanitation and infested with rats. Inevitably, plague put a stop to pretence that it could look after itself. A Sanitary Board was formed and was the embryo from which municipal government grew.

When the New Territories were leased, it was the stated intention of the British Government, apart from providing an umbrella of law and order, to leave them more or less as a settled rural community. It was not thought that there was a need for any form of municipal body, a council, to oversee them and to establish some form of local government. The villages had their representatives, and there was an Advisory Council, the Heung Yee Kuk, for the whole New Territories. District Offices substituted for local authority, and cleansing, sanitation, medical and other services were gradually provided by government departments and extended as the need arose. But there was no overall municipal council with public representation. Indeed, there was a wholly anomalous situation whereby qualified voters living in the New Territories had no council of their own but could vote for the Urban Council of Hong Kong, whose remit was the island of Hong Kong and Kowloon up to the encircling mountains, but nothing beyond them.

New towns had been built with populations of several hundred thousand, and although each town and district now had a management board, there was no coordinating body to provide municipal services. The essential question was whether to extend the Hong Kong Urban Council to the New Territories or to create a special council. Several factors had to be weighed; extension of the Urban Council would have involved fresh elections; each town already had its distinctive features, and as with the post-war Mark Young proposals, an overarching Urban Council would have created, in effect, a powerful Greater Hong Kong Council overpowering a weakling non-elected legislature. The least contentious solution was to create a New Territories Regional Council which avoided all these pitfalls. Time was of the essence. The plan to set up a Regional Council with municipal responsibilities was announced with little fanfare and only token muttering in the spring of 1984.

The people had been told by Chinese leaders that Hong Kong people would be ruling Hong Kong. There were few, if any, firm ideas emerging as to how this would come about. Those of us who were drafting the proposals did not have a free hand. We had to work within the system as it existed and what we did had to be capable of rational and unexciting explanation. It was desirable for it to be published and publicly accepted before the text of the much bigger question of the overall agreement with China about the future was finalised. There were still thirteen years before 1997; the pace of change had to be steady and incremental if it were not to risk intervention by China and put economic prosperity in jeopardy, and it had to maintain a stable political environment.

The White Paper of November 1984 followed the April Green Paper and set out the intention to make a start in 1985. Hong Kong was set on the road to implement the ambiguous words in the agreement with China that the Legislative Council 'would be constituted by elections'. It promised that in 1985, twenty-four members would be elected by functional and residential constituencies, elected members would slightly outnumber those appointed by the Governor, and although there were to be ten official civil servant members, they would be in a minority. In other words, it would be possible for elected representatives to unite to defeat government proposals. The White Paper promised a review in 1988. The events surrounding this review are described in chapter 20.

14

Behind the Headlines

The rubric 'positive non-intervention' is much used to describe Hong Kong's economic philosophy. It came from Sir Philip Haddon-Cave, Hong Kong's Financial Secretary from 1971 to 1981. However, it is forgotten by those who parrot it that Haddon-Cave qualified his words with the caveat that in times of dire necessity, the rule should not put the economy in a straitjacket. Each year his annual budget address to the Legislative Council had us shifting wearily in our seats for between three and four hours as he justified with labyrinthine analysis the short-term and long-term aspects of government finances and prospects for the economy. But Sir Philip was far from being a dull man; alongside his keen intellect, acid tongue, impatience with ineptitude and firm control of our finances dwelt a lively sense of humour and the spirit of a bon viveur.

But the philosophy of encouraging private initiative and investment to which his rubric alluded was deeply embedded in the culture of Hong Kong. From the beginning of settlement in the nineteenth century, Hong Kong's transport system, its buses, trams and ferries were organised and funded by private subscription; so, too, were its electricity, gas and telephone services. The government's role was to provide an infrastructure of roads, drains and water supply, law and order and the regulatory framework in which business could operate; and to collect sufficient taxes, fees and charges to pay for it all. Schools and hospitals were largely sponsored by community organisations and religious bodies, and were subvented by the government which tried, as far as possible, not to become involved in management. Intervention took place when there was an outbreak of plague or some such cruel reminder to the government to rouse itself as, for example, when it provided housing when fires burned down the squatter settlements of refugees from the civil war in China. Otherwise the government tried, without picking winners, to stimulate and create the conditions in which entrepreneurs could flourish.

Hong Kong society in the years after the Pacific War changed profoundly and became more travelled and worldly wise. In each of the districts into which Hong Kong as a whole was divided there was a sports organisation and an arts association, and youth groups were expanding. Funds were raised for squash courts, football pitches and swimming pools, and the Jockey Club, from its charity fund, built concert halls. Ballet classes took hold and district Chinese orchestras were formed. From skills learned at the Outward Bound Training School, mountaineering, canoeing and sailing became new leisure activities for Hong Kong's young people. Tens of thousands of Hong Kong's students were being educated in schools and universities overseas. Hong Kong was becoming more cosmopolitan and more international in outlook.

While on holiday in the summer of 1980, sitting on boulders in the clear air of the mountains in Kashmir, Jane and I thought about the housewives in our new towns living in tiny high-rise flats, sometimes twenty or thirty storeys above the ground, looking after their children far from their ancestral villages, old friends and neighbours. Back in Hong Kong I gathered together a group of young women from the housing estates, university lecturers, and so forth, to discover whether there was a need for an organisation similar to the Women's Institutes or Townswomen's Guilds of the United Kingdom, which would provide a social nexus for the women from the housing estates. There was little argument about the need, the only question was when. In about a month the first organisation was formed. Others followed and are still working successfully today, bringing new skills and interests and new friendships into the lives of these high-rise housebound wives.

Island House, where we lived from 1973 until 1985, was a perfect setting in which to uncover and stimulate these energies for change. The great trees which flanked the lawn, the strange house with its light tower, the terrace looking eastward down the harbour with its fringe of velvet green ridged hills fading into distant blue, all these created a special atmosphere conducive to loosening inhibitions, putting present anxieties behind and thinking about the future. Meeting after meeting took place there, and every so often the Governor would come, in shirtsleeves, to join in discussions about current problems and the future. These were evenings which inevitably sparked off discussion about political development in Hong Kong, questions of the future, and what was happening across the border in Guangdong.

Overseas visitors, Members of Parliament, Ministers and members of the Royal Family included Island House in their itinerary of visiting the new towns. The Young Fabians, led by Baroness Eirene White, were somewhat discomfited to discover that we were doing so much without a political creed and without a heavy tax burden. A surging economy, low rate of tax, no subsidy for public utilities and a 'consumer pays' principle enabled Hong Kong to provide many of the benefits of socialism within a capitalist economy. Education and medical services were cheap and available to all, and a non-contributory social service safety net was part of the system we took for granted, together with cheap housing for half the population. We had a Fabian connection in my brother-in-law, Dr R. S. Pease, whose grandfather had been one of the founders of the movement, and we were able to remind them of their motto, 'Pray devoutly, hammer stoutly', which might have been used to describe Hong Kong. These were occasions at which I tried to dispel the pejorative laissez-faire 'anything goes' label we had acquired over the years, by describing the positive and progressive social policies of the government.

After the opening of China to the outside world in 1978, visitors from the mainland were added to our guests. These were lunch parties at which conversation flowed freely and interestingly. It was a life of great variety. In a single week in September 1980, Timothy Raison, Minister for Home Affairs, came to lunch, followed by a group of nuclear physicists who were on their way to the South-Western Physics Institute in China; the Provost of Worcester College, Oxford, Lord Asa Briggs, came to find out what was happening in Hong Kong; Members of Parliament from Westminster came to see what was being done – but talked mainly about their own work in Britain!; commissioners and leaders of the Guides and Scouts joined in a social barbecue; and the week was rounded off with a tea party for a troupe of Hong Kong girl folk dancers who had been a hit in London.

Gurkha battalions were stationed in a number of permanent barracks in the northern New Territories, and since the Sha Tau Kok incident in 1967, when they had relieved the Hong Kong police from their border duties, they had been guarding and patrolling the border against illegal immigration. By the eighties the tanks which used to roar, rattle and screech their way to the firing range through the streets of Yuen Long were gone. Gone, too, were the artillery which frightened motorists out of their wits as they practised their shooting from firing points close to the main road.

The civil administration enjoyed the added dimension to their lives and work provided by the army who were ready, as part of their training, to help with community projects, in floods and typhoons and in building roads. All enjoyed their warm hospitality at mess dinners on ceremonial occasions. On Tuesday, 28 October 1980 a dinner was held at Government House for the departing Second Battalion 2nd King Edward VII's Own Goorkhas, the Sirmoor Rifles. This was a grand occasion at which, after dinner, the champion piper of the Queen's Own Highland Regiment strode piping behind the seated diners, to the bewilderment of the Chinese guests unfamiliar with this tribal ritual.

Lieutenant Colonel Jackman, Commandant of a battalion of the Sirmoor Rifles, wrote me a letter dated 2 September 1980 which reveals, from personal experience, the extent of the contribution the battalions made during the time when the border was under pressure from illegal immigration, particularly during the period at the end of the seventies and early eighties before the border fence had been built into a formidable barrier. In his own moving words he tells part of the proud history of the battalion, the historic significance of the day they left the border with bugles playing, the cooperation between all of us who worked in the New Territories at that time, and the surge of illegal immigrants struggling to reach home base in Hong Kong:

> Since the Battalion's return to Hong Kong from the UK in April 1977, 3 1/2 years or forty months ago, it has spent 20 months on anti-illegal immigration operations. In the last 16 months alone 13 months have been spent on these operations. The Battalion has apprehended 18,000 illegal immigrants, with 17,000 being arrested in the last 16 months. Five awards for bravery have been received and one soldier has died on operations.
>
> On 14 September 1980 the Battalion will come off the frontier for the last time before it moves to Brunei in November for two years of duty there.
>
> 14 September is a significant day for 2nd Goorkhas for it was on this day in 1857, during the Indian Mutiny, that the Regiment was finally relieved after holding the main piquet on Delhi ridge for over three months. During that time 327 men were killed or wounded out of a total strength of 490, including 8 out of 9 British Officers. They were the highest casualties of any Regiment or Corps engaged in Delhi. To this day the Regiment celebrates Delhi Day on 14 September every year.
>
> In the Days of the Raj when the Regiment returned from operations on the North-West frontier of India, it was customary for us to march home from the nearest railway station to our lines to the accompaniment of drums and bugles – there being no band in those days. It seems most fitting therefore that we should celebrate Delhi Day this year, and mark our relinquishment of Border duties, by marching from Lok Ma Chau, the western end of the Frontier, into our lines at Cassino to the accompaniment of our bugles.

These touching words more than ever recall the contribution made to the life of Hong Kong, particularly the New Territories where we spent so many years of our lives, by the officers and men of the British Forces, during the great changes that were taking place and the challenges that were being faced between the end of the Pacific War and reunification.

15

Xiamen

Our first visit to China had taken place in 1973. Later, in the seventies, I visited the fast-developing city of Shenzhen, on the other side of the river from Hong Kong, and accompanied the Hong Kong soccer team to Guangzhou for the inaugural football match of what was to become an annual event. The match took on a greater significance as it marked the return to normalisation of relations between the ordinary people of Hong Kong and the rest of Guangdong. The mostly male spectators packed the stadium wearing the blue jacket and caps of the past, all smoking so heavily that the still air of the stadium filled with a pall of blue smoke.

When travel to China became almost commonplace in the years following 1978 and the opening of China, almost alone among senior government officials, my wife and I took the opportunity to travel there as often as we could. I include accounts of some of these visits in order to paint a picture of the changes taking place in China and to put events and changes in Hong Kong in their wider context, and to show that the two places had begun to move closer together well before the conclusion of the agreement with China about Hong Kong's future.

The economic reform programme, and the opening to the world of opportunities for investment in China as part of the reforms, meant that in 1982 we were able to visit Fujian province, home of the Hokkien dialect which I had spent two years, nearly thirty years previously, learning under the whirling fans at the Chan family ancestral hall in Kuala Lumpur. Our companions on the journey had been born and brought up in Fujian many years before and were returning home for the first time. It was as though I, too, were going home, so deeply incised in my memory were the descriptions of Xiamen I had learned by rote, and so thoroughly had I been steeped in the language and lives of my teachers.

Fujian is isolated from the rest of China by mountain ranges through which runs a single-track railway line. Partly because of this isolation, its spoken dialect has developed differently from the rest of China, and within Fujian province itself the language of the capital, Fuzhou, is different again from the rest of the province. The Fujianese are a proud, separate and determined people, fine-tuned by isolation and hardship. As we arrived in Fuzhou, the provincial capital, we were taken to visit Yung Quan Si, a Buddhist monastery on Wu Shan overlooking the town. The road looped up the mountain through the trees, where here and there, seeking the sunlight, wild white roses, red azaleas and purple rhododendrons skirted the way. It was the time for family groups with their baskets of offerings slowly to wend their way up the slope to their family graves. Passing them, we went on higher into an ancient forest of moss-covered trees to a temple rising up the slope on platforms, with dusty-red, pillared cloisters and yellow roofs against the green of the forest. Flagged paths led to far pavilions and great boulders laid bare by the stream were deeply inscribed with the thoughts and remembered poetry of travellers and worshippers. On one huge stone a single ideogram for Buddha the Enlightened One covered the surface, deeply carved and picked out in red so that it stood in three dimensions, making its dramatic statement.

At dinner that evening the Vice Governor stressed the importance of improving the transport infrastructure and about the work going on to develop the ports and airports at Fuzhou and Xiamen, and spoke surprisingly openly at that early date, in 1982, about the role of Hong Kong in improving relations with Taiwan just across the straits from Fujian.

From Fuzhou a steam train took us up the valley of the brown Mang River to An Ping, passing villages with tamped mud and wooden walls beneath dark-tiled, curved roofs. At An Ping, while we loaded up the cars to take us to Wu I mountain, a small crowd collected to catch a glimpse of these curious arrivals from another world: one of our friends had a striped suit, my wife had auburn hair, and a third had silver-painted toenails and curly hair.

We were whisked away, hurtling through the countryside, horn blowing, scattering pigs and chickens and swerving dangerously past growling and obstinate timber lorries. In the river beside the road, a raft of logs was being poled slowly down with the current, against an enduring background of rice fields and small conical mountains.

After a night on hard boards we were up early the next morning to the loud, scratchy, recorded broadcast of revolutionary songs which acted as the muezzin call to work in the communes. Breakfast was in the great barn of the commune with its peeling walls. The peasants, ready for the day's work, sat at round tables with a continuous fixed bench, bent low, slurping great bowls of noodles. We ate more sedately of rice gruel, egg cake, preserved cabbage and 'wool' made from slowly frying pork which is stirred until it breaks into fibres. Outside, to our surprise, the public wall newspapers in their glass cases announced the resignation of Lord Carrington as Foreign Minister. News of the Falklands War had reached furthest Fujian!

Breakfast over, we were off in the sunshine to climb and stroll around the great stone cliffs of Wu I. Far down below, the waters of the winding river were blue and green, bordered by the brilliant spring leaves of neatly coiffed tea bushes. We rode on bamboo rafts with curled bows, and were poled through rapids and across deep clear pools. We walked ancient stone paths, past statues lying in the grass waiting for restoration and through terraced tea gardens, and wondered at boat burials hundreds of feet above us in a carved-out hollow in the cliffs.

While Fuzhou is the capital city of the province, the former treaty port of Amoy (E-mng in Hokkien and Xiamen in Putonghua), because of its deeper water and its road connections to Guangdong, has overtaken Fuzhou commercially and as an attraction for investment. In 1982 it was quickening to the call of economic reform. Many shops were still boarded, there were few vehicles on the street and the predominant colours were blue and grey, but down at the airport it was a different scene. Hundreds of workers were working with rudimentary equipment, picks, shovels and wheelbarrows, building for the future, to make Xiamen one of the show places among the coastal cities.

No one should leave Xiamen without crossing by ferry over the mile or so of water to Gulangyu, a humped island lying across the front of the main town, home in imperial times to the treaty port officials, the customs officers, the consuls and the rich, retired sugar, rubber and tin merchants from South-East Asia. We strolled past the burnt remains of the British Consulate and the foreign cemetery with its gravestones broken during the angry emotions of the Cultural Revolution. We peered past the pillars into the empty shell of a tycoon's house, surrounded by other houses where his wives had lived; the billiard table was still there with torn baize, an ancient Hoover was propped against a wall, and the marble statues still stood on the newel post. We could almost hear the tinkle of champagne glasses and the cocktail chatter of earlier days. We found the houses in which our friends and companions had spent their childhood, and perhaps we passed the bungalow in which our Governor, Sir Murray MacLehose, had lived before the war, while learning Hokkien.

Ours was a memorable visit. We were fortunate to be able to see this world at an early stage in the process of change and modernisation and, from what we had seen and the frank conversations we had had, to come away reassured about the reforms taking place in China and by extension, Hong Kong's own future, heavily dependent as it was upon China's stability and its opening to the world outside. We had had an opportunity to talk with provincial leaders, to see life in the countryside, to witness the construction of new roads, and to walk and talk among the ordinary people. It was many years yet before reunification, but here were the visible signs of the China to which Hong Kong was to be restored. China seemed set on a path of reform and change in the lives of its people from which there would be no turning back.

This visit was also important for me personally because it meant that when I later took part as a member of Hong Kong's Executive Council in the negotiations about Hong Kong's future, I did so with more confidence in the eventual outcome than those who had not had an opportunity to see China at first hand. It was an outcome which, having seen what we had seen, we could now contemplate with more confidence.

In 1982 I believe it is fair to say that there was a still a good deal of scepticism about the reforms and changes taking place in China. I shall never forget how, in one of our visits to Hangzhou, we stood and toasted noisily with local leaders who said of the Cultural Revolution, 'It will never happen again!' People in Hong Kong, however, many of whom had lived through the early days of the People's Republic, had a less sanguine perspective. The view of Hong Kong's future seen from the West and also by doubters in Hong Kong was that it was going to be 'taken over' by the communists and that the People's Liberation Army would come marching in.

This visit to Fujian was the first of many visits to China with our Chinese friends during the following years. We flew to the far north-east to Jilin province and visited the corner of China where the borders of China, North Korea and Russia meet. We travelled in a minibus for thirteen days along the Silk Road from Lanzhou to Kashgar and later from Lanzhou down through Sichuan to Chengdu. We visited the former British naval base at Weihaiwei and paid our respects to the grave of Confucius at Chufu. We stood on the summit of many mountains and saw the scenery which has made China famous, Gweilin, Huangshan, Taishan, Ermeishan, and the mountain ridges at Jinggongshan where China's leaders had planned the Long March. And of course we watched Shanghai and the towns and cities around it become transformed from the dim-lit grey buildings of the past into the modern world.

16

The Beginning of Negotiations

*T*he departure and arrival of Governors are punctuation marks in the life of a colony; you are never quite sure what the next man will be like. There is certain to be a change of style, and no Governor is like another. Just as in elected governments, the civil servants provide continuity and for better or worse put a brake on revolutionary change; and perhaps what is more important, they provide a collective memory, an invaluable aid when contemplating dramatic changes in policy. Each of Hong Kong's Governors, and now Hong Kong's Chief Executive, could not have been more different from one another. After ten years with Sir Murray MacLehose, in 1982 Hong Kong was due for a change.

Sir Murray had arrived in 1972 when Hong Kong had not fully recovered from the direct challenge of the disturbances of the Cultural Revolution. Government House had been beset by rioting mobs waving the red book of Mao's thoughts and the Governor had been abused by demonstrators. Confidence had drained away, and though citizens voiced their support for the colonial government, there is no doubt that Hong Kong had been made rudely aware of the looming presence of China.

By 1972, although the turmoil in China which had begun in 1966 was continuing, Hong Kong gave a great sigh of relief when immediate danger seemed to have passed. The stock market, which had been held in check, boomed. Released from fear, housewives, amahs, professional people, clerks and civil servants were caught up in investment fever. Inevitably, the balloon burst as quickly as it inflated, leaving luckless investors to pick up the pieces. It was a restless time, full of anxiety, directionless. Sir Murray, coming to Hong Kong, gave it a rudder and steered an unwavering course through years that were difficult, not only for Hong Kong, but more widely for the world economy. This was particularly so during the crisis in the mid-seventies brought on by escalating oil prices, when Hong Kong chartered a monster oil tanker to hold some oil in reserve and tried without success to think of ways and means to deal with the problem of growing unemployment. Here the bosses and their workers cooperated to share the work out rather than have their co-workers laid off. But all in all Sir Murray's programmes of reform helped Hong Kong weather these storms and brought stability, prosperity and, above all, pride to the people at their achievement

Ten years had passed, and it was time to leave. After weeks of farewell visits, speeches, lunches and dinners and at the climax of departure, Sir Murray was taken ill. He recovered surprisingly quickly and after a splendid send-off display by massed bands, parading troops and dancing children, he shook hands with the members of his councils at the Queen's Pier, crossed the harbour in his launch and quietly departed.

Sir Edward Youde, a distinguished diplomat and scholar, who each morning first read the Chinese papers, had been British Ambassador in Beijing. He was quiet, patient and unwavering, kind, considerate and humorous, and, second to his family and his work, liked nothing more than to retreat to the rewarding solitude of Hong Kong's wetland bird sanctuary. He took over at a time when the government machine was running smoothly and the economy prospering. Sir Murray's visits to China had broken the ice with Chinese officials. The subject of 1997 was no longer taboo. All thoughts were now on how to engage China in serious discussion.

Sir Edward and Pamela, his wife, also a Chinese scholar, arrived on a fine windy day on 20 May 1982. From the beginning, their warm friendliness impressed the media, those they met at the airport and all involved in the welcoming ceremonies. They stood on the foredeck of the *Lady Maurine*, the Governor's launch, a miniature royal yacht, small, white and immaculate as she made her way slowly across the harbour with bands playing, fireboats spraying their fountains, and helicopters trailing red, white and blue smoke.

As they neared the Queen's Pier a playful wind blew the launch away from the landing, and the waiting guests twice readied and relaxed, but finally the new Governor, in starched white, plumed hat and sword, stepped confidently ashore. As he walked along the lines of assembled councillors and reviewed the Gurkha troops, while guns boomed out their royal greeting, he gave no sign that, some time earlier, the screw holding the feathers had somehow come loose and had been boring into his sparsely covered scalp!

The members of Executive Council, in morning dress, and the Chief Justice, in breeches, ruffs and scarlet, were assembled in a semicircle on the red-carpeted stage of the City Hall for the oaths of office, the speech of welcome from the Chief Secretary, Sir Philip Haddon-Cave, and the Governor's address. Sir Edward spoke of the future with the following words:

'It is not surprising, given the circumstances of the lease, that this issue should now be raised. I believe there are good grounds for confidence and that the omens are good. The commitment of Her Majesty's Government to Hong Kong and the interests of its people remains firm. The relationship with the People's Republic of China on which so much depends, has never been more cordial.'

He went on to say that there was: 'a common recognition of the vital importance of the continued prosperity and stability of the Territory and a common wish to preserve them.'

These measured words put the people of Hong Kong on notice that the issue of the lease was something that had to be addressed. His words did not raise false hopes, but alluded to the meetings and visits which, after thirty years, had broken the silence of Hong Kong's relationship with the mainland and echoed the view, shared with the Chinese government, that stability and prosperity were all-important. As we were to tire of hearing over the next few years, his address implied, in Deng Xiaoping's words, 'Tell your businessmen to put their hearts at ease and not to worry.'

I had been appointed a member of the Governor's Executive Council in 1978 and so became one of the cabinet of advisors to the new Governor. Some years previously, as Secretary for the New Territories, I had met Sir Edward Youde when, while British Ambassador to China, he paid a private visit to Hong Kong. We had travelled by boat from the harbour to Castle Peak, passing the container port and the new town of Tsuen Wan, to yet another new town, Tuen Mun or 'fortress gate', which was being built around a long established settlement with many hundred years of history.

We had driven up a steep track through pine trees to a vantage point beside an ancient temple overlooking the new town, passing under the arch where Sir Cecil Clementi, Governor in the 1920s, had inscribed a salutation. Sir Edward saw the new town and also caught a glimpse of historic Hong Kong, and could see that, although we were busy expanding and developing, there were deeper currents to be recognised and respected. The temple was itself a reflection of two beliefs, Taoist and Buddhist, with the buildings interlocked, and not surprisingly, it was the source of an insoluble dispute between the trustees of the two parts who were struggling to obtain title to the valuable lands owned by the monastery and needed for development. The monastery, beneath the branches of a great banyan tree and protected by giant boulders, had seen better days, but was redolent of an age when, high up the side of the Castle Peak, it kept watch over the small market town and the fishing fleet at shelter in the bay.

We went on to visit the village of Sha Tau Kok at the eastern end of the boundary where the colony and mainland China met in the middle of the street and where, in 1967, militia had opened fire on the Hong Kong police post. In Sha Tau Kok you entered the world of unchanged China, decaying shops lined the road to the pier with their pots and pans, bamboo brooms, hard, dried shrimps and strings of withered, salted fish, rice in great sacks and numerous beans. We travelled out on a police launch to a small island busy with the week-long rituals of ten-year propitiation ceremonies. Vegetarian food is eaten and there are continuous hours of exhausting prayer ceremonies which have never been fully explained.

On this early visit the man who was eventually to become our Governor already had seen the container port, being entirely developed by private enterprise companies who were quick to perceive the revolution that was taking place in transport by sea. Within months, areas of the sea had been sold, filled and piled, and a port for the new ships built. Sir Edward had seen the giant cranes which within a few years were to develop Hong Kong into one of the greatest ports in the world, ready to deal with the demand placed on it by the explosive economy of southern China. He had seen a new town from the steps of an ancient monastery; he had walked carefully down the Hong Kong side of the street in view of the border defence soldiers of China; he had seen the serene beauty of the eastern coast, with its emerald islands, clear water, and distant blue mountains; and he had witnessed the solemnity, the ancient ritual and the joyful expectation which are part of a successful propitiation of innumerable gods. It was a useful preparation for his appointment as Governor.

Sir Edward Youde administered calmly and quietly, reading his papers and files, talking to many people and visiting widely to see for himself the housing estates, squatter villages, and factories, as well as his departments of government. Throughout his tenure, and despite the pressure of negotiations about the future, he continued to do this unobtrusively. As the years passed, his unremitting work and travel and his quiet friendliness worked its way deep into the affections of a people who take their time to make up their minds about a person and build up their assessment of his character episode by episode.

At the behest of his predecessor, McKinsey Management Consultants in 1973 had put their stamp on the government machine, dividing the administration into policy branches and striving for a clear separation between the ivory tower of policy and the departments in the trenches. In practice the separation was blurred, and from the start did not fully take into account the existence of literally hundreds of government advisory bodies where policy issues received their first airing. As the years passed, working relationships had to be adjusted to new requirements, the growth of government, physical and political development, the expanding population, and the emergence of care for the environment. And gradually the changes brought about by McKinsey were eroded. Despite this, Sir Edward inherited a well-oiled and responsive civil service.

Another million people had been added to the population during Sir Murray's ten-year term as Governor and six new towns were in varying stages of development. District Boards had been formed and elections were in the offing. The members of the Legislative Council, although still appointed by the Governor, were now a more representative reflection of the various aspects of the life of the community and of its social structure.

Sir Edward had arrived in Hong Kong when the question of the future was at the top of the agenda of Executive Council, and there it stayed until his tragic death in 1986. The decision by Sir Murray, with Foreign Office agreement, to raise the question of the shortening term of New Territories lease and of downstream property leases has been much debated and criticised. This criticism borders on the absurd. How long could Hong Kong go on pouring money into the development of the New Territories without knowing what would happen when the lease expired? Although Sir Murray's suggestions had been met with a negative response in China, they had raised at the highest level of the government of China the looming and serious practical problem of the shortening lease. It was disappointing, but inevitable, that Sir Murray's suggestion that this problem could be solved by administrative measures taken in Hong Kong carried with it the implication that the British were proposing a course of action which would have blurred the question of sovereignty and the return of Hong Kong to China. But it was worth a try, and to have put forward more radical solutions straight away would have resulted in even more criticism.

Sir Murray's repetition to investors on his return to Hong Kong of Deng Xiaoping's phrase 'put their hearts at ease and not to worry' did exactly the reverse, and served only to fuel the fires of speculation. Doubt and uncertainty continued. The months and years passed and it was not long before even casual conversations on the street turned to the question of the future, 'What do you think is going to happen?' The nine-point plan China had offered to Taiwan in 1981 had been brought up again as a way forward during the visit to China by Humphrey Atkins in the spring of 1982 in preparation for the autumn visit of the Prime Minister, Margaret Thatcher. Although there was no spontaneous reaction to this suggestion at that time, for those who had ears to hear, the idea that the British should study the plans for Taiwan gave the British government something to think about. China was also telling its frequent visitors from Hong Kong that Hong Kong could enjoy the measures held out to Taiwan, retaining a high degree of autonomy and keeping its economic and other systems intact. It would not have to follow the socialist policies of the mainland or local communist party leadership. As Deng Xiaoping had said, it would be 'one country, two systems'. It was at this point, with the long-awaited visit by Mrs Thatcher to Beijing just a few months away, that Sir Edward Youde took over the reins in Hong Kong.

Expansion of teenage education, changes taking place in the economy, increasing sophistication and exposure to the world brought about not only by travel but by the ever-increasing number of students returning from overseas, were changing Hong Kong. There was a large gap between the number of elite schools and the number of children seeking places in them. Year after year many thousands of young people went for education overseas, to the United Kingdom, Canada, the USA and Australia, and many returned, adding to an increasing political awareness. Some of those who returned formed a group called 'The Observers', whose views were published in thought-provoking articles in the *South China Morning Post* and were in the vanguard of subsequent political debate.

Millions were travelling to mainland China. Imperceptibly and with increasing momentum, Hong Kong and China were becoming more interdependent. My notes record visits and lunches at Island House for visiting delegations of high officials, deputy governors from our neighbouring provinces of Guangdong and Fujian, and a very enjoyable lunch with a delegation in 1981 led by Wang Daohan, then the charming and lively mayor of Shanghai, who, as I write, is People's Republic representative on ARATS, the Association for Relations across the Taiwan Straits .

More of Hong Kong's people, too, because of the changes taking place within China, were beginning to be less apprehensive at the thought of eventual reunification with the mainland. To some this was a welcome rediscovery of patriotism and identity, while others were nervous but already sensed the inevitable conclusion that there was going to be an end to British administration; yet others sought a guarantee of a safe haven, which forced husbands and wives to separate in order to acquire foreign residency. There were few, if any, heretical voices calling on the British to stay. Some were later to accuse Britain of deserting Hong Kong, but these accusations turned rather on the withdrawal of their British resident status than the eventual reunification with China and the expunging of what was, to the Chinese, the degrading nineteenth-century surrender of national territory.

In retrospect it may seem to have been completely unrealistic, but at the time it was inevitable that Whitehall, Westminster, Government House and the members of Executive Council should argue for the retention of British administration. While acknowledging Chinese sovereignty Executive Council had the lives of five million people to worry about and could not let go lightly a government and administration that they knew well, without having a clear idea of what would replace it. While understandable, this caused the Chinese members of the Executive Council to be castigated for being unpatriotic. But remember the year — it was during the Cold War and the world was divided into two camps separated by curtains of iron and bamboo. Nothing comparable to the return of Hong Kong to a communist country had occurred in history. This was the starting point of negotiation, not the righting of the wrongs of history. There was world opinion and the mind-set of the media to consider. A retreat to the ceded territory of Hong Kong and Kowloon, a kind of 'fortress' Hong Kong, was even considered for a time. This absurd idea came from minds ignorant of the fact that the boundary between the ceded territory and the territory leased in 1898 ran through the middle of Kowloon and that more than a million people lived on the other side of Boundary Street, and that the lifeline, the airport, conveniently situated in Kowloon, was actually in the territory whose lease would expire in 1997. So, too, were power stations, reservoirs and the container port.

Hong Kong did not stop work while the diplomatic storm clouds gathered. In 1982 the first part of the railway to the border was electrified, creating a new, fast suburban train service, and the Mass Transit Railway, Hong Kong's underground, was connected to the new town of Tsuen Wan. Behind our house the level crossing of the railway had been replaced by a new road bridge and the first tower blocks of the new town of Tai Po were appearing over our treetops. Great projects to improve the infrastructure and build housing, offices and factories were being advanced, no matter what was going on the political front. Here was no sign of an administration running down but rather a quickening of the pace of change and development. Hong Kong was lucky that during this period of drawn-out negotiations about its future, it enjoyed a period of sustained economic growth; the government coffers were full and it was able to invest in these reassuring developments, thereby creating a feeling of 'business as usual' in the midst of extremely serious political concerns.

On our island a tailor bird was weaving its nest from a hibiscus leaf, a white-eye was building its tiny cup in the apricot tree, the orioles had returned from their southern migration, herons and egrets plundered the foreshore and a cheeky kingfisher dived into the swimming pool. At an international festival, choirs from Finland, Iceland, Puerto Rico, the Philippines and our own Children's Choir sang their hearts out.

Soon after his arrival, on 26 June 1982, the Governor and Lady Youde came to supper at our Island House to meet a group of young people who were moving ahead. Guests included Christine Loh, who was to become a Legislative Councillor, Anna Wu, who was to become a Legislative Councillor and later chairperson of the Equal Opportunities Commission, Margaret Ng, who became a barrister and was later to represent the Legal Functional Constituency in the Legislative Council, Andrew Li, who became Chief Justice in 1996, and so on. This was one of many relaxed evenings at Island House for the Governor to meet young people. They spoke, without mincing words, of their hopes and fears for Hong Kong in the weeks leading to Mrs Thatcher's visit to China and before negotiations which were to decide our future were to begin in earnest.

These evenings had begun ten years before during the MacLehose era and were to continue for several more years, the last taking place shortly after the arrival of the last Governor, Christopher Patten. Conversation was uninhibited and private and in no instance was confidence breached. They gave the Governor a useful insight into the thoughts and worries for the future of a group of intelligent, articulate young people, and when he returned to his desk, helped him shape his own search for a solution, knowing that it would either command support or fail for the lack of it. In the years of negotiation with China which followed, these get-togethers became increasingly important. As the drama unfolded it was essential to listen to particular worries and opinions and to the reactions to information being relayed by Chinese officials to visitors to Beijing.

Sir Edward Youde joined the British officials who accompanied Mrs Thatcher into the Great Hall of the People on 24 September 1982. The main purpose of this meeting was to get agreement to start negotiations, and this was achieved, although some months then passed before meetings began. The high ceilings, huge pillars, great austere spaces for greeting, and vast meeting rooms each assigned and decorated in the style of one of China's provinces, are awesome. Chairs are arranged to reflect the gravity of meetings so that the principal speakers have to talk uncomfortably sideways to one another with the interpreters sitting behind, which does not put visitors at ease for a cosy chat but rather resembles a set-piece with the others in attendance silently facing one another in a horseshoe shape.

For the British Prime Minister this was a discussion about sovereignty and administration. For the Chinese there was never any question about the recovery of sovereignty. This had already been said many times to many people and was even said again by the Prime Minister Zhao Ziyang to the press assembled on the route into the meeting room. However, MrsThatcher emphasised, in Beijing and in a later press conference in

Hong Kong, the validity of the treaties ceding Hong Kong and Kowloon and leasing the New Territories. This rubbed salt in the wounds by, in the words of the Chinese, 'providing ironclad proof of the nature of British imperialism in the nineteenth century'. For China and for Chinese everywhere, the Hong Kong treaties were a symbol of China's weakened state during the alien and faltering Manchu dynasty. This was now a new, confident, strong China dealing with imperialist concessions extracted from the Manchus who, centuries before, had positioned their officials throughout China speaking and writing a different language much as our colonial officials did! The recovery of sovereignty was a sacred mission, and to continue to allow foreigners to govern a part of China was abhorrent. The lines were drawn for the negotiations which were to follow.

After visiting China and before her press conference in Hong Kong, the Prime Minister met with the official members of Executive Council. We were told the negative outcome of her discussion with Deng Xiaoping. The problem now facing us was to persuade Chinese leaders that Hong Kong's prosperity and the confidence of the international community rested on British law and administration, and that the ultimate authority for this came from the British parliament. At that early stage we were not visionary or trusting enough to think of a solution which would keep the systems intact, the civil service working as before, the Common Law in operation with our own Court of Final Appeal, and membership of international organisations continuing. That came later, after a long slog of two years' negotiation.

Throughout these years, Executive Council was fully informed about the negotiations, which otherwise were a closely guarded secret. Instead of the weekly Tuesday morning meetings, the agenda of Executive Council was divided into two. On Tuesdays, the ordinary business of Hong Kong was dealt with and on Wednesdays, the future. Towards the end of the period, with the approach of the deadline of September 1984 given to the negotiators by Deng himself for bringing an end to discussion, Executive Council met daily, a special room being set aside so that we could read sensitive papers in complete security.

Much has been written about the twists and turns of the negotiations themselves. There is not much more to be said. The two years between the arrival of Sir Edward Youde as Governor and the initialling of the Joint Declaration divide into two. The first year was spent defending a position unacceptable, at the very outset, to the Chinese government. This led to a hiatus in the autumn of 1983 and to the solution to the impasse put forward by Sir Percy Cradock.

Negotiations were getting nowhere. Hong Kong knew from visitors to Beijing, articles in the press and talks with Chinese officials in Hong Kong that British obduracy was the stumbling block. It was a time of great anxiety and crisis. There was a run on the Hong Kong dollar and panic buying in the supermarkets. Hong Kong's Financial Secretary, Sir John Bremridge, in New York for a meeting of the International Monetary Fund, was, as luck would have it, on a launch preparing to watch the America's Cup when the news came recalling him to Hong Kong. He had spoken out strongly against a fixed exchange rate and embarrassingly did so at the airport on his return to Hong Kong, not knowing that while he had been away other officials in Hong Kong had agreed to a plan to do just that put forward by John Greenwood, an economist with the GT fund management group. Subsequently, at meetings between the Prime Minister and Bank of England officials in Washington and after a visit by officials to Hong Kong in 1983, the Hong Kong dollar was linked to the US dollar and continues to be linked to this day.

The run on the dollar brought home just how fragile confidence was and, although the currency was stabilised, people were not. They were tired and anxious and wanted an end to waiting. It was soon to come.

17

Negotiations Concluded, 1983–1985

I n December 1983 the Governor and Executive Councillors travelled to London without his officials for an urgent meeting with the Prime Minister, Mrs Thatcher, Foreign Secretary Sir Geoffrey Howe, Sir Percy Cradock, and other ministers and officials, to discuss the impasse the negotiations about the future had reached.

Time was running out. In September 1984, if no agreement were reached, China's own twenty-point plan for Hong Kong, which had already been published, would be implemented. The twenty points were seductive but contained nothing on the detail of Hong Kong's legal system and governance, its economy and social system, and no guarantees that the twenty points would materialise and that Hong Kong's way of life would be maintained. At this point, Sir Percy Cradock supplied the intuition, the imagination, and the words to bridge the gap between the two sides.

Sir Percy had returned to London from being Ambassador in Beijing to become Mrs Thatcher's foreign policy adviser, and it was he who supplied the formula which was to break the deadlock and to lead to agreement. His proposal was to take the Chinese proposals, the twenty points, and other statements which had been made and to see whether, using them as a base, a solid structure could be built which would ensure continuing autonomy, freedom, stability and prosperity for Hong Kong. If this could be done the Prime Minister would be willing to recommend to Parliament the transfer of sovereignty to China and the accompanying arrangements for the administration of Hong Kong by China. On this basis down-to-earth negotiations began.

As we entered 1984 there were only nine months in which to put together the detailed description of Hong Kong's government and way of life, with the solid backing of a legal system and administration to preserve it. This was required if any agreement was to survive and be acceptable to Hong Kong people and world opinion.

Sir Edward Youde worked tirelessly, making visit after visit to Beijing and when necessary to London, as a member of a negotiating team led by the British Ambassador to China, Sir Richard Evans, who had replaced Sir Percy as Ambassador. Another team worked in Hong Kong and later in Beijing, sending papers backwards and forwards between the Hong Kong and Macao office of the Ministry for Foreign Affairs, Executive Council in Hong Kong, and the Foreign Office in London.

Against this edgy background there was an unexpected diversion. Unmindful of the touchiness of taxi drivers to anything affecting their livelihood, the government gazetted legislation to increase taxi registration and licensing charges. Taxi drivers have a hard life; their shifts are long, their nerves stretched and rewards meagre. Hearing about the legislation, they reacted forcefully and predictably, encouraged, no doubt, by having seen on television a few months previously how effectively French lorry drivers and farmers succeeded in holding their government to ransom by blocking roads. Since they were already on the streets, the drivers parked their cabs at busy intersections in Kowloon, bringing traffic to a halt. Kowloon was gridlocked. On 13 January, unable to reach Kowloon because the only road from the New Territories was blocked, I queued with thousands of others to squeeze onto packed trains into town. The drivers were unmoving.

The government stance was not to allow itself to be blackmailed. As the evening of the 13th wore on, the main crossroad junctions in central and north Kowloon were blocked. It was impossible to tow the vehicles away and security vehicles were unable to move freely. Tough young men from the crowded tenements of Mong Kok and Yau Ma Ti, known for dealing in drugs, prostitution and gambling, taunted the police; a petrol bomb was thrown against a bank, and rioting and looting followed. I held meetings with the drivers' leaders and gave my advice to Legislative Council and to the government that the taxi drivers had a stranglehold on Kowloon and that worse disorder would follow unless the situation could be brought under control by withdrawing the legislation. A strong group of Legislative Councillors had come to the same conclusion. They informed Sir Philip Haddon-Cave, acting Governor in the absence of Sir Edward Youde who was in London for talks with the Foreign Secretary. The legislation was withdrawn, and the taxis reversed away from the junctions and melted into the night.

The year 1984 brought with it month after month of grey skies and cold weather. Spring came and went almost unnoticed. It was as though the heavens were reflecting the sombre mood, the anxiety and strain of the drawn-out negotiations. Meeting after meeting took place in Beijing, the Governor continued to shuttle backwards and forwards, the public were in the dark about what deal was being made, and I made speech after speech optimistically reminding the audiences of the fundamental strengths which would see us through. There were visits by Members of Parliament, among them George Robertson MP, who was to become Minister for Defence in the government of Prime Minister Tony Blair; Sir Richard Luce, minister responsible for Hong Kong; and Sir Geoffrey Howe, Foreign Secretary, who briefed Executive Council on his visit to Beijing, and said in plain words at a press conference that sovereignty and administration would pass to China. It had taken a long time to get these words out.

As the weeks passed nerves were frayed, minds were tired. China was exasperated with the pernickety care the British side were taking to get the eventual agreement as comprehensive and detailed as possible. We preferred quite properly to get things down in black and white. To heighten mistrust, Jardine Matheson, one of the companies which had been involved in the landing in Hong Kong in 1841 and a pillar of the commercial community, announced the removal of their legal domicile to Bermuda.

China was equally furious when Sir Roger Lobo, Executive and Legislative Councillor, proposed a motion in the Legislative Council that any agreement had to be acceptable to the council. The combined councils had also written a manifesto to which China took grave exception. China held firmly to the constitutionally correct view that the negotiations and agreements were the perquisite of the sovereign powers and not for the humble citizens of Hong Kong, since China had never abandoned the view that Hong Kong was part of China. Although innocent of this manoeuvre by Sir Roger, Britain did not escape blame for not curbing what appeared to be an orchestrated campaign by unruly councillors. Against and despite this unpropitious background, by the end of March 1984 the shape and even some of the wording of the final text was emerging.

There was a moment of high drama when the proposal from the Chinese side to establish a joint commission (see *Experences of China*, by Sir Percy Cradock, John Murray 1994) to oversee the transition to Chinese rule was seen as smacking of Chinese interference in Hong Kong even before the transfer. It seemed eminently sensible to me that the two sides should cooperate about the working arrangements of government which would straddle 1997. Such a proposal would ensure that both sides would work together to sort out and decide matters in which both governments had an interest, and deal with a host of minor practical matters which, if ignored, could have given rise to misunderstandings and delays which would still be unresolved when reunification took place. I have never quite been able to understand the opposition to this proposal. It reflected once again the basic lack of trust that existed between the two sides, and provoked a strong reaction from other Executive Councillors who saw it as an early surrender of sovereignty and interference in the running of Hong Kong. Mine was a lone voice in its favour. Eventually, however, the proposal was amended and accepted, the introduction of the joint commission delayed until after the final ratification of the agreement, and arrangements for its meeting in Hong Kong postponed until 1988. It was also agreed that the two sides would continue to meet and talk for three years after the transfer. This extension was a useful tidying-up period, but it was also cosmetic, and by extending the operation of the Joint Liaison Group, as it came to be called, it applied a Band-aid to the handover.

As the last paragraphs of the final agreement were being written, an intervention by Sir Geoffrey Howe led to the inclusion of a vitally significant few words in the text of the Joint Declaration: these were that the Legislative Council of Hong Kong would be 'constituted by elections'. On these three words depended the steps Hong Kong was to take in the years ahead towards a democratically elected government.

18

Signatures and Celebrations

*T*hroughout the long, hot, summer days of 1984 discussion about the agreement with China had continued in Executive Council, and at times less formally around the table in Government House. The agreement was to take the form of a declaration by both governments, followed by an elaboration of China's basic policies towards Hong Kong to be contained in a number of annexes.

We were all caught up in the drama of those days of secrecy as the text and its annexes emerged section by section after the drafts had been passed round from Hong Kong to London and Beijing and had been finally amended and approved. The Governor, on his visits to London, was sometimes accompanied by non-official members of Executive Council, and at other times he travelled alone between all three places, explaining and pleading and filling in the gaps which the bare words of telegrams failed to do.

At times, in discussion, I took a different tack from my colleagues based on what I thought the people would want us to do, what they would accept and what I thought their reactions would be to particular bits of the agreement. I was optimistic that the result was going to be much better than when we had started on this long journey. We seemed to be getting the best of both worlds. The administration, the government, would continue as before but it would no longer be administered by the British but by the Hong Kong people themselves. The civil service and all the systems which had been developed over the years would continue as before

— the Common Law, an independent judiciary, and basic rights and freedoms. What could be better than that? And as I write in 2002, several years after the return of sovereignty, who would have believed that by now there would still be expatriate British officials sprinkled throughout the administration and the police force, who were allowed to continue in their employment by the government of the Hong Kong Special Administrative Region of China.

Finally, in the early morning of 26 September 1984, the Governor flew to Beijing to be present at the initialling of the agreement by the leaders of the delegations, H.M. Ambassador Sir Richard Evans and Vice Minister Zhou Nan, and then to fly back in the afternoon when distribution began of the booklet containing the Draft Agreement. It was a draft only insofar as it had not yet been ratified by the British Parliament — that would take a further few months — but it was not a draft in the usual sense that it was open to amendment. There could be no further change in the agreement which had been reached. This was the finished work. In three days, two million copies were distributed and were acclaimed, almost without exception, as a remarkable achievement. 'Much better than we had hoped' was the universal comment. It was a comment that night at a dinner party at the Kowloon Club which I had founded some years before. Guests and waiters alike all said they accepted it.

It so happened, and no doubt this was Deng Xiaoping's objective in urging us on, that the thirty-fifth anniversary of the founding of the People's Republic was to take place on 1 October 1984, following the initialling of the agreement. Sixteen delegates from the Hong Kong government, led by the Executive Council, were invited to Beijing to take part in the celebrations. Beijing was changing. So much was newly built, so much being built, and there was a relaxed feeling and liveliness among the people strolling the pavements of the capital. The last time I had been in Beijing was that cold February in 1973, during the great Cultural Revolution. Then we had stayed in the Peking Hotel with its draughty doorways letting in whistling blasts of freezing air and its long, gloomy corridors and echoing dining room. Now we were in the latest hotel with a glass-walled elevator tube, comfortable atrium-lounge and ornamental garden.

Leaves in the mountains on the way to the Great Wall were yellow, red and copper-gold in the autumn sun. Orange persimmons were ripening on the trees and the heavy, drooping heads of the second grain crop were waiting to be harvested. The streets of the city were lined with flowers and its buildings decked with lights. The Premier at a banquet for four thousand guests in the Great Hall of the People spoke with satisfaction of the agreement for the return of Hong Kong .

The morning mist cleared for the grand Thirty-Fifth Anniversary Parade along Chang An Avenue, passing the Tiananmen gateway. The square was filled with 200,000 young people, who with their coloured flip-boards created an immense carpet of colour and at a flick of the wrist spelled out different messages of greeting and congratulation. Deng Xiaoping, a sturdy figure in an open limousine, passed down the ranks of the procession calling out greetings to the troops, 'Tung zhi men ni hao?' ('Comrades, are you well?'), at which they roared a guttural 'Hao' in reply. For two hours the procession passed Tiananmen, for two hours we stood with other dignitaries at the foot of the wall leading to the Imperial Palace watching the spectacle of troops, tanks, rockets, dancers, athletes, floats and miracles of precision marching and bursts of colour. For we Hong Kong visitors it was a remarkable climax to the years of waiting.

Hong Kong had been promised fifty years of no change to its fundamentals, its way of managing the economy, law and way of life. These were set out in general terms in the Joint Declaration, but Hong Kong needed its own detailed road map for life after 1997. Hong Kong had accepted the deal, there were no demonstrations, and life in the streets of Hong Kong was normal. Things were out in the open, gone were the meetings behind closed doors, the future was decided. It was now a matter for representatives of Hong Kong and China, rather than the sovereign powers, to draft a Basic Law, based on the agreement, which would become part of China's own constitution. This was to take a further five years, longer than the agreement itself had taken. Meanwhile, the British in the Liaison Group were to work with China, mutually to sort out what needed to be done to introduce changes to systems so that they could continue to function, and so that laws would have effect after the handover.

Hitherto, the ultimate appeal by aggrieved litigants from judgements of the Supreme Court in Hong Kong had been made to the Privy Council in London. After 1997 this would stop. However China, with extraordinary magnanimity, had agreed that Hong Kong should have its own Court of Final Appeal. Here was real evidence of China's determination to make explicit the separation of the two systems. Remarkably and generously, China went a step further and agreed that 'as required', judges from other Common Law jurisdictions could join the Hong Kong judges on the court. Here China was agreeing that, for example, that Australian judges could take a seat in the Court of Final Appeal in Hong Kong. This 'as required' phrase gave rise to prolonged mistrustful wrangling by Hong Kong lawyers as to how many judges this meant at any one time and delayed the setting up of the court and the withdrawal of the Privy Council of Great Britain from the procedure on appeal from decisions of the Supreme Court of Hong Kong. China was going out of her way to demonstrate sincerity, but there were those in Hong Kong without the same generosity of spirit and trust.

One morning a few weeks later, in Sir Edward Youde's study at Government House, he told me that I was to take over the post of Chief Secretary in 1985 when Sir Philip Haddon-Cave retired. This was unexpected. All my postings had been so full of interest, full of excitement, full of opportunity that we had never schemed or planned to move on to higher things, never thought about promotion. Since the cold, blacked-out wintry evening in 1945 when I had left home to join my ship in Hull, life had flowed from one thing to another; not without punctuations of anxiety, but inevitably. 'When you are ready you will know what to do.' A new chapter of life was beginning.

The year 1984 ended as it had begun. Members of Parliament, before they had to vote in the Commons, wanted to see for themselves how the people were taking the agreement which had been reached without their participation. They went away surprised and satisfied. There were other visits too. Prince Philip spent two hours chatting in the lounge at the airport with members of the World Wide Fund for Nature, whose Hong

Kong chairman I was, and enquiring about progress with our wetland reserve; I greeted the Olympic Volley Ball Team from China and the gymnastic team from Guangxi, and wedged between lunches and dinners, gave a garden party for a hundred guests on the lawn of our Island House. The media, too, unleashed from the embargo of the past two years, hung on everyone's word to try now to unravel the future beyond the agreement.

After the past weeks of excitement we went to Bangkok to recover our breath. Memories came flooding back of 1947, when I had spent a year as third mate of the M.V. *Kola*, a 3,000 ton coaster running between Singapore and Bangkok. In Singapore we had anchored with the other coastal vessels and Bugis schooners in the inner harbour off Collyer Quay, behind the protecting mole. We loaded odd things, musty gunny sacks full of empty bottles or onions, and at Pulau Bukum, the oil terminal island off Singapore, shiny four-gallon cans of kerosene. The journey to Bangkok took three and a half days, three and half days were spent in port at either end, and the round trip took two weeks. Our deck crew were Malaysian, the engine room crew from Pakistan, Chinese stewards fed us and looked after our cabins, and loading the cargo was left to Chinese compradores, who in return were allowed to carry thirty tons of cargo for themselves.

Our pretty little ship had chugged through the Straits and turned north up the east coast of Malaya past the green, inviting islands of Tioman, now a tourist destination but then largely uninhabited, and on into the open waters of the Gulf of Thailand. This was a delightful journey for most of the year but in the winter, when the north-east monsoon blew from China, the sea piled up on the coast and then rolled back making our journey rolling, pitching and tortuous and blind in squalls of tropical rain. After days of creaking and lurching we found shelter and relief near the green-hatted limestone islands and brown waters at the entrance to the river leading to the city. Our ship had been especially built for the coastal trade and crossed the bar at the river mouth, barely churning its way over the mud and leaving behind a frothy, cocoa-coloured track.

The journey up the river had been dreamlike as we glided between the narrowing banks through the brown water with its little islands of water hyacinth, slowly flowing to the sea. We tied up at the wharves of the Bombay Burmah Company to load our cargo of long-grained Siamese rice for the return journey. Heavy sacks were carried on the sweating, calloused shoulders of a stream of Chinese wharf workers, a dirty sweat-cloth twisted round their heads, thin muscular legs trotting up long bouncing planks, and with a deft shrug dropping each sack into place. Ashore in 1947, the shopkeepers had not discarded their traditional broad, black, shiny trousers, turned and belted at the waist over a white vest. In the city the French-built trams ran, and in the bars were cane chairs and slow circling fans troubling the hot and humid air. Klong waterways overhung with great branching flame trees bordered the quiet suburban streets. Now nearly forty years later, I returned to Bangkok to the memory of these forgotten things, and to look from afar at the future lying in wait for Hong Kong. The wheel had turned full circle. What a strange destiny had brought the third mate of the *Kola* in 1948 back to that same place to begin another turn of the wheel.

19

Chief Secretary

The announcement that I was to succeed Philip Haddon-Cave as Chief Secretary at the beginning of June 1985 brought more than twenty years of life in the New Territories to an end. Unlike my colleagues I had never cut my teeth on the cloistered disciplines of establishment, economics and finance, and there was, no doubt, some muttering in the corridors about the unusualness of my appointment.

We would have to leave Island House, which had been our home for twelve years. It had been home for the officer responsible for the government of the New Territories and its affairs since the beginning of the century and, because it was situated among the people he administered, had become an important symbol of government's concern for the separate identity and welfare of the New Territories. As it happened, and perhaps emphasising the closer integration of the New Territories with urban Hong Kong, Island House was never again to be the residence of a government official.

It took a few weeks to disengage from years of work close to the people. Cabinets of personal papers had to be destroyed, including years of speeches and barrow loads of mementoes of official occasions, and I had to make a sad farewell to my Chinese secretary, Mrs Tam Ho-yin, who nearly always worked in the evenings in the office long after I had left. She was word-perfect in English, helpful to her colleagues and a friend to so many. She was firm with my shortcomings and admired by all for her generous capability. She was a true representative of many thousands who contribute so much to the efficient running of Hong Kong. They are the unsung heroes.

Just before we said goodbye to Island House, there occurred an election day for District Boards on 7 March 1985. In these elections nearly half a million people voted and elected two-thirds of the members of each board. The boards were not local government and have been criticised because they had no executive responsibility, for example for employing staff to clean the streets and building and managing buildings. Instead they could make their voice heard about anything affecting the lives of the people in their district and criticise the policies and decisions of central government. More important, and symbolically, on the edge of what the foreign media still referred to as 'Red' or 'communist' China, we were holding one person, one vote elections for an organisation which could criticise the policies of its government.

This anomaly and the reassurance it gave to those who were willing to see its significance and the hope it held for the future nevertheless did not appease those who did not wish to be comforted. For me, the elections were a pleasant reminder of the two terms I had spent at the University of Kent studying the strengths and weaknesses of forms of local government. Here in Hong Kong we had done away with the restrictions which hampered discussion in more conventional local councils, whose ambit of responsibility and discussion was restricted by law. In place of a vacuum with no representation, no sense of belonging and responsibility, we were building a structure which would, hopefully, bind the districts and their people together.

Industrialisation and exports during the previous twenty years had placed Hong Kong, although not a nation, among the top ten trading nations of the world and had earned us membership of the world body of the General Agreement on Tariffs and Trade, GATT. To serve this trading empire the government established representative and trade development offices in Geneva, Brussels, Washington, New York and Tokyo. Before returning through China to Hong Kong to become Chief Secretary, I had a useful opportunity to visit these offices, to talk with ministers, to speak to academics and learned societies, to appear on television, and by spelling out what the agreement with China had achieved, to attempt to allay some of the widespread worry about the return of Hong Kong to a China which was little known, less trusted and seldom visited by Western leaders and opinion-makers.

The tour ended in China, and my wife flew to join me in Beijing. We stayed in the Embassy and enjoyed the warm hospitality of Sir Richard Evans and his wife Grania. I left the Embassy one morning to have a friendly talk with Vice Minister Zhou Nan, later to replace Xu Jiatun as head of the New China News Agency, which represented the Chinese government in Hong Kong, and who had led the Chinese team in negotiating the agreement with the British. Later in our travels we were accompanied by a young assistant from the New China News Agency, Qiao Zhonghuai, who in 2001 became a Vice Minister of Foreign Affairs.

On the morning we left for Shanghai there was time to walk round the quiet, leafy enclosure of the Embassy garden with its relics, half-hidden in the shrubbery, from the legation burnt by the Red Guards in 1966; the font from the chapel, some statues, the memorial tablets to those killed during the Boxer rebellion, and the plaque to the memory of Sir Robert Hart, who, in the last decades of the Qing dynasty, had founded and run the Chinese customs service.

Shanghai in 1985 was still a run-down city of crowded terraced houses in the former foreign concessions of France, Germany and Britain with their exotic tiled roofs, mansards and dormers, cupolas and gothic towerlets, each now the crowded home of many families. Here and there, the gardens of wealthy merchants could be glimpsed through trees. The heavyweight commercial buildings on the Bund facing the slow brown river had not yet woken from almost half a century of slumber. In an office in the former Hong Kong and Shanghai Bank building I met Mayor Wang Daohan, who had once lunched with us at Island House and who gave me an outline of the plans which, by the end of the century, were to transform Shanghai once more into a great modern international city.

We flew on to Xiamen for a second time. Fujian province had lost no time since modernisation began in 1978, building bridges, railways, deep water ports, industrial parks and airports and lining its streets with trees and flowers. The grand villas of wealthy rubber, sugar and tin merchants from South-East Asia on the island of Gulangyu were restored and painted. Along the coast, past Xiamen's famous university, there was even a strange relic of a forgotten war, an enormous green-painted Krupps 1891 naval gun, 16 inches or more, stripped of its mechanisms, pointing blindly seaward on its traverse and making use of the round fort of an earlier century. Close by, a dance hall and restaurant now put to use the empty tunnel of an abandoned air-raid shelter.

Guangzhou was the last of the cities on our southward journey, and we stayed in the White Swan Hotel looking over the murky waters of the Pearl River at a grey, tired city of crowded narrow streets shabbily awaiting renewal. Once more we experienced the strange emotion of entering Hong Kong from mainland China, gliding slowly by train through the rich green rice fields and fishponds of the delta, crossing the broad brown rivers, passing from a world which had been closed for so long to the other world of Hong Kong.

Arriving in Hong Kong's Central Government Offices, I sat in a small room across the corridor from my future office reading files and papers. Sir Philip Haddon-Cave, saying little, went on with his work until, on 20 June, he poked his head around the door and said he had finished clearing out — and left. Two weeks later, on 5 July, Sir Edward Youde, the Governor, went on vacation for six weeks. I was sworn in as Acting Governor by the Chief Justice in the Executive Council chamber, reciting the oaths of office in the presence of the other councillors, and in a few solemn words was reminded of the burden and responsibility of office.

The design of the Chief Secretary's house, Victoria House, had been supervised by Lady Maurine Grantham, the American wife of Sir Alexander Grantham, Governor in the 1950s. It was a gracious American colonial house built with entertainment in mind. From the terrace the ground fell away for hundreds of feet and we looked across the dense city buildings of Victoria already reaching up to pierce the skyline, to the harbour full of lighters, bumboats, liners, tankers, visiting destroyers, ferries, tugs and barges, and then, raising one's eyes, Kowloon with its steep encircling hills, the distant mountains of China and the shining waters to the east and west of Hong Kong. The suddenness of this stretching panorama, with its sharp contrasts, as you walked through the house to the lawn, took the breath away. Around the house, despite the passage of so many years and so many occupants, the garden had not been a principal concern of previous Chief Secretaries. We set to work to dig a fishpond and brought in trees and boulders, and during the hot summer months of 1985 dared to disturb the ordered flowerbeds and the expanse of grass with new planting.

With the agreement signed, almost at once Hong Kong and British officials started on the next thirteen years of their liaison meetings. They met alternately in Beijing and London, and later in Hong Kong, trudging the corridors in their dark official suits, convening their anxious assemblies, gathering and dispersing with their files, telegrams, grapevines, second-guessing and whispered surmisings.

The Liaison Group made it a priority to decide the form and wording of documents to be used in land dealings whose validity would last for fifty years. Here was ready proof that the Chinese government meant it when it said that things would remain unchanged. The expiring land lease of the New Territories had been the reason for starting negotiations about the future. Now the property developers could put this worry behind them. Land had played a dominant role in Hong Kong life since the settlers in the 1840s had squabbled over who was to have the best bits of foreshore. Revenue from land sales, property tax, stamp duty on dealings in land, bank profits and taxes on the income of property companies accounted for 50 per cent of the government's revenue and played an unreliable and unhealthily dominant role in the economy. This became a serious worry in the future when the economy went into recession and property prices slumped, and with them, too, government revenue. Land leases even occupied a special annexe of the Joint Declaration. China, concerned that the British were going to run off with the people's patrimony and squander precious land resources before the post-1997 government had its hands on the controls, had stipulated that the total amount of land to be granted during the period leading to 1997 should not exceed 50 hectares a year and that the revenue from land disposal during that period should be shared equally between the British Hong Kong government and the future government of the Hong Kong Special Administrative Region.

Fifty hectares was an arbitrary figure plucked out of the air. It seemed enough at the time but was not, and by the time government's plans and policies had been met there was never sufficient land to meet the appetites of private development or for a balanced housing programme. Because of this short supply and because of an accelerating economy, land increased in value to astronomic levels. Additional land could not be sold to try to bring the price down and home buyers were forced to pay absurd prices for their apartments. The concomitant was that, through wise investment by a Joint Land Commission set up to supervise this part of the agreement, taking a half share of land sale proceeds, the incoming government in 1997 gained a dowry of billions.

Liaison between Britain and China was intended to ensure that the British handed over Hong Kong in good working order. Senior expatriate civil servants had to be replaced, and laws had to be translated and, where needed, disengaged from the laws of England. This was a task for the Hong Kong government, but an organisation overseen by the Chinese government had to be established to draft the Basic Law for the incoming Special Administrative Region binding Hong Kong to the central People's Republic government and removing Her Britannic Majesty, the Queen, from rule of Hong Kong at midnight on 30 June 1997.

Annex 1 of the Joint Declaration had this to say: 'The National People's Congress shall enact and promulgate a Basic Law of the Hong Kong Special Administrative region of the People's Republic of China ... stipulating that after the establishment of the Special Administrative Region the socialist system and socialist policies shall not be practised in the Hong Kong SAR and that Hong Kong's previous capitalist system and life-style shall remain unchanged for fifty years.'

A drafting committee was appointed by the Chinese government, consisting of a selected group of Hong Kong representatives together with lawyers and leaders from Beijing. To give credibility to their work, the Hong Kong members assembled a consultative committee of over 150 people to advise them. Within this number, a group of business and professional people who shared similar views coalesced, known as the Business and Professional Group, which grew in size until it became known as the Group of 89. They played a pivotal role in bringing the drafting to a widely accepted conclusion in January 1990, four and a half years later, and were to form the nucleus of a Federation of Business and Professional people, the BPF, after 1997, when the drafting was over.

The composition of the Legislative Council which was to take office in 1995, for the last two years of colonial Hong Kong, was of particular importance. If it were elected in conformity with the Basic Law, it could then hold office both before and after the transfer of power in 1997. This concept of a 'through train' for elected councillors was agreed by China, and was a coup for the drafters of the Basic Law and behind-the-scenes persuasions. It demonstrated how far China was willing to go to ensure a seamless transition between British Hong Kong and its post -1997 identity. It was quite remarkable to have reached agreement that councillors, elected under British administration by the colonial government, could continue to hold office in part of the People's Republic of China for two years after reunification and until the next elections were held in 1999.

The train, alas, was to be derailed at the frontier of transition because of British determination to pursue a scheme for elections developed by the last Governor, Christopher Patten. His objective was to increase the size of the constituencies which represented special interests and professions in a way which did not conform to the original intention when these constituencies were first introduced. Nor did it conform to the intention of the drafters of the Basic Law. This gave rise to a prolonged dispute which could have been settled by asking those of us who had written the Green and White Papers on representative government which had created these constituencies, and the drafters of the Basic Law who lived in Hong Kong, what their intention was when they wrote the law. But this opportunity was ignored in pursuit of ingenious schemes to broaden the electorate which, as China warned, were doomed to fail.

20

A Fresh Chapter Begins

*I*n the months and years following the signing of the agreement the Governor continued his frequent travels to London and Beijing, forcefully putting his point of view on the many questions raised in its implementation. Each time he left, as Chief Secretary and his deputy I took over as Acting Governor, and when he was away I chaired the meetings of Executive Council and was president of the Legislative Council.

Meetings of the Executive Council took place in the government secretariat in an unadorned room around a long marmalade-coloured teak wood table, with no distracting pictures on the walls, no concession to comfort. At 9.30 every Tuesday morning the Governor entered through his door at the end of the table as his clerk announced 'His Excellency the Governor'. Members then sat and discussion of the agenda for the week began, starting with the approval of the decisions of the last meeting to be signed by the Governor. These were not a record of who said what or how a decision had been reached, merely the decision itself. The private record of who said what was kept for the archives by the Clerk of Councils, who sat quietly in a corner taking notes. Officials who were needed for discussion of agenda items waited their turn to be called, entered and sat, 'boding tremblers', at the other end of the table. There they waited apprehensively for questions on their presented papers, but otherwise did not join the discussion.

Legislative Council meetings, on the other hand, took place in the colonnaded former Supreme Court of Hong Kong, constructed in the first years of the twentieth century on land reclaimed from the harbour, next to the cricket ground and to the right of the Hongkong and Shanghai Bank so as, incidentally, not to obstruct the bank's view of the harbour! The Governor sat where the Chief Justice had previously sat, on a canopied, penitential, hard teak wood throne salvaged from a former marine court.

Hong Kong moved on as the economy and society adjusted to changes in the Chinese and world economy, and made use of the opportunities it afforded for our entrepreneurs to invest in China. There is a thrusting ambition, clever adaptability, and a desire to outwit and to excel which make themselves felt even walking the pavements of Hong Kong. The government is caught up in this restless excitement, projecting and planning, building and demolishing, with senior officials working in their offices long after business has closed for the day.

There was now a new and closer relationship with China as we began on the twelve-year journey to transition. Now a new topic had entered popular discussion and a new need arisen to be kept unofficially informed of the progress being made in drafting the Basic Law. It was to take five years to draft the Basic Law, and during this time I had many long and fruitful discussions and conversations with members of the drafting committee.

It was a time of adjustment and an acceleration of the changes set in train by the reforms and the opening of China to the outside world. The stream of investors, industrialists, lawyers, accountants, and at a different level, family members travelling to China swelled to a flood. Hong Kong was doubly blessed that the return to China coincided with the change from a closed communist China to one of economic reform in which the country thirsted for contact with the world outside. How different and difficult it would have been if things had been as they had for the previous thirty or so years: a China of campaigns and 'struggles', of the Cultural Revolution, and a China closed to the outside world. Suppose we had had to carry on until the expiry of the New Territories lease waiting for China to begin discussion about the future?

The omens were good. Those who, to be on the safe side, had obtained a foreign domicile, returned to Hong Kong, finding that their qualifications were unsuitable to gain employment or to practise overseas, or that there were no vacancies, or that they could not stand the food any longer! Most of the older generation found that when all was said and done Hong Kong suited them best; they missed their friends, the food and the pleasure of walking about their own Chinese city.

Britain was to administer Hong Kong until responsibility was handed over to China, but at the same time it was to cooperate with China to ensure a smooth transition. These two requirements did not always march happily together and tended to be interpreted differently by the two sides. The British took a rather robust view of their independent responsibility, the Chinese were ever-anxious that there was not a hidden motive, a hidden agenda behind the British and Hong Kong government actions and policies. Hong Kong's new relationship with China brought into the open differing views of our communist neighbour and how far we could rely on the promises made about the future, and for the unbelievers, a desire was revealed to erect barriers and to seek international support for them.

As I have related, in the seventies the Hong Kong government had begun inching forward with its plans for minuscule political change. A Legislative Council which had previously been dominated by a majority of the Governor's officials had given away its majority to an increased number of members chosen from among the public and appointed by the Governor. The building of new towns in the rural New Territories for families displaced or resettled from the crowded slums of Kowloon had led to the creation of the District Boards as a sounding board for criticism of government and a way of releasing any simmering discontent, as well as to make proposals for needed improvement to the lives of people living in the crowded buildings of the city and in the decaying villages. In May 1984, at the height of the negotiations leading to the agreement, ignoring the tense atmosphere and after eighty years of direct colonial administration, the government announced its plans in a Green Paper to increase the elected elements in these local boards.

The ink was scarcely dry on the Joint Declaration before these proposals in the Green Paper became firm policies in a White Paper. This underscored the statement in the Joint Declaration that 'the Government of the United Kingdom will be responsible for the administration of Hong Kong [until 1997] with the object of maintaining and preserving its economic prosperity and social stability and that the Government of the People's Republic of China will give its cooperation in this direction'. However, it could be said by China, with some justification, that the changes that were proposed in the White Paper were also covered by the agreed function of the Joint Liaison Group, 'to discuss matters relating to the smooth transfer of power in 1997'. Political reform certainly had a bearing on a smooth transfer of power. There had been no discussion of this sensitive area, and this gave rise to the first outburst of displeasure from China after the signing of the agreement.

The director of the New China News Agency in Hong Kong, Xu Jiatun, wagged his finger and accused the British of deviating from the agreement. A month later, the director of the Hong Kong and Macao Affairs Office in Beijing, Ji Pengfei, visited Hong Kong. He met District Board leaders and came to lunch at our house on the Peak, but declined an invitation to visit Legislative Council, thus underlining the fact that China regarded the council as an advisory body without legislative authority. Ji said that in order to comply with the Joint Declaration it was best to change as little as possible, and not to change the political system unless it would be beneficial, again giving a strong hint that there had been a lack of consultation with China over political reforms. The deputy director of the Hong Kong and Macao Affairs Office, Lu Ping, also spent some weeks in Hong Kong in early 1986, meeting principally with the Basic Law drafting and consultative committees.

In January 1986 the Foreign Office minister responsible for Hong Kong, Timothy Renton, speaking in Hong Kong, added fuel to the flames when he suggested that Hong Kong people were free to choose what government they wanted! Throw-away lines like this sowed the seed for years of doubt and controversy which lasted until the transition to China in 1997. But there were other things to worry about.

The illusion of a great happy family of people across the globe living under the care and protection of the British flag belonged to an age when to travel from the far-flung corners of Empire, and particularly India, meant an arduous and expensive journey by sea. The difficulty and the cost alone kept the millions of 'children' of the Empire from flooding to the family hearth. In contrast, officials, armies, merchants, and in some cases their wives and children, were transported at their employer's expense thousands of miles from Great Britain, to be employed in the various responsibilities and rewards of Empire. They travelled 'home' at long intervals, first by sail and then by steam. The British India Steam Navigation Company, which I had served for a brief four years, played an important role in this transport; it had specially designed troop ships and was a regular carrier to the Far East.

After the Pacific War times were hard in rural Hong Kong, particularly in the villages that depended on the meagre returns from one crop each year of brackish-water paddy, grown in the north-west of the New Territories. A glut of rice from the cheap rice-producing countries of South-East Asia drove the farmers of Hong Kong from the land. They found, with peasant perspicacity, that so long as they could prove that they were true family members of that great commonwealth of nations, the British Empire, they could obtain a passport and travel to England, and later to continental Europe. For a villager, this was relatively easy. In the Land Registry of the District Offices were the proofs ready to hand that applicants were bona fide descendants of families living in the New Territories at the turn of the century. A simple declaration sworn before the District Officer enabled them to obtain a passport to travel to England.

Never slow to miss a trick, in the sixties a company was formed by an ingenious village leader from that same area of poor paddy land in the north-west, to charter jumbo jets on regular flights to Heathrow to carry villagers and their families cheaply back and forth. So from the rice prices of Asia and cheap air fares began the burgeoning of Chinese restaurants in Western Europe. The deserted village paddy fields they had left behind became vegetable, chicken and pig farms, managed by new arrivals from the mainland, many of them illegal immigrants, while indigenous villagers armed with their British passports found a more profitable occupation satisfying the appetites of the West for a more adventurous cuisine.

During the next twenty years there were migrations to the United Kingdom of Asians from Uganda and people from Pakistan, from India and from the West Indies. One by one the loopholes to immigration were plugged by legislation in Parliament, and the former easy assumptions of citizenship disavowed. This issue came to a head during the years of negotiation about Hong Kong's future. Hong Kong was not like other former colonies where, on acquiring independence, their citizens acquired the nationality of a newly independent country. It was stated by some in crude, uncomplimentary terms that Britain was handing over several million people to communist rule.

There was an understandable worry in London that there would be a mass exodus. Seen from another angle, Britain did not wish to be seen encouraging people to leave when the sole purpose of the negotiations was to secure a stable and prosperous future for Hong Kong and to enable people to remain there. Nevertheless, for many people in Hong Kong, this was one more step into an uncertain limbo. Those that had the means and were unwilling to accept the assurances of the future either went themselves, or sent their wives and families, chiefly to Canada, the USA or Australia to acquire residency and a passport, the husbands shuttling backwards and forwards, 'spacemen' as they were called in Chinese, whenever they could spare the time from work. Some wives went to the USA to give birth to their children, but the mass of the people had nowhere to go. There was talk of betrayal and abandonment without recognition of the reality of how Britain could deal with a mass influx of people. That was Britain's problem. (This was an attitude mirrored in 1999 and countered in similar fashion by restrictive legislation, when Hong Kong itself was threatened by a possible influx of over a million kinsmen from the mainland claiming right of abode in Hong Kong.)

At a more popular level there had been discontented grumbling for a number of years over nationality. With the withdrawal of the privileges of passports and citizenship from its colonial territories, Hong Kong citizens had ended up with the accurate but disparaging description of British Dependent Territories Citizens. If that were not bad enough, Explanatory Note 64 of the Joint Declaration said: 'since Hong Kong will no longer be a British Dependent Territory after 30 June 1997 it will not be appropriate for those who are British Dependent Territories Citizens by virtue of a connection with Hong Kong to be described as such after that date.' They were to be called British National Overseas Citizens, whatever that meant, and would be entitled to use British passports describing them as such, but nevertheless, would have to stand in the pejorative alien queue on entry to Britain. What now, they said, of the long ties of loyalty, friendship and responsibility?

The change gave rise to many questions which were to take some years to resolve, but it also sparked off other, additional questions. What would become of the ethnic minorities? Hong Kong's Indian population had been loyal citizens of Hong Kong for many generations and would now become stateless. What, too, about the widows of servicemen who had fought valiantly and had died fighting for Hong Kong? Which countries would recognise the new passport? Were millions of people in Hong Kong going to find there was nowhere to go after 1997? These feelings, some rational, some irrational, are easily understood. Here the Liaison Group demonstrated its usefulness. In July 1986 agreement was reached that British National Overseas passports would contain an endorsement to the effect that the holder had a Permanent Identity Card and the right to live in Hong Kong. In other words, they were not 'stateless' and if need be could be returned to Hong Kong. After some time, countries recognised the BNO passport and after months and years of petitions and pleading an acceptable solution was found for the widows of soldiers who had fought for Hong Kong, and for the ethnic minorities.

Despite the earlier misgivings, eventually the BNO passport became a well-accepted, second-best travel document and, with its issue established, half the population acquired this status and the passport that goes with it, and have it to this day.

21

Light and Nuclear Power

*T*here were other more practical happenings to scratch the nerves of an already anxious community. Two measures of the growth of Hong Kong are the need for more and more water and the building of power stations. Factories work around the clock, and the lights of office towers burn into the night as analysts and others work midway between the financial markets of America and Europe. The brilliant shop signs of the crowded streets are symbols of a city that never seems to sleep. The two power companies, Hong Kong Electric and China Light and Power, which supply Hong Kong and the islands and mainland Kowloon and the New Territories respectively, each built new giant stations, models of their kind whose smokeless chimneys poke like giant joss sticks above the skyline of the hills. It was not enough. When nuclear power was less an object of protest than it is today, time was spent looking around the colony to see whether, in its small compass, there was a remote corner where a nuclear station could be built. But it was a fruitless quest, as there was nowhere to be found sufficiently distant from towns and villages, neither in the remote north-east nor the far south-west. The idea that Hong Kong should have its own nuclear station was dropped.

Sir Lawrence (later Lord) Kadoorie, chairman of the China Light and Power Company and a man of vision, understood the precariousness of Hong Kong's position as a capitalist colony and a tiny bit of empire on the coast of the Chinese giant. He saw that the future lay in building strong links of mutual interest with China. He realised, too, that industrialisation of the Pearl River delta and modernisation of the cities of southern China would all require immense supplies of power. Hong Kong itself would need more power, but before the full capacity of a modern power plant could be used in Hong Kong, electricity surplus to local requirements could be supplied across the border to the Pearl River delta where it was in short supply. A start had already been made by 1980, when overhead power lines began carrying electricity from Hong Kong north across the border into the grid of the Guangdong Power Company. And in the course of discussion to interconnect the transmission network further, the question was raised of constructing a nuclear power station to supply both Guangdong and Hong Kong. By the end of 1980 the technical feasibility of the idea had been confirmed. Discussions about the future of Hong Kong had not yet begun but here already was specific evidence of how important China viewed her future role and relations with Hong Kong and the future.

The two Hong Kong power companies separately enjoy a monopoly in their basic supply areas of Hong Kong Island and Kowloon and operate under schemes of control limiting profits and ensuring that they meet their obligations to serve the needs of the growing population and economy. When the feasibility of constructing a nuclear power plant some distance across the border in mainland China had been confirmed, agreement to proceed was reached between the UK, China and Hong Kong. A joint venture company would be formed in which Hong Kong would have a 25 per cent interest and take 70 per cent of the power. The nuclear island of the station would be French and the conventional island, the generators, British. It was estimated to cost US$ 3.5 billion. But specifically it was to be a Chinese power plant built in China.

The political significance of this giant project, which involved so many participants, put a stamp of confidence on the future, and it underscored China's commitment to Hong Kong. Here was power flowing across the border, first from Hong Kong to the mainland and then, with the completion of the nuclear station, from the mainland to Hong Kong. Britain and France were helping to build the station and then later to manage the plant for a period, to train and work alongside Chinese scientists and operators. And if Hong Kong had no long-term future as a separate capitalist entity and yet was expected to continue to pay the going rate for the power it consumed, why was China investing in such a long-term project? Lord Kadoorie saw the significance of this, but for those who had no ears to hear it was pushed to the background as just another part of Hong Kong development.

Public interest was low key and focused on the safety aspects, coming mainly from those who did not trust China's competence to build and maintain a nuclear power station. The management and maintenance of buildings in China was poor: 'Look at the hotels,' they said. Then in April 1985 came the Chernobyl meltdown with its disastrous escape of radiation. Now there was justifiable anxiety, and street protests and mass signature campaigns followed, led by some teaching staff of the Chinese University. Processions were organised, led by Legislative Councillors. However, Allen Lee Peng-fei, one of the Legislative Councillors, took a contrary view and was reported as saying that 'Daya Bay has been skilfully exploited by activist groups in fanning the citizens of Hong Kong into a frenzy of fear'.

Things came to a head during the summer of 1986 while I was Acting Governor and when the Legislative Council was not in session. A fact-finding mission of councillors led by Executive Councillor Ms Tam Wai Chu was circling the globe visiting nuclear installations. Before the mission returned and could report, some members of the council, flexing their muscles and trying to sideline the fact-finding mission, pressed me to recall the council for a special debate. This request would have raised the temperature without contributing to informed discussion. I refused to recall the council until the mission had returned and until details of the operation, monitoring and safety measures of the plant were known. When these were made public, when hundreds of visits to the plant while under construction were taking place and when people were able to talk to the serious and reassuring Chinese engineer in charge, there were no more protests. Eventually two debates took place in the Legislative Council; the first attempted to stop the construction and was heavily defeated, the second took a more balanced view and concentrated on asking for safety measures to be scrupulously pursued by the government.

Countries like France, the supplier and builder of the reactor, depend upon nuclear energy. Hong Kong has serious air pollution, and the Daya Bay power station, 70 per cent of whose electricity flows into Hong Kong, helped stave off the need for further polluting fossil fuel plants; moreover the electricity was cheaper to produce. A special communication line crossing the border to the Hong Kong Observatory was installed to monitor radiation levels. Everything possible was done to reassure. In December 1993, thirteen years after the idea had first been discussed between Chinese officials and Lord Kadoorie, the plant began supplying power to the Hong Kong grid.

The smouldering worries about Daya Bay served to bring politicians together and gave an added impetus to the need to reach a consensus on the clauses to be included in the Basic Law dealing with the political system after 1997. In the summer of 1986 a coalition of drafters of the Basic Law, Legislative Councillors, academics, lawyers, District Board members and municipal councillors agreed on a future legislature of sixty members, half of whom would be directly elected, the other half to be divided between representatives of functional groups and those elected by an electoral college. When the draft was finalised in January 1990, this was the agreed formula to be implemented phase by phase, up to and after 1997. The views were moderate; there were no angry demonstrations, no shaking fists, no banners demanding instant democracy, but rather a sombre realisation of what was attainable in the face of China's often-expressed concern for stability. This concern was described officially, but boringly for the impatient fist-shaker, as 'gradual and orderly progress'!

About this time I was returning one day from a helicopter survey of our new town development and flew over terraced steps cut into a rocky hillside which had been intended for the barracks of a battalion of Gurkhas to stem an earlier surge of illegal immigrants crossing to Hong Kong, and which became the victim of British budgetary defence cuts. The site sloped steeply down to the water and the bare terraces looked out on a scene of islands floating in an empty sea. We circled the site while I photographed, and I carried the photos back to the Governor. It was the Governor's ambition to build a third university to meet Hong Kong's need to concentrate more on science and technology. The site was chosen and the University of Science and Technology was built in a record three years; since its opening in 1994 it has become one of Asia's leading universities.

My work as Chief Secretary was fast coming to an end, but there was no let-up in the stream of ministers, councillors, professors, young leaders, lawyers and journalists who came to breakfast, lunch and dinner. First it had been the agreement, now the topic moved on to what was going to happen in 1997. We had endlessly to reassure, to point out that we had a detailed agreement with China, ratified by both governments and registered with the United Nations. Hong Kong would continue its membership of world organisations, the legal system would remain intact, the capitalist economic system would continue, land leases would be renewed and new ones issued for fifty years, and if a symbol were needed to reassure and to signify improved Sino-British relations, Her Majesty the Queen and Prince Philip had been welcomed in China. The auguries could not have been better, but disbelief continued.

22

Loss of Sir Edward Youde

On Friday, 6 December 1986, a fine peaceful morning in early winter, Emily Lau, a journalist and contributor to the *Far Eastern Economic Review* and later a popularly elected Legislative Councillor known for her sharp and wide-ranging criticism, had come to breakfast at Victoria House. We were sitting looking out across the harbour quietly chatting about current affairs when the phone rang. My personal assistant asked me to come to the office immediately as news had come that Sir Edward Youde, who was on a visit to Beijing, had died in his sleep at the residence of the Ambassador, Sir Richard Evans.

The Governor had been accompanying a trade mission and had completed a last day of talks with Zhou Nan and Li Hou at the Hong Kong and Macao office. He had died peacefully in his sleep, to be found in the early morning by his personal assistant, Richard Hoare. Lady Youde and Dame Lydia Dunn were visiting Xian and were flown back to Beijing. The Ambassador moved to clear away barriers of regulations to allow Sir Edward to cross international boundaries and be brought back to Hong Kong. In the absence of the Governor in Beijing I was already Acting Governor; suddenly the sole responsibility as Governor was mine.

Sir Edward was not supported by a political party and a gaggle of politicians. He stood alone. Now he was lost to Hong Kong in the midst of delicate and ongoing discussions with China about the Basic Law, about the development of the political structure, about passports and about a nuclear power plant being built on our doorstep. But Sir Edward's death meant much more than the loss of a quietly determined leader. In his unassuming way he had identified with the people and was held in great affection by them. This was demonstrated by the crowds which greeted him when he made his weekly visits to housing estates, hospitals and schools. There was no one to step into his shoes; for that we would have to wait months. I was due to retire and meanwhile would have to keep up the momentum of government.

Executive Councillors met and I told them the sad news. Sir Mark Heath, a huge man, Director of Protocol and a former Ambassador to the Vatican, David (later Sir David) Ford, who was to take over from me as Chief Secretary, bearded Alan Scott, Deputy Chief Secretary, quiet and authoritative General Boam, Commander of the British Forces, efficient Alistair Lang, Clerk of Councils, their staffs and many others arranged the details of an unscripted ceremony for the funeral in his own territory of the first Governor to die in office. All Sir Mark could discover was that a thousand troops could march in procession and that a seventeen-gun salute could be fired. Arrangements were made to bring from London the Minister for Hong Kong, Timothy Renton, Sir Patrick Wright, Permanent Secretary at the Foreign Office, David Wilson, also from the Foreign Office and responsible for Hong Kong, and the Ambassador, Sir Richard Evans, from Beijing.

British servicemen were regularly flown to and from the United Kingdom in RAF transport planes and it so happened one of these was in Hong Kong. Approval was quickly and readily given by the Chinese authorities for it to fly to Beijing to bring Sir Edward, his wife and companions back to Hong Kong the following day.

We waited on the rainy tarmac in the evening, together with members of Executive and Legislative Councils, in black silent lines as the coffin was lifted from the aircraft with skill and precision by Coldstream guardsmen. Then we drove in slow procession through the streets, eerily emptied of traffic. Thousands of people lined the pavements and pedestrian bridges to see their much loved and respected Governor pass. To them he had worn himself out with years of shuttling backwards and forwards between Hong Kong, London and Beijing, working for them and future.

The flag-draped coffin lay in state in the ballroom of Government House. All day Sunday and Monday many thousands of people, young and old, rich and poor, wound their way up the hill in long lines to sign the condolence book and pay their respects.

On Tuesday morning I presided at an Executive Council meeting with the Minister, Timothy Renton, in attendance. The funeral then took place. The coffin was lifted from Government House by guardsmen and placed on an open carriage. In the bright December sunshine we went slowly down the hill to St John's Cathedral, Gurkha troops with arms reversed slow-marching to the regular beat of muffled drums, Sir Edward's insignia carried on velvet cushion, Lady Youde and her two daughters in the car with its Crown insignia, myself and Jane walking behind followed by councillors and other principal mourners and more troops.

As a young Third Secretary of the British Embassy in Nanjing, Sir Edward had played a conspicuous role at a dramatic moment. During the last stages of the civil war he was despatched by the Ambassador to work his way through the troops of the People's Liberation Army lining the river, to talk personally with Mao Tse-tung to secure the release of the frigate *Amethyst* and allow it to steam down the Yangtze to Shanghai. He had lived and worked for four separate periods in the capital Beijing and had a wealth of valuable experience behind him. His years of governorship had been dominated by negotiations over the future and that these had been brought to a successful conclusion owed much to his wise and firm counsel. He worked without sparing. For recreation he retired either to Hong Kong's wetland sanctuary at Mai Po with telescope and tripod to watch birds, or to walk among the mountains in the north of the New Territories. Hong Kong had lost both a Governor and a dear friend.

Analysts, speculators and soothsayers had a field day weighing the chances for who was to be appointed to replace Sir Edward. Gradually the field narrowed down to David Wilson, the Foreign Office official heading the British team on the Joint Liaison Group. He, too, was a Chinese speaker, had been a previous political adviser to the Governor and was a member of the British team during negotiations about the future. He was no stranger to the hotchpotch of topics which the future was throwing up and the minefields he would meet along the way.

Meanwhile, until Sir David's arrival, Hong Kong's problems were my problems. I moved my office to Government House and David Ford moved into mine as Chief Secretary.

David Ford had first come to Hong Kong in 1967 as a specialist in psychological warfare to help with measures to counter those who were attempting to destabilise Hong Kong during the Cultural Revolution. He was to serve under both Sir David Wilson and his successor, Christopher Patten.

A review of the next steps in developing the system of representative government had been promised for 1987 in the 1984 White Paper. Concurrently the Basic Law drafting committee was drawing up its recommendations for the composition of the government to take office in 1997. Obviously working from separate angles, the two approaches had to converge and coincide. It made no sense to introduce reforms which would be swept aside at the handover. It would have had serious consequences and would have meant pressing ahead with change during the last remaining years leading to the handover against a torrent of criticism from China and a probable breakdown in communication. The effect on the economy would have been dire, resulting in a flight of capital from the markets and erosion of the people's savings. It was an unthinkable scenario. Despite these foreseeable consequences, there are those who criticise the British for timidity and failure to take this last-minute chance to introduce a fully fledged one man, one vote democratic system, disregarding the danger to the agreement which had been reached with so much effort.

Suspicion of what the British were up to came from another unexpected quarter, from a musty piece of legislation. As long ago as 1865 the British parliament had passed a Colonial Laws Validity Act. This act stipulates that whenever half of a colonial legislature is elected it shall become a 'representative legislature' which shall have full power to make laws — in other words, to become virtually independent. This was ammunition for the democrats and a legitimate cause for concern to the Chinese.

In February 1987 Mr Lu Ping, deputy director of the Hong Kong and Macao Affairs Office, put down a marker. In a clear warning to the British side, any political reforms, he said, if introduced before 1997, must be in line with the system laid down in the Basic Law, and if not, any representative system would be abandoned in 1997. People generally were uninterested in what they saw as arcane posturings: in January, a public opinion poll conducted for the *South China Morning Post* showed that 42 per cent of the public were just not interested in election procedures while a mere 39 per cent said that there should be some form of direct election to the legislature. The British had agreed the need for convergence with the Basic Law but the timing of a review in 1987 could not have been more unfortunate, coming as it did before there was any clear idea about what was likely to be in the law. These predicaments were what had sent Sir Edward Youde shuttling between the three cities and were the inauspicious background against which the promised review was to take place later in the year.

Political reform was not the only worry. There were suggestions about reducing the number of British troops in Hong Kong with still ten more years to go before the handover. Executive Council was concerned about the effect this would have on confidence and stability and Britain's commitment to stand by Hong Kong until the return of sovereignty. Troops of the garrison had taken over responsibility from the civilian police for patrolling the border during the disturbances of the Cultural Revolution in 1967, and had been an effective deterrent to illegal immigration. Some time before the transfer of power, the police had to be eased back into position on the border. It was too early for withdrawal but not too soon to be thinking about this and other means to reduce the size of the garrison. The question of reducing the garrison brought home the reality of 1997, and councillors were concerned that the removal of their protective umbrella would send the wrong signal to residents.

Meanwhile all was not well in China. In Shanghai. In December 1986, social tensions caused by the impetus of economic reform had unleashed unseasonable calls for political reform which had swollen into quite serious demonstrations by students and workers. There was a smaller demonstration in sympathy in Shenzhen across the border from Hong Kong. This unrest provoked a strong reaction from the leadership in Beijing against liberals within the Party, who were roundly denounced. The *South China Morning Post* of 12 January 1987, quoting unspecified sources, wrote that Deng Xiaoping had said that further protests must be dealt with severely and that he had ordered a crackdown on liberals: 'We have been too lax in curbing the tide of bourgeois liberalism.'

The General Secretary of the Chinese Communist Party (CCP), Mr Hu Yaobang, had not been seen for some days, because, it was said, he was worn out. He had actually quit office on 16 January 1987. Various other officials and academics lost their positions. Miss Deng Lin, Deng's daughter, speaking earlier in Hong Kong in support of her father, deplored the demonstrations, drawing attention to improvements that reform had brought and calling for patience and stability. These events happened long before the prolonged disorders and subsequent crackdown of 1989 and are now generally overlooked, but the firm way in which they were handled should have sent an unmistakable warning to later protesters.

23

The Walled City

Now that we were on speaking terms with China and before the arrival of David Wilson there was an opportunity to solve, thankfully for the last time, the vexed question of the Kowloon Walled City. Before the signing of the lease of the new territory in 1898, the northern half of the Kowloon Peninsula was governed and administered by the Chinese. So, too, were the surrounding hills, the spectacular rocky feature resembling a crouching lion, Lion Rock, and the land and villages surrounding the bays to the east and west of the peninsula. This farmland was dotted with tightly clustered grey-tiled roofs and whitewashed walls of Chinese villages and their accompanying and numerous temples.

In the east of Kowloon a walled and fortified village, which became grandiosely known as the Kowloon Walled City, was the seat of Chinese officialdom and housed a garrison of a few hundred Chinese troops. A paved granite track led down from its gatehouse to a simple landing place in Kowloon Bay where Chinese fighting ships could anchor. It was agreed, when the lease of the New Territories was negotiated, that within the city of Kowloon Chinese officials should continue to exercise jurisdiction and that they could continue to use the road from Kowloon to San On in Guangdong, and that the landing near Kowloon could continue to be used for the convenience of Chinese men-of-war, merchant and passenger vessels. However, this accommodating attitude did not persist. It was only a short while after the leasing in 1898 that the continued presence of

Chinese officials within the Kowloon Walled City created an anomalous and unacceptable situation for Hong Kong's rulers and was seen as 'inconsistent with the military requirements for the defence of Hong Kong'. British jurisdiction had been extended to the whole of the new territory by an Order in Council given by the Queen, so why should the Walled City be excluded? Contrary to previous understandings and agreements, it was peremptorily taken over on the 16 May 1899 and the Chinese troops and officials were told to pack their bags and depart.

Following its seizure, this walled 'city' or village was treated no differently from other villages in the leased territory. As it was owned by the villagers it was left alone. Development of surrounding farmland took place, and as the years went by, except for the Walled City, gradually even the villages of Kowloon themselves were either acquired by the government or by private developers for urban development.

Kowloon was a growing township, the Walled City was a uncontrolled and malodorous slum. In 1933 the Hong Kong government made a vain attempt to take control. The residents took their protests to the government in China, which reminded the British of the convention and the fact that according to its terms it remained under the jurisdiction of China even though Chinese officials were no longer stationed there. The British decided to leave well alone.

Later, during the war years, the Japanese marched prisoners of war from their camp in West Kowloon, bedraggled and emaciated, to take down the fortifying walls of the city and use the granite blocks and bricks for the improvement of the Kai Tak airport. Squatters later assisted the process of demolition and built their huts where the wall had been.

An attempt to clear the Walled City was made again in 1948. On this occasion the response reflected the deteriorating situation caused by the civil war in China. The Chinese government in Nanjing politely and firmly required the British to release people who had been arrested, to pay compensation for damage done, and to remove the police, and conveyed a strong hint to the British not to rock the boat which was, by then, in danger of capsizing altogether. The British acquiesced.

Conditions deteriorated. Buildings in the Walled City, which towered as high as fourteen storeys, were built without plans and without proper foundations, and dark, dank and cavernous alleyways followed the pattern of the narrow lanes of the former village. It was a haven not only for drug addicts and prostitutes but for unlicensed doctors and dentists and for thousands of immigrant families who could not afford even the rent of a bedspace elsewhere in Kowloon. It was a no-go area for government officials; however, welfare groups could go in, and soon after our arrival in Hong Kong in 1957 my wife, Jane, joined a welfare group which went each week into its dark interior and distributed vitamins and milk to a long queue of thin, wan-faced children.

To make matters worse, and to add to the misery, the Walled City was almost under the flight approach to the airport and at busy times, every five minutes jet planes screamed and roared their way to land, skimming the rooftops of this crazy collection of skyscrapers leaning dangerously against one another. Exasperated, in 1963 the Hong Kong government made yet another attempt to clear the 'city' and resettle the residents. It succeeded no better than previously.

In 1997 the whole of Hong Kong was going to come under Chinese jurisdiction, including the wretched Walled City. In 1986 relations with China were good and, looked at objectively, there were persuasive reasons for allowing the British to clear up this disgraceful blemish on Kowloon, and not to leave the problem to be solved by China. Compensation would have to be paid to owners, residents, shopkeepers, hawkers, factories, doctors and dentists. Hong Kong had the money and rehousing could be found for all legitimate residents. The suggestion was put to the officials in the New China News Agency and they in turn quietly sounded out the Kaifong (residents) Welfare Association. They satisfied themselves that the complex problems of clearance would be handled with sensitivity and that a committee, to include representatives of the Residents Association, would be formed to advise on specific issues. After rebuffing the British so many times, China now agreed that they could go ahead.

I held meetings in Government House with a tight group of officials on whom was impressed the need for total secrecy. Secrecy was essential, otherwise the clearance and demolition would have become the subject of local debate and international interest and a probably unmanageable political football. Building clearances are planned long in advance, and so great is the demand for decent housing that if news of a clearance leaks out, there is a rush to fill up and stake a claim to every spare corner and bedspace in buildings to be cleared.

With the Walled City there was a double need for secrecy, both practical and political. There were no leaks. To maintain secrecy, squads of officials who were to do the screening of residents and businesses were told that they were going to a different destination until they were about to board the trucks in the early morning which took them to the 'city'. Surprise was complete and by the end of the day the initial screening had been completed. We then knew that the clearance and demolition would involve housing and compensation for 33,000 inhabitants.

And so the Walled City was cleared. There were businesses such as unlicensed dentists who had left China, some with a qualification which was not recognised in Hong Kong, operating in stalls along the roadside; there were the buildings which had been used by Chinese officials. There were prostitutes and drug addicts and endless variations of the human condition to be sorted out, compensated and resettled. Gradually the gaunt grey buildings were emptied and demolished and, in its place, as part of the agreement with Chinese officials, there is now a pleasant Chinese garden containing a few relics of the past eventful history.

24

The Arrival of Sir David Wilson and Retirement

*T*he first months of Hong Kong's year pass quickly. Celebrations for the New Year, reckoned by the lunar months in January or February, follow the winding-down of business and the settling of accounts. Family reunions send hundreds of thousands away from Hong Kong to visit their relatives in their native villages in the mainland; others tour scenic spots in China and the world. Workers from Chinese restaurants in Europe return to their native villages in the New Territories. Workmen down tools, quiet descends on building sites, barges and boats are docked, ships sail away, and for once the sea is as empty as before an advancing typhoon. Hong Kong, once in a year, is quiet.

This welcome interruption to the frenzy of normality follows close on the heels of Christmas and the Western New Year. Qing Ming, the spring grave-sweeping, and Easter then arrive with another long break. The memory of those days is one of flower markets, fireworks, ornamental orange trees, peach blossom, lucky red packets, and an encouraging message delivered by me as Acting Governor which was to be televised. Against this auspicious background there were flickers of political sheet lightning.

'Britain and China Clash over Voting' was a February headline in the *South China Morning Post*. 'Pro-Beijing sources' were quoted as saying there might be no direct elections to the Legislative Council before 1997. Lu Ping, deputy director of Beijing's Hong Kong and Macao Affairs Office, had said that political reforms, if any, introduced before 1997 must conform to the Basic Law which would not be completed until 1990. To counter this it was reported that on his last visit to Beijing, Sir Edward Youde had warned Chinese officials that two 'heavyweight' Executive Councillors might resign if direct polls were not approved. These were warning shots, and the way ahead on political reform would have to wait for the arrival of Sir David Wilson.

Meanwhile there were other more frivolous anxieties. Several months before, we had generously succumbed to the persuasions of a film company to allow Victoria House, our residence in my former role as Chief Secretary, to be used for a party scene in the filming of James Clavell's book *Noble House*. We had not moved to Government House for the few months before the arrival of the new Governor, and guests who would normally have stayed there now came to Victoria House to stay with us.

So it was that Kenneth Baker, British Minister for Education, and his wife, who had earlier been invited to stay with the late Governor, were now our guests, and their visit coincided with the commotion of the shooting of the scenes designated for those particular days. The situation called for careful planning.

Carpenters had fitted a flimsy new and 'grander' entrance to the house and the signal to start filming was given as we whisked the Bakers off for an evening of racing under the floodlights. As the Crown car wound its way along the narrow roads of the Peak, the pink, gold, blue and black Rolls Royces which had been pressed into service for the filming from the rich and famous swept smoothly up the drive and filled the car park. The filming of the party scene of 'taipans and tycoons', with 'extras' provided by family members, their friends and our staff in their starched white and black, began with the opening of the newly magnificent front entrance and moved inside to where tables were spread and 'champagne' flowed. We endured an anxious evening entertaining the Bakers in the Governor's box at the races, and returned to the house. The cars were gone and the cables, generator and paraphernalia removed as though nothing had taken place while we were away! The next day the cameras returned as our guests were once more away on their official visits; Pierce Brosnan, the star of the film, swept in and out of the prop front door in dramatic fury until it, too, collapsed from exhaustion.

On a more serious front, there were ideas to stretch the imagination. The need for a new airport had been a topic of conversation and concern not only in Hong Kong but for all travellers who landed at Kai Tak. Planes roaring in flew along the hills which bounded Kowloon to the north and then at a few hundred feet above the roofs and executed a sharp banking turn to the right over the washing lines, peering into the windows of the elderly, greying apartment blocks, before hitting the runway. Kai Tak had seemed capable of almost indefinite expansion as bits and pieces and more parking bays were added to the terminal. But expansion meant more and more planes were flying over crowded Kowloon. There had been talk of building a new airport for years, but the ideal solution could not be found.

In 1987 a brilliant, visionary engineer, Gordon (now Sir Gordon) Wu, chairman of a major construction firm, in alliance with a Who's Who of property and development firms, put forward a proposal to build an airport island in the sea to the west of Hong Kong, with shipping berths and land for development of new towns and road and rail links to the border. 'Tycoons Unite on Second Airport', ran the headline. The Hongkong and Shanghai Bank and the Bank of China were said to be ready with finance and so, too, were mainland Chinese investors in Hong Kong. It was a grandiose scheme and the emergence of such an alliance spoke of confidence.

It was really too much for the government, too imaginative, probably full of snags, but it made those at the top do some serious thinking. Some questioned why an airport should not be built on the boundary with China to serve both Hong Kong and the mainland. This seductive idea had earlier been scotched because it would have meant aircraft of countries with which China had no diplomatic relations overflying the mainland. Later, in 1987, it was equally impractical because it would have meant aircraft flying over the emerging town of Shenzhen, where the Shenzhen Special Economic Zone, getting in first, was building its own airport. The decision which was announced came down to a sparsely inhabited island, Chek

Lap Kok, to the west, lying just to the north of the larger island of Lantau, to be reached by highways, bridges and a railway from the centre of the city. Even then the final decision to go ahead did not come until two years later, in October 1989, and it was used as a morale booster for Hong Kong which was still coming to grips with the tragedy of Tiananmen.

I flew to London in February 1987 to brief Sir David on what to expect when he arrived and to give my view of the political turn of events and the warning signals about democratic reform which had been coming from Beijing. I also spent half an hour with the Foreign Secretary, Sir Geoffrey Howe, and with Sir Patrick Wright, head of the Foreign Office, met Members of Parliament and talked to the media.

Sir David Wilson maintained tradition and arrived on 9 April 1987 in full fig, with helmet, sword, feathers flying, sailing across the harbour in the Governor's launch, greeting the members of his Executive Council and inspecting the guard on the Queen's Pier before taking the oaths of office in the City Hall in front of the assembled dignitaries of Hong Kong. His matter-of-fact inaugural address pledged his determination to maintain the pace of progress and not to neglect anyone in the process. Of the review of the system of representation, he said: 'These are serious issues with far-reaching consequences. We must approach them calmly and with common sense. If there is to be change it should be prudent and gradual.' The fat was already in the fire. To maintain momentum, the Green Paper, 'Review of Developments in Representative Government', had been published just before Sir David arrived and the British Foreign Secretary had been able to give the Chinese Foreign Minister, Wu Xieqian, an idea of its contents at a meeting just before in Berne in early April 1987.

I now ceased to govern and was appointed the Governor's adviser for six months. I descended to a huge empty room in the lower ground floor of Government House, read and wrote papers on Hong Kong politics, and from time to time talked things over with Sir David. In particular I came across the axiom that strong party government generally leads to a decline in committees and weak government means more. Certainly Hong Kong then, and in later years, was no exception: there was no strong party government so that whenever there was a problem a committee mushroomed like magic and, since there were (and are) so many, there were not enough individuals with the necessary talents to be found to sit on them. Each member, therefore, wore many hats and dashed frantically from one meeting to another, breathlessly, arriving late and leaving early. In the final analysis there had to be an end to this never-ending consultation and a more decisive form of government had to take its place.

Leaving my dungeon in Government House, I travelled to Brussels and Vienna and made reassuring speeches to sceptical audiences who thought they knew all there was to know about the communist bloc and did not want to hear a message that there might be something different happening in the Far East. No one wished to know that China was changing. The contrast for Western audiences with their experience and emotions caused by the Cold War was too great. How could such an agreement have been reached with a communist power?

In 1987, the wettest summer in Hong Kong's history, we moved from the spacious, colonial grandeur of Victoria House to another government eyrie, a pink bungalow higher up the Peak from which the ground fell away precipitously, almost to the harbour's edge. It was one of those houses dotted about the cooler, grassy slopes of the Peak, in the earlier years before the roads were built, linked by paths along which sedan chairs passed, dogs were walked and businessmen hurried to the Peak Tram.

They stand, those houses, in the early photographs of Hong Kong — England, Surrey in Asia — picnic parties among the grass and rocks, hats, long skirts, parasols, and in the background, hovering houseboys. Now the houses, if they still survive, are enveloped in trees and those that have not survived have been developed into terraced houses and apartment blocks. The Peak, like the rest of Hong Kong, has had to succumb to the greedy demands of a thrusting economy; but as a sole concession to the past, the rise and fall of the ridgeline has to be preserved in the profile of its ubiquitous, low-rise apartments.

I was anxious that we should not lose momentum in the building of relations with Guangdong which had been started by Sir Murray

MacLehose and continued by Sir Edward Youde. It was too soon after his arrival for David Wilson himself to visit, and it was arranged that, as his personal adviser, I would lead a party of senior officials to exchange views and ideas about future infrastructure development, roads and railways, with our counterparts in the provincial government. My hope was that this would establish the foundation for close and regular cooperation.

We travelled by train, meandering slowly and comfortably through the wet landscape of the delta, seeing the first signs of double-tracking of the railway, half-completed highways and urban expansion. Guangzhou (Canton), too, was expanding and developing and feeling the strain, and, despite our escort in their security vehicles, barking staccato commands and waving flags, ordering all before to wait obediently by the roadside or in the gutter, we moved only slowly through traffic jams.

It was over-optimistic of me to hope that in 1987 we would be able to break down the psychological barriers in Hong Kong created by the years of colonial rule and exposure to Western culture. Hong Kong remained strangely uninterested in the great economic resurgence taking place on its doorstep, and what began as a great hope for high-level future cooperation and regular meetings remained a topic of discussion between officials from Hong Kong and Guangzhou until the turn of the century, instead of turning into decisive action to solve common problems. Meanwhile highways, railways and great bridges span the rivers of Guangdong and criss-cross the delta. Large towns and industrial and science parks have sprouted where, until the reforms of 1978, there were country towns, quiet villages, fishponds, vegetable farms and paddy fields.

Economic reform in Guangdong had its ugly side. Local authorities, anxious not to miss out on the gleam of prosperity, were able to acquire land from villagers in excess of the need for measured expansion to meet real demand, and as you drove along the delta roads, scarred hillsides lined the route and former paddy fields lay fallow beneath a burden of bright, brown infertile soil, waiting for industry. The skeletons of abandoned building projects were a stark reminder of the failure of excessive enthusiasm. However, ten years later, by the turn of the century, the delta was showing signs of becoming a coherent development area of forty million people.

This was the last time I would visit China as an official. It was time to move on and begin a new life, and time to say goodbye as an official to many friends. The Wilsons held a dinner party for us in the ballroom of Government House, young musicians from the Academy of Performing Arts played, and for the first time in that venue Hong Kong shed a bit of the formality of its colonial past.

25

A New Home

I
t had been arranged that I would remain as Sir David Wilson's adviser for six months after his arrival, but we needed to move out of the house provided by the government into a home of our own. I had earlier said to Sir Edward Youde, when he told me that I must follow the rules and retire at sixty, that I intended to stay in Hong Kong. Few, if any, civil servants had had a career similar to mine. For us it had been normal to be posted from one appointment to another, not to spend too long in any one place or post. Most civil servants worked in the urban offices of the government and lived in apartment blocks scattered around the city, and moved into larger, more comfortable apartments as promotion came their way. We, on the other hand, had spent years living in the New Territories where there were houses with gardens for District Officers, close to the people in their district care. (Things have changed. None of the houses are now lived in by District Officers, which tells the story of a changing society: one became an education centre and nature trail for the World Wide Fund for Nature; one became a centre for recuperation from AIDS; one bungalow has been demolished for multi-storey redevelopment; and another is the viewing platform from which visitors photograph the great bridges spanning the islands to lead to the airport.)

We were fortunate to have lived in the country as it developed from market town, ancient villages, paddy fields and vegetable farms to satellite towns, highways and railways, sorrowfully accepting the planned obliteration of a way of life and a living environment and working to ameliorate some of the deleterious effects of development. Now in 1987 we needed our own home and once more looked to the New Territories.

In the years before and immediately after the war, the ambition of many of Hong Kong's Chinese managers and professionals had been to own a bathing pavilion along the shoreline stretching out from Kowloon to the west, and for the wealthy to build a country retreat for weekend enjoyment, to entertain their friends to tennis, to swim, to play mahjong and to indulge their fondness for growing miniature trees. Gradually the bathing pavilions were put to more popular use by clubs and societies and the houses were rented to those who were bold enough to risk living in semi-isolation in a society which was less secure than in the past.

With the help and advice from a friend we looked up the overgrown driveways of the houses to the west of Kowloon. Most had already been bought by property developers for redevelopment into apartment blocks. There was one which could not be redeveloped into a high rise because of planning restrictions and was, therefore, of no interest to real estate developers. It stood alone, deserted, vandalised and overgrown: Dragon View. It had not been lived in for a number of years and in Hong Kong's tropical climate the tendrils of creepers and bursting vegetation had enveloped the driveway and blanketed the paths and terraces of the old house. The doctor who had decided in 1953 to build on this hillside spur had liked its isolation, its uninterrupted view of mountains and sea and its scope for gardening. Now the doors were missing, windows were shattered, ceilings were lying on the floor. But my wife was convinced it was the place for us. We visited the house, bringing gardening tools to cut our way through branches and creepers until we could look out to the blue mountains facing us across the seaway and to the islands of distant Hong Kong and nearer Lantau. Then miraculously on a tree in the overgrown garden for a brief moment I saw a rare and brilliant green-blue bird, Verditer's flycatcher. This seemed to be an omen. We decided to contact the owner.

Madam Lee, widow of Dr Raymond Lee Yeo Hsuan, an eminent former citizen, was living in Canada. Dr Lee had been a member of the British

Army Aid Group operating in China during the Pacific War and had made an epic journey of about a thousand miles across war-torn China to take charge of a famine relief operation in western Guangdong. On return to Hong Kong he continued a distinguished career and had become an Urban Councillor, and subsequently left for Canada to join so many of his compatriots in retirement. He had lavished attention on the garden of Dragon View, building pathways into the hills, terraces and pavilions, with benches carefully placed to watch the lateen-sailed junks as they tacked their way along the quiet channel between his garden and the clouded peaks of the island of Lantau. The house took its name from the Chinese village along the road, Tsing Lung Tau, 'the head of the green dragon'. This is an important element in the geomancy of Feng Shui: the green dragon and the white tiger rest on either side of a location, which is 'good feng shui'. The dragon's vein ran down the line of the nearby hills and rested in the sea.

We contacted Dr Lee's son, Edmund, also a doctor, who was acting for his widowed mother. He wrote to us as follows (and I include his letter in full in view of what took place in an attempt to calumniate me some years later):

'Many thanks for your letter enquiring about the house at Castle Peak. It belongs to my mother and I can only speak on her behalf. As you probably know the house is in a state of disrepair due to repeated vandalism from nearby villagers. However structurally it is still pretty sound. Certainly it needs rejuvenation. If you are interested please feel free to inspect the house and its environs. We have received several enquiries recently and the price of $1.5 million has been suggested.'

We replied to his letter that the cost of putting the house in a liveable condition would require at least $260,000 and asked if he would consider a slight reduction. He agreed to a small reduction and a price of $1,425,000. We had never met and were only to do so in the office of the solicitors to complete the purchase.

The land on which the house was built had only been roughly surveyed at the beginning of the century on what were known as demarcation sheets prepared by the surveyors from India. The lease plan looked like a child's drawing done with a setsquare about half an inch in size, and when measured more accurately the house had been built quite a few feet south of where it should have been. We needed to rectify the boundaries to put the house in the midst of its land by giving up land behind and receiving the same amount in front. It had been sold, too, rather extraordinarily, without any driveway to get from the house to the nearby road. In return for a fee we were then granted a right of way to the road, but no ownership to the land over which it passed. We were to live there for almost fourteen years until we, too, ironically, were in the way of the widening of Castle Peak Road — the very same road, as it passed through Tsuen Wan, from which I had helped to move a whole village in 1959.

After months of hammering, sawing, plastering, painting and rearranging, the house was ready. I had finished six months as the Governor's adviser and we moved in on 11 November 1987 at one o'clock, the date and time having been carefully selected by a Feng Shui master by consulting our horoscopes, cross-referenced to the Chinese cycle of years and the lunar calendar. A friend arrived with a suckling pig on a wooden platter, basted with honey and roasted to a crisp and freckled rich brown. The gods were satisfied and we were free to celebrate in the usual manner. Gradually, as the years passed, despite our hot and humid summers and long dry winters, the garden became a treasure land of unusual plants flowering throughout the year and was much visited by fellow horticultural enthusiasts.

26

A Change of Life: 1989

*D*ragon View was a delight, perched on its hillside spur above the narrow Castle Peak Road, which passed between it and the sea. It was half-hidden by the overhanging branches of two sprawling Flame of the Forest trees (*Delonix regia*) whose vivid scarlet flowers in the spring announce the return of the sun to the northern tropics. Through the house, the sudden vista of the sea, the steep, mountainous islands beyond and distant Hong Kong brought a gasp of delight from visitors. The ground sloped steeply upward behind the house through dark woodland, home for snakes and spiders, with long trails of purple bougainvillea, gordonia with flowers like poached eggs, and mauve bauhinia. A trickle of water, which after rain became a torrent, fed a small pond in a sanctuary of creepers, branching fern fronds and wild ginger, a retreat for five shy terrapin.

As we settled into our new life it was not long before there were offers of things to do. We were already busy with voluntary work: Jane was Chief Commissioner of more than 36,000 Girl Guides and I was chairman of the World Wide Fund for Nature, president of the Outward Bound Trust and chairman of an Oxford scholarship fund for Chinese research students. I became chairman of the film star Jackie Chan's charitable trust and of Operation Smile China Medical Mission, which sends medical teams to China to operate on children whose faces needed corrective surgery, particularly for cleft lips and cleft palates which are common in rural China.

There were boards and committees of schools, hospitals and sports organisations, and after a break to ensure that there was no conflict with my government work, I became a non-executive director of a number of companies, one of which gave me an opportunity to travel to Australia and also to make numerous visits to meet officials in the Finance Ministry and insurance industry of China. But most interesting and important of all, in 1988 I was asked to become the first chairman of a newly independent Housing Authority now freed from government chains.

Many years before, on Christmas day 1953, the ashes were still smouldering from a disastrous fire which, in the tinder-dry winter air and gusty north winds, had raged through a shanty town of squatters. Fifty thousand people were homeless from the inferno. Realising that the immigrants were in Hong Kong to stay, and that more and more were continuing to arrive, Hong Kong began to build. Once begun there was no stopping. Forty years later, half of Hong Kong's population, three million people, lived in high-rise housing blocks built in response to the fires of the fifties. Before building could begin, squatters were cleared into other tin-shed shelters until they could move back into high-rise permanent homes. Despite this tremendous effort the situation never seemed to get better. Hong Kong's population was growing by at least a million every ten years through both natural increase and the steady stream of immigrants, legal and illegal, from the rest of China. The estates built in the crisis years of the fifties and sixties, after twenty-five years or so, were now substandard and had to be demolished and rebuilt and their families housed in newer estates. The wealthier residents of rented new estates had to be enticed out to buy newly built modern flats. Meanwhile, there were still well over a hundred thousand families — half a million people — on a waiting list. These, for the most part, were families living stoically in rundown tenements subdivided into tiny cubicles. It was not possible to increase the pace of building because of the paragraph in the agreement with China which restricted the disposal of land by the government before 1997 to fifty hectares a year. For some things, such as expansion of the container port, universities and so forth, the limit was waived, but the restriction imposed unnatural constraints on the disposal of land for housing.

I led a delegation from the Housing Authority to see housing development in Beijing, Shanghai and Guangzhou. All those years of living apart from the mainland, apprehensively viewing China as it went through its turbulent years of political upheaval, and at that time with no particular wish to visit villages from which they had long been separated, had created on the part of some Hong Kong people a reluctance to recognise the changes that were now taking place and an unwillingness to acknowledge the reality that, following reunification, the border would become a mere boundary. Some were lacking in curiosity, or were putting off the inevitable as long as they could. Some members of the Housing Authority shared this lack of curiosity, and so our visit was planned with the aim of breaking down the barriers.

In each of the cities we visited, new monster housing estates with comprehensive facilities were being built. There was much to admire — things, too, to criticise — but the direction of change was easily seen and sensed. Shanghai had picked up some ideas from Singapore in its approach to some of its housing and rehousing problems, and each city was stirring with energy, vitality and change.

Meanwhile, across the border in Shenzhen, glass-walled tower blocks were peeping over the hills, visible from Hong Kong. Shenzhen had already grown into a well-developed city with crowded traffic intersections, broad, tree-lined avenues, parks and gardens. (These later were to earn it a prize as the Garden City of the World!) The airport at Huang Tien in Shenzhen was now serving forty cities in China and was linked to Hong Kong by fast ferry. Further to the west, construction was due to start on a new bridge at the Bocca Tigris, Humen, at the mouth of the Pearl River, where the first battle of the nineteenth-century opium wars had taken place. The development of Shenzhen from a small township, villages and paddy fields to a great city took twenty years, and in that time it had grown to an incredible size of nearly seven million. It not only rivalled Hong Kong in the size of its population but, because of its low prices, was a place to shop, to eat and to have your clothes and curtains made. But in the early nineties, very few wished to see the writing on the wall.

27

Political Development 1987–1990:
Tiananmen and the Boat People

W hen Sir David Wilson arrived in 1987, the Green Paper review of Hong Kong's political system had just been published in an atmosphere unfavourable to bold initiatives. China had said that anything unacceptable to China and not in conformity with the Basic Law was doomed not to survive the transfer of sovereignty. The public response to the review was muted except from the few who were especially interested in political development. The majority preferred to keep well away from politics. The main point at issue concentrated on whether Hong Kong should have elections in 1988, before the drafting of the Basic Law was complete, or wait until 1991 when the Chinese position would be clear.

Signature campaigns were held to obtain support for early direct elections. Anonymous opinion surveys also conveyed the same message. An independent Survey Office to advise on the response to a public consultation paper decided to take signature campaigns as one submission and individual signed letters as separate submissions. Mass signature campaigns are a simple way to engender support and demand very little thought and responsibility from those who are pressed to sign as they hurry on their way to work, whereas individual letters, although produced wholesale on a copier, were judged to have a greater legitimacy. That was the view of the Survey Office.

It was no surprise that the White Paper published in 1988 to report the result of the survey and finalise recommendations for change concluded that submissions were generally in favour of direct elections, but that views were divided over the timing of their introduction. However, when it was discussed in Executive Council it was finally decided that elections should be held in 1991 when what was in the Basic Law would be known. There was strong criticism of this decision, cries of chicanery, and ridicule for the independent findings of the Survey Office. It is not possible to predict in what way China would have reacted if Hong Kong had gone on to hold elections in 1988, but we can be certain that it would have been very damaging to relations in the lead up to 1997 and to the cooperation so desperately needed if the transition was to be smooth. The decision was not changed.

Despite these excitements, in general things settled down. The economy was booming and the drafting of the Basic Law was progressing well. This latter required much effort, for not only were the essentials of Hong Kong's way of life, law, social and political system and economy being spelled out, but the drafters were tightening up much of the hurriedly prepared wording of the Sino-British Agreement. But the period of calm did not last long. The committee continued its painstaking work in 1989 against a background of increasing disquiet about events in China. On 6 April, the anniversary of the Shanghai demonstrations in 1976, Hong Kong newspapers reported that students in Beijing had defied a ban on meetings to discuss how to speed up democratic change.

There was political unrest elsewhere in former communist countries. Reformers in Russia had defeated communist party candidates in parliamentary elections. In Poland the independent worker's movement, Solidarity, was legalised, while on television there were nightly scenes from Seoul of students and workers locked in combat with riot police. As fate would have it, Hu Yaobang, a Chinese leader who had sided with the students in the 1976 protests, died. Wreaths were laid at the monument to the People's Heroes in Tiananmen where in 1976 they had been laid to commemorate the death of Zhou Enlai. There were reports that marches had also taken place in Shanghai. By 20 April 20 the crowd of workers and students in Beijing had swollen to 100,000 and there had been protests and attempts to break in to Zhongnanhai, the seat of government. Funds and tents were collected and sent to the demonstrators from Hong Kong.

Hopes of a peaceful outcome were kindled and then as rapidly, extinguished. The Russian president Mikhail Gorbachev visited Beijing at the end of a thirty-year break in relations, and to the humiliation of the government, was unable to enter the Great Hall of the People by using the grand entrance, but had to go in through the back door. On 18 May the Chinese Premier warned that 'if the movement did not end it would be more chaotic than the Cultural Revolution'. The situation was serious 'not only in Beijing but throughout the country and bordering on a state of anarchy' (*South China Morning Post*, 19 May 1989).

On 19 May, before the final disaster, troops began to move into the capital, meetings were banned and martial law declared. The occupation of the square by the students not only continued but efforts were made to barricade the roads leading to it. On 23 May troops moved closer to the centre of the city. Students then voted to leave on 30 May, but decisive leadership to accomplish this was lacking and, grievously, many were still there when the army opened fire during the night of 3–4 June and, using tanks and troops, moved in to clear the square.

The effect on Hong Kong was traumatic. Wearing the black and white colours of mourning, marchers filled the streets, shoulder to shoulder by hundreds of thousands, and cars, taxis, lorries and buses tied black streamers to their aerials. To share in their distress we travelled in by train from our home in the New Territories and joined the mass of quietly moving crowds on their way to the racecourse — the only large open space in the urban area. The racecourse was filled by a mass demonstration, and everyone converged there to hear harsh words of condemnation and to sing patriotic songs. After a while, with heavy hearts and troubled minds, we left for home.

The events of Tiananmen are long remembered. An Alliance for the Support of Democracy in China was formed. Some members left the Basic Law drafting committee in protest, never to return. Reacting to the public mood, the Governor, Sir David Wilson, once again raised with the British government the question of providing an escape route, a passport for the people of Hong Kong. He could do no less, but once again this was rejected. Three things were, however, promised. A privileged fifty thousand families of the professional and managerial classes were selected and obtained British passports; a Bill of Rights was introduced into Hong Kong; and the construction of a new airport to boost morale was announced.

There were other distractions. While a privileged few were constructing their escape route out of Hong Kong, a new flood of refugees from Vietnam was pouring in. Hong Kong had already done its bit to help deal with the refugee crisis which immediately followed the end of the war in Vietnam. Accounts of Hong Kong seldom mention the long saga of Vietnamese refugees which was the troublesome, costly and continuing backdrop to all the other things Hong Kong had to worry about and lasted for twenty-five years, until the end of the century.

It had begun when, following the fall of Saigon in 1975, the *Clara Maersk*, a Danish cargo ship, scooped up boatloads of refugees from the sea as she steamed in the direction of Hong Kong. She arrived with nearly four thousand men, women and children crowded on her decks and superstructure, lining the rails and looking anxiously for refuge. Many a rusty and broken small boat at the end of her working life followed that dramatic beginning, and helped by a tattered sail, limped and chugged her way up the coast to sanctuary.

Later, shortly before Christmas 1978, the *Huey Fung*, a rusting cargo ship, had been 'chartered' by corrupt officials who sold tickets to freedom. Gold, paid to the captain, was later discovered hidden in the engine room. Hong Kong was reckoned to be a soft touch. The ship was ordered to anchor in the open sea near islands to the south of Hong Kong and told to proceed on her voyage to Taiwan. The captain called Hong Kong's bluff and refused to move, and the ship stayed there, pitching and rolling, well into January while the critical world watched. It was cold, wet and stormy; there was no alternative but to let her enter with 3,300 sick and hungry refugees who had been living for over a month in hellish conditions and without sanitation in the holds.

By the end of that year, 1979, there were very nearly 100,000 boat people in Hong Kong. As succeeding years passed these numbers rose and fell; some were resettled, others came. But in 1989, when we were anxiously watching events in Beijing, we also had to patrol the seas to the south where more boats were arriving than in any other year since 1979. These were not those fearing reprisal from the new regime but people duped into seeking an easier life overseas.

The world had developed compassion fatigue and turned its attention away from Vietnam to even more serious and intractable problems in Africa. Hong Kong was tired and exasperated by this endless flow of migrants. It had had enough. This time they were not given the same welcome as previous arrivals, but were locked behind barbed wire in closed camps and with few exceptions categorised as economic migrants. These were people who were escaping from the hardship of the regimented economy of communist Vietnam, just when that economy was being reformed and liberated. Over the next few years they were loaded onto planes and sent back, at first carried on board protesting and then walking on less reluctantly as life in Vietnam gradually improved.

By the middle of January 1990, the drafters of the Basic Law had just about completed their five years of work. All that remained to be done was to reach final agreement with China on the development of the political system after the return of sovereignty and also in the years leading to it. This latter point was important because, provided the system and the composition of the Legislative Council in 1997 was in conformity with the Basic Law, it could, upon confirmation by a Preparatory Committee to be established in 1996, become the first Legislative Council of the Special Administrative Region after 1997. This was the 'through train', the imaginative contribution to the smooth transfer of sovereignty.

With the objective of securing this agreement on the development of the political structure before and after 1997, unbeknownst to Hong Kong, the Secretary of State for Foreign and Commonwealth Affairs, Douglas Hurd, began a correspondence in January 1990 with the Chinese Foreign Minister, Qian Qichen. The British were anxious to secure as many directly elected seats to the legislature as possible in response to what was perceived as an overwhelming demand in Hong Kong: 'failure to do this would risk severe damage to British authority in the period before 1997.' Other subjects in the letters included the formation of an electoral college to elect a number of seats, a restriction on the number of foreign nationals who could be elected and separate majority voting for the passage of bills and motions by those representing functional constituencies and those elected by direct elections and by the electoral committee.

Any exchange of letters between foreign ministers is extremely important. These letters were no exception. They narrowed the difference between the two sides, and ended with the Foreign Secretary writing to the Chinese Foreign Minister agreeing to limit the number of directly elected seats in 1991 to 18, on the understanding that there would be 20 in 1995, 24 in 1999 and 30 in 2003. The Foreign Secretary went on to say that he agreed in principle with the arrangements for the electoral committee proposed by China. He continued to express his concern about the restrictions on foreign nationals participating in the legislature and on the separate voting system. On the voting system, China believed that this would provide a necessary check and balance. On the participation of foreign nationals in the legislature, China said this was a necessary restriction because of the number of foreign passport holders in Hong Kong, and in any case it was far more liberal than in other parliaments. China was, however, willing to recognise that apart from expatriates, many Chinese in Hong Kong hold foreign passports, and to exclude them entirely would have deprived the legislature of some of her leading citizens.

Although they knew something was delaying the conclusion of their work, the members of the Basic Law drafting committee in a plenary session were kept waiting in China to finalise the draft until the exchange of letters between the foreign ministers was complete. Only then did they sign off on their nearly five years' work. For reasons which have never been adequately explained, this correspondence was not made public until its dramatic production by Chinese officials during the visit of the Rt. Hon. Christopher Patten, who had taken over as Governor, on his visit to Beijing in the autumn of 1992.

28

Sir David Wilson

Each Governor had his style, and just as each governorship was distinguished by the problems and anxieties of the day, so the solutions depended on the Governor's particular personality and leadership qualities. Sir David Wilson, who was Governor now, inherited a different and difficult set of problems just two years into his governorship.

He brought with him a quiet, thoughtful style and the calm and diplomacy needed to balance the sometimes conflicting demands of the administration of Hong Kong with the need to cooperate with China. The explosion of discontent and dissatisfaction in Beijing in Tiananmen took place in the middle of 1989, just two years into his governorship. David Wilson had to calm Hong Kong and restore confidence that Hong Kong's future did not lie in ruins.

Viewed from the outside, Tiananmen seemed to spell an end to all the progress that had been made in social and economic reform, an end to the opening of China to the outside world, and to mark a return to the hard-line policies of former years. Happily, this was not to be so. Deng Xiaoping's policies continued as before, even while the rest of the world was recovering from the shock and horror at what they had seen on their television screens.

One of the morale-boosting initiatives was the government's decision, four months after Tiananmen, at long last to build a replacement airport, which Sir David announced in the Governor's policy address at the beginning of the 1989–1990 legislative session.

The construction of an airport capable of handling a throughput of 80 million passengers a year would entail the reclamation of an airport island from the muddy depths of the sea, and would involve the building of immense bridges, tunnels, highways, and also a railway. There was no disguising it would be a stupendous engineering feat, costing US$16 billion.

The Chinese leaders, recovering from Tiananmen, reacted predictably to this decision. There had been no discussion; what were the British up to now? What had happened to the promise of cooperation? The equally predictable response was that this was a decision within the administrative power of the Hong Kong–British government. The Chinese questioned where Hong Kong was to find the money. Would the incoming government in 1997 be left with an intolerable amount of debt? Had all the options been explored? These may have been reasonable enough questions, but nevertheless Hong Kong needed to push on. Having already spent years in the bureaucratic sifting processes, it did not wish to face interminable discussion with Chinese officials which would have resulted in further delay and would have taken the shine off this bold initiative. It might well have pushed the project into the period stretching up to and beyond 1997, then to be overshadowed by the change of sovereignty. The announcement had to be made now or never; the political fall-out could be dealt with later. Fall-out there certainly was.

There followed almost two years of patient but determined negotiation before an Airport Agreement was signed between the two governments; and even then the wrangling did not stop. Meanwhile, as luck would have it, with an expanding economy and rising revenues, Hong Kong's fiscal reserves improved dramatically. Even though more direct capital was injected into the airport, it became clear that it was far from draining Hong Kong's reserves. In 1997 the Hong Kong Special Administrative Region, because of a flourishing economy and astute investment of its surplus revenues, would inherit foreign currency reserves which were among the highest in the world.

The airport negotiations were brought to a head with a visit from the

Prime Minister, John Major, to Beijing in September 1991. He was the third government leader to visit China after Tiananmen, following the Japanese and Italian prime ministers. It had taken two years for the international quarantine, which had been imposed on China after the events of 1989, to be lifted. The British Prime Minister accepted this invitation to visit Beijing despite the obvious criticisms he could expect from his parliamentary colleagues and the media. But not only did his visit ratchet the airport forward, it helped show Hong Kong's own leaders and people that sanctions and ostracism were unhelpful in encouraging the reform programme in China, which was continuing as though Tiananmen had not taken place

Although much criticised as a period lacking in decisive government, looked at more objectively there was much on the credit side. During David Wilson's governorship further progress had been made in the development of the political structure; agreement over the 'through train' concept for legislators had been achieved; the drafting of the Basic Law had been completed; and the negotiation over the airport had taken place and an agreement signed. The events of 1989 in China had been an unexpected set-back to the period of much-vaunted 'gradual and orderly progress'. They put into a temporary deep freeze of mistrust the improving relations with the West brought about by the previous ten years of reform and openness.

Some criticised the Governor for being weak and indecisive for not pushing ahead with elections when in fact he had, with the support of the British Government, fought hard to increase the number of directly elected members to the Legislative Council and had supported the 'through train' whereby the elected councillors of 1995 would continue to hold office after 1997. He had also, after Tiananmen, voiced a hopeless recommendation to the British Government to restore citizenship to the over three million British Dependent Territories citizens of Hong Kong. But rumours were rife that he was to leave, fuelled by reports from London that the Prime Minister himself had been lobbied by Conservative and business circles in London to replace him.

These speculations surfaced after the Prime Minister's visit to Hong Kong on his way back to London from the airport talks in Beijing. When asked, the Prime Minister replied, shortly and enigmatically, that 'there is no vacancy in Government House'. This seemed to put the matter to rest; and it was therefore a complete shock to Hong Kong to read on New Year's Day, 1992, that there was indeed a vacancy, that Sir David Wilson was to leave Hong Kong and would be given a seat in the House of Lords. Hong Kong reaction was that he had been treated shabbily and peremptorily by the British Government. More particularly, there had been no warning to Hong Kong's Executive Council, no consultation and no opportunity to remonstrate. It would have been more acceptable if there had been an announcement as to who was to replace him, but a decision about that was not made until after the British elections in the spring of 1992, and the new Governor did not arrive until 9 July.

Despite the despondency following the mass demonstrations and military crackdown in China, and despite the preoccupation with politics and constitutional affairs and discussion of the airport development, the bread and butter work of governing Hong Kong continued uninterrupted. The record of social and economic development in the Wilson years, 1987–1992, is impressive. The superstructure of the crystal tower of the seventy-storey Bank of China, designed by I. M. Pei, was completed, container cargo throughput exceeded that of Rotterdam, one of the largest hospitals in the world was opened, a light rail system began operating, and a second harbour tunnel connecting Kowloon with Hong Kong was completed.

It is an understatement to say that Hong Kong had been slow to respond to the need to be more active in promoting education. Primary education became compulsory only in 1971, 130 years after the founding of the colony. Three years of secondary education for all was added a dilatory seven years later in 1978. The number of students who were able to go on to study for a degree at Hong Kong's two universities in 1997 was hopelessly inadequate. All in all, Hong Kong's educational system had fallen far behind the standard needed to meet the challenges of the future and a changing economy. In an almost desperate attempt to catch up, the expansion of university places took place during Wilson's term of office, to provide greater opportunities for Hong Kong's young people to stay in Hong Kong to study rather than to travel overseas. However, because secondary education had lagged so far behind, it was at first impossible to find sufficient students with the necessary standards to enter university. The expansion and effort to catch up established a target for the future and drew attention to the problem, but true improvement was to take many more years.

These random few instances are selected from the achievements and progress which kept Hong Kong, despite its lack of natural resources, on a path of uninterrupted growth during a period of great uncertainty. But they were not enough to satisfy David Wilson's detractors and were disregarded by ill-informed critics. Christopher Patten, a Conservative Member of Parliament and long-serving Cabinet Minister, had lost his constituency seat of Bath in the spring of 1992. John Major's question of who to appoint in place of Sir David Wilson had been answered. This solution satisfied those who thought that it was time to take the job of government away from officials who had made a life's work of studying China and Chinese and put a politician in place: someone who would 'stand up' to China in a penalty shoot-out over elections.

29

Another Voice

*T*he Governor's launch, the *Lady Maurine*, tiny among the fire floats squirting their fountains, edged across the harbour. At the quayside behind the Queen's Pier, once again the customary troops and bands were waiting, swords poised to salute and bayonets glittering; arms were presented with a smart clatter and councillors and their ladies were introduced. But no more white drill, epaulettes and fluttering feathers of office, no more morning dress; the Governor, to mark the change from official to politician, wore a suit like the rest of us. It was the beginning of the end of the old colony: time to change.

Curiosity is the principal emotion which the arrival of a new Governor arouses, and so we flocked to the City Hall to see and hear what the new man had to say. After his swearing-in by the Chief Justice, Christopher Patten spoke, flattering Hong Kong for its achievements, talking of the challenges in the years remaining before 1997 and noting what he termed the hallmarks of the Hong Kong system: the rule of law, freedom, democratic participation by the people at every level and an open market economy. He vowed to improve and strengthen government, to maintain and improve competitiveness, to continue to build the infrastructure and to battle against inflation, to safeguard the low tax economy and to use our wealth to help the less privileged, to be relentless in the fight against crime and, having heard that the relationship between Britain and China was still bedevilled by misunderstanding and lack of trust, to work to remove obstacles and to cooperate with China. He concluded by saying that as Hong Kong's Governor he had no secret agenda. In fact he seemed to have brought with him opinions about Hong Kong which were shared by his predecessor.

They were stirring words, words carefully chosen, words with sharp edges, with no prevarication, no blurring the message. The speech was rousing and well received. Now, the audience thought, we are going to have the crisp, decisive government needed to get us ready for the even bigger change to come in 1997. There was no hint of the constitutional changes to be developed secretly with the help of a few trusties during the summer months of 1992, which were to be laid out in his policy address to the new session of the Legislative Council in the autumn and to a shocked and bewildered China.

Following his swearing-in ceremony, the Governor left the red-carpeted stage and mixed with the assembled notables, shook hands and spoke a few words to as many as he could. To me he said enigmatically, 'I have heard a lot about you', smiled, and passed on.

As chairman of one of the principal quasi-government organisations, the Housing Authority, I was invited to see Mr Patten during the early part of the summer. I spoke to him about the difficulty elected members of Legislative Council who were also members of political parties experienced if they were appointed to Executive Council, in having to accept the concept of collective responsibility for Executive Council decisions when they ran contrary to their party's politics. I also thought he should visit China, and said so. But the secret brew being cooked up in Government House during those summer months to disrupt the 'gradual and orderly progress', the measured principle of change prescribed in the Basic Law, made a visit to China at that time quite out of the question. Chinese officials would be sure to raise the sensitive question of elections, about which the foreign ministers had reached an agreement by correspondence. Indeed, China was already nervous because of an earlier suggestion by Alastair Goodlad, the new minister responsible for Hong Kong, that perhaps the Basic Law could be changed, and also by the appearance on the steps of number 10 Downing Street alongside the Prime

Minister, John Major, of the Hon. Martin Lee and Yeung Sum, newly elected
Legislative Council members, who both represented the United Democrats
and were both members of the Alliance in Support of Democracy in China,
which had called on Prime Minister Li Peng to step down.

Members of Legislative Council who broadly represented the business
community and who sought to develop a cooperative working relationship
with Beijing had formed a group of councillors which they called,
mysteriously, the Cooperative Resource Centre (CRC). At the end of June
1992, in time-honoured way, they trooped to Beijing for a meeting with
President Jiang Zemin. China, already apprehensive at what the politician
Governor was up to, blandly but pointedly told Allen Lee Peng-fei, the
leader of the CRC delegation, that the route map of the Basic Law was to
be followed. The message was clear. China wanted a smooth transition
and a smooth transfer of sovereignty. Allen Lee responded that they would
like to see the two sides sitting down to discussions. But while firing
these warning shots China proceeded as though her defences were
invulnerable, that the solemnly invoked Basic Law was already complete
and comprehensive. In fact it was capable of different interpretations,
and there were spaces and terms in it which assumed, from what had
gone before, what was meant now, without further explanation. The
drafters had never imagined that someone would go through it with a
fine-tooth comb to discover ways of getting round its provisions. Even
the representatives of different political groups in the Legislative Council
had never looked at it in this way.

Meanwhile problems with the airport financing provided background
music. One of China's 'principled' objections to the project from the
beginning had been that it was so grandiose, so expensive, that this last
folie de grandeur of the departing colonists would drain Hong Kong's coffers
dry. China asked for what was a ridiculously small sum to be left in the
treasure chest when the flag came down. Hong Kong's reserves were huge.
China's fears were summarily and gleefully dismissed by the government.

A change to the membership of Executive Council in the summer of
1992 was needed to clear the way for the changes to be announced a few

weeks later in the Governor's policy address. The Hon. Dame Lydia Dunn, Chinese, articulate, glamorous and forthright Senior Member of Executive Council, suggested to her fellow members, some of whom also sat in the Legislative Council, that in order to give the new Governor a free hand they, including herself, should resign en bloc. This they did, thus ending a long-established custom that some members would sit in both the Legislative and Executive Councils. The new-broom, lively Young Turks brought in to Legislative Council some years before by MacLehose had, after a few years' apprenticeship, been promoted to Executive Council. There they had worked out a route map for future political development at private meetings with David Wilson. They were now removed by their own honourable gesture, leaving Dame Lydia Dunn to be reappointed and to continue her leadership of the council. There was talk of a backroom deal, but in one stroke the cross-membership with the Legislative Council came to an end, and Martin Lee, member of Legislative Council, popular leader of the Democrats, whether he was willing to serve or not, thus became ineligible for membership of Executive Council. Thus without a shot being fired the Governor was able to rid himself of troublesome councillors who had been involved in the drafting of the Basic Law and who would certainly have opposed, in Executive Council, what was to happen next.

On 7 October 1992, Christopher Patten, speaking to the opening session of the Legislative Council in the former Supreme Court building, which had been erected to commemorate the Jubilee of Queen Victoria, titled his address , 'Our Next Five Years: The Agenda for Hong Kong'. He spoke in crisp, plain words of Hong Kong's enduring qualities — stability and prosperity, minimal government, the link to the US dollar, the formation of a Business Council, teacher retraining, more and better teachers, smaller classes, whole day schooling, a comprehensive social security system, and the pursuit of economic growth rather than increasing taxation to provide the funds for these social policies. He spoke of accountable government honouring performance pledges, the environment, and law and order. These were all things the man in the street wanted to hear. During the next five years some were achieved, some made a start, and some were dropped, while years later many remain as will-o'-the-wisp objectives dancing ahead of Hong Kong's power to achieve as population growth and unexpected challenges push them out of reach.

A substantial part of the address outlined proposals for constitutional reform. Some of these, such as the lowering of the voting age to 18, were not controversial. Others were. Elections for the Legislative Council were due in 1995. Mr Patten proposed exploring how to build up democracy without contravening the Basic Law and the Joint Declaration. The Basic Law had taken five years to write and those who had worked on it firmly believed that they had squared the circle and settled the system which was to take Hong Kong through the transition, and that would allow the Legislative Council elected in 1995 to carry on through the handover in 1997 until 1999. It was not to be so.

The two municipal councils and the nineteen district boards each included members appointed by the Governor. This was to enable them to include community leaders who were disinclined to stand for election because of age, occupation or profession. They were those to whom the community had looked for leadership for many years. They had demonstrated their usefulness on the boards and were welcomed by the elected members. Now they were to be abolished.

The functional constituency members in the Legislative Council were anathema, not only to Westminster politicians, but to political commentators world wide, as well as to the pro-democracy faction in Hong Kong. Functional constituencies had developed from the previous informal system whereby the Governor had appointed members to represent a wide range of professional and occupational groups 'through which much specialist knowledge and valuable expertise had been provided to the Council' (May 1987 Green Paper). In practice, although the system was working, the functional constituencies were an anachronism. Some had a minuscule electorate and could be open to manipulation, so were easily the butt of criticism for their elitism and for the advantage they gave to special groups. These criticisms obscured, and continue to obscure, objective evaluation. Whether they were performing well and serving a useful purpose was of no interest to their critics. Some were and some were not, as with all councillors however elected or selected. In 1992 there were twenty-one functional constituency members, and nine more were due to be added by 1995. The concept was so well known in Hong Kong that those drafting the Basic Law did not bother to include a definition of a functional constituency in the law. In fact Sir Edward Youde had made their definition clear in addressing the Legislative Council when they were introduced in 1984: 'by this we mean organisations representing commerce, industry, the law and other aspects of our social and economic life.' The key word here was 'organisations'.

The remainder of members appointed by the Governor was to be abolished, and Mr Patten now proposed to fill these nine additional supposedly functional seats by replacing the appointed members with members whose aggregate franchise would include the entire working population. This was a revolutionary departure from the system representing organisations which had been defined by Sir Edward Youde, and a clever manipulation of the opportunity provided by a lack of definition in the Basic Law in effect to give two votes to about two million people.

China assumed that in Annex II of the agreement between the two sides, which dealt with the setting up of the Joint Liaison Group, there was a safeguard to deal with any oversights and omissions. The two sides had agreed that to achieve a smooth transition, there would be a need for close cooperation during the second half of the period between 1985 and 1997. 1992 was well into the second half and the smooth transition of the Legislative Council held out in the Basic Law was a matter for such cooperation. The Governor preferred to speak first, to pull the public to his side and agree to cooperate later on what he had said.

Reactions to his address were drawn along familiar lines. The *Times* was quoted by the *South China Morning Post* as saying that he had made a brilliant and eloquent debut, a firm commitment to democracy as a philosophical ideal and as an essential part of economic progress, and that this had been done with political audacity and tactics which suggested a lawyer's cunning. The *New York Times* described his open style as a refreshing change from the remote Foreign Office functionaries who preceded him. These contemptuous words displayed a total ignorance of the far from remote, shirt-sleeved, down-to-earth style of MacLehose and his many achievements, nor did they account for Youde's enduring popularity and Wilson's strenuous efforts at a most difficult time.

China had short notice of what he intended to say, and in a report in the *South China Morning Post* the Governor is quoted as saying that a message that he should not make his speech at all had come to him in a number of ways from China, one of them directly. These requests he firmly rebuffed and the extent of his determination to introduce the changes was spelt out in a reference he made to the transfer of sovereignty: 'I don't think any one would want a through train to run carrying discredited goods.' This was new terminology for the system which his distinguished predecessors had fought for and had been working on for many years.

Shortly before he went to China on 19 October for his first and last meeting with Lu Ping, the director of the Hong Kong and Macao Affairs Office, the Governor came to our house for supper with a small group of academics and professionals. The party included Leung Chun-ying, who subsequently became Senior Member of Executive Council, and Professor Lau Siu-kai and Professor Joseph Cheng Yu-shek, with whom I had regularly discussed the political challenges facing Hong Kong and who had joined in discussions with governors since 1974. Speaking from years of experience and study of politics in Hong Kong and the mainland, they advised, at this first meeting, a cautious approach which gave face to China. But 'face' was not a concept which had any part to play in the vigorous expression of the Governor's strongly held views.

Officials in China and all Chinese put themselves to considerable trouble and inconvenience with greetings and farewells. This was Mr Patten's first visit to China as Governor, but he was not met at the airport by the director of the Hong Kong and Macao Affairs Office, and bearing in mind the warnings before the address was delivered and the ferocity of the Chinese response to it, it was not surprising that the atmosphere at the meetings which followed was formal and firm. In a more normal course of events the meeting would have continued the dialogue, the unfinished business which previous governors had been conducting with Beijing, and hopefully it would have brought fresh thinking to bear on outstanding issues. Instead, the meeting was taken up with the Governor's constitutional proposals, and towards the end of the discussion, as Mr Patten relates, letters which had been exchanged between the two foreign ministers were introduced across the table by Director Lu Ping.

When the letters became public knowledge, the Governor said that he had not previously seen them. This carried the implication that before he took up his Governorship, neither Foreign Secretary Douglas Hurd, nor Prime Minister John Major, nor his officials in Hong Kong, had mentioned the letters and their relevance to Hong Kong's constitutional development. Such an omission would have been extraordinary. How could it be explained that they didn't come up in conversation when the Governor visited London later that summer when, presumably, he briefed the Foreign Secretary on his proposals — surely it must have rung a bell? It was said by the British side that the letters were not legally binding. But what about an Englishman's word? Or if it had been decided to go back on them, why not write to the Chinese Foreign Minister and say that times had changed and that Sir Douglas Hurd had had second thoughts? This is all history now, but it was, to say the least, an unsavoury and negligent episode and was a bad start to the next five years.

There was an immediate clamour for the letters, which were not in the public domain, to be made known. Both sides released them, and the chorus arose from all directions, 'It's in the Basic Law', 'Oh no, it's not', 'It's contrary to the Joint Declaration', 'Oh no, it's not', 'The letters mean this', 'No, they don't', 'Yes, they do'. The subject was serious but the dialogue held strong echoes of Gilbert and Sullivan.

Letters between foreign ministers are used to bring some finality to difficult points at issue which cannot be solved by officials. The very introduction of a Legislative Council constituted by elections had earlier been dealt with in this way. The bitter disagreement which now divided the two sides and split opinion in Hong Kong mainly concerned the composition of the committee formed to elect ten members to the Legislative Council. The Governor in his address had proposed that they be elected by an electoral college consisting of the combined strength of the district boards and municipal councils. This was quite different from the system mentioned for later detailed discussion in the exchange of letters between the foreign ministers, which had spoken of an electoral college chosen from four sectors of the community. The Chinese Foreign Minister had replied in 1990 that the draft Basic Law already contained a provision for such an electoral committee representing four sectors and that this should be followed. The Foreign Secretary, Sir Douglas Hurd, had responded clearly and unequivocally that he agreed 'in principle with the arrangements which you propose for an Electoral Committee which could be established in 1995. The precise details of how this should be done can be discussed later'. While the legal experts who were consulted were to say that this was not an agreement, it cannot be denied that the words contain an unmistakable commitment to the principle, while allowing for later discussion about the detail. It is not difficult to understand why the Chinese government, and Director Lu Ping in particular, whose reputation was at stake, felt bewildered and betrayed.

I had been involved in local political development almost since arrival thirty years before and had had first-hand experience of discussion with Chinese officials. It was not possible now, when the future of Hong Kong's political development and the prospect of a smooth transition were endangered, to abandon my views and knowledge of what had gone before. In the five years which followed the signing of the agreement I had been involved in the follow-up, first in government and then after retirement, as one of the advisers to the Business and Professional Federation (BPF) which had been formed out of the members of the Basic Law drafting and consultative committees. Among the other BPF advisers were former executive councillors Sir Chung Sze-yuen and Sir Lee Quo-wei, who had been on the council during the drafting of the agreement with China and had first-hand knowledge of what could be achieved and what not.

Against this background of experience and involvement going back many years, the BPF made its position clear in a statement and a press conference on 9 November 1992 shortly after the Governor's visit to Beijing. We had debated long and hard before making our views public. David Gledhill, former chairman of Swire, a leading British company in Hong Kong, Michael Somerville, community leader, Sir Chung Sze-yuen, and I sat alongside the chairman, Vincent Lo, a member of the Basic Law drafting committee, to make our views known. Local and international press and television were present in force. The BPF said that with regard to the election committee, discussion should resume on the basis of the principle agreed in the letters between the foreign ministers, namely, that the nine new functional constituency seats should follow the principles established for the previous twenty-one seats and the 1984 White Paper and be based on recognised organisations, associations and institutions. These suggestions were set out in a letter to the government's Secretary for Constitutional Affairs in February of the following year.

Some weeks later, the BPF was invited to meet the Governor, but our discussion with him bore no fruit beyond the familiar response, 'It's not in the Basic Law: show me where it is.' This was technically correct: it was not there in so many words because everyone in Hong Kong knew very well what was meant by a functional constituency, and hadn't Governor Youde spelled it out? I suggested that the best way to find out what was intended by the Basic Law was to ask the people who had had a big hand in drafting it. They were, after all, leading members of the Hong Kong community, not officials who had been sent from Beijing. The suggestion was not taken up. I also proposed this in a paper (which was later published) for a planned symposium on the way ahead for Hong Kong, which was to have been presided over by Ji Pengfei, the Chinese minister responsible for Hong Kong, at the end of October 1992. His visit to Hong Kong and the symposium fell victim to China's reaction to the Governor's proposals. The proposals were ingenious and, as the *Times* said, politically audacious, but doomed from the outset. The BPF made it clear that in its judgement, which was based not only on long experience but on personal acquaintance with the officials involved, China would not change its position, and that the result would be that the Legislative Council would not survive the transfer in 1997 and that fresh elections would be needed. The 'through train' would crash; and so it did.

30

The Years Between, 1992–1997

*T*he disagreement over the changes to the electoral system had unhappy consequences. China took the dispute so seriously that threats were made not only to derail the 'through train' but that contracts and agreements entered into by the government before the transfer would have to be re-examined after. On reflection it was realised that this would damage both Hong Kong's and China's interests and the threat was allowed quietly to evaporate, but not before it sent the stock market into pessimistic decline.

The Jardine Group, however, was singled out for its rumoured support for Mr Patten and for earlier shifting its domicile out of Hong Kong. China objected to the participation of the group in the consortium to build the next container terminal. As a result, this huge undertaking was held up for many years until a rearrangement of consortium members took place and a compensatory arrangement for Jardines had been agreed. Even now as I write in 2002, the sea is still being filled in for the terminal!

This heightened political atmosphere spilled over into our own lives. Five years previously I had been appointed chairman of the Housing Authority by Governor David Wilson on the recommendation of his Chief Secretary, David Ford, and so I was a left-over from the pre-Patten era. I had thought for some while that the time had come for a Chinese chairman to take over the appointment to an organisation responsible for housing half the people of Hong Kong. The government had replaced expatriates with Chinese for most important appointed chairmanships.

I was linked to the colonial period. The problems we were dealing with might not be any easier for a Chinese chairman to solve — making those who could afford it pay double rent, finding flats for single people and the elderly, rehousing squatters and dealing with a long waiting list — but the hard solution to these questions might be more acceptable and believable coming from one of their own people. There also had been hints, in order to silence me, that as chairman of the Housing Authority I should not speak out on political development as I had been doing. In any case my views were not welcome to the government and I now had little or no contact with the Governor or the Chief Secretary.

My departure was precipitated one day when we returned from a visit to Beijing. A journalist called to inform me that two Democratic Party councillors, Yeung Sum and Szeto Wah, had called for my resignation from the Housing Authority and that if I did not resign they would introduce a motion in the Legislative Council to force me to go. The journalist reported Yeung Sum as saying, 'The sooner we see the back of him the better!' I turned to Jane and said, 'All right, I will resign,' and sent a letter next day informing the Governor. He accepted my resignation, briefly thanking me for my work.

Our next challenge was more serious. Since my first posting to the New Territories in 1978, I had been involved with Hong Kong's political development and relations with post-Mao China. I had negotiated with China's officials the building of the first permanent bridge across the river which divided us from the mainland, then the return of illegal immigrants across the completed bridge. I had visited the embryo city of Shenzhen with Sir Murray MacLehose and had joined in the discussion, following our visit, with the head of the New China News Agency. I had been part of Executive Council during the years leading up to the substantive discussions on our future and during the negotiations themselves. When they were over, during the five years of drafting the Basic Law, both before and after retirement, I had been in close and regular touch with those involved in its formulation. We had been companions on a long journey, struggling to reach an understanding of what was possible as we edged our way towards the realisation of the concept of 'Hong Kong people ruling Hong Kong'. I had worked closely with three Governors, MacLehose, Youde and Wilson. Jane and I had enjoyed many evenings together with them from the seventies until 1992, exchanging thoughts with young people who were prominent opinion makers. We were going to stay in Hong Kong. I could not turn my back on so many friends, so many shared conclusions and so much experience; and if we remained, I could not keep silent.

Now I was to be put to the test. It was rumoured that I was to be among a second batch of Hong Kong Affairs Advisers to be appointed by China. I could either refuse and opt out of political life, or stand by my convictions and faith in the future, and join my friends knowing that this would expose me to criticism from the 'stand up to China' hardliners who were spoiling for a fight.

Some say, I believe, that civil servants should not meddle in politics; others say that when expatriate civil servants retire they should hotfoot it out of their territory and never return — no 'staying on'; and others say, 'My country right or wrong.' In becoming a Hong Kong Affairs Adviser to China, I seemed to be breaking all three canons. When I was first appointed to work in the New Territories, Sir Ronald Holmes, the District Commissioner, said that first and foremost District Officers were political officers. Certainly we were involved in grass-roots politics from the word go. Later I had been deeply involved in setting up a more politically representative system in the New Territories, then later at the Legislative Council level, and finally as a member of the Executive Council in the negotiations with China. Subsequently I had been privileged to have discussions with friends who were drafting the Basic Law. Jane and I had stayed on because after so many years away, with our parents no longer alive, and being heavily involved in the local community and numerous local organizations, Hong Kong and not England had become our home. I had been keenly interested in political development for many years, and this interest had been sharpened by my time at the University of Kent. I was on friendly terms with the members of the Hong Kong and Macao

Affairs Office, having met and discussed Hong Kong affairs with them in the past. More so than most, we had travelled widely in China and had seen at first hand the changes that were taking place. We had seen enough to make us confident that China meant what she said. It was the most natural thing to lend a hand and join my friends as one of the advisers.

When it was put to me I said that if I were invited, I would accept. The die was cast. I was on the list with forty members of the community, including academics, prominent businessmen, political leaders, the two Vice Chancellors and the two bishops, all of them friends. But naively, in joining my friends I had not bargained for the malevolent and unreasoning attacks from the British press. I was a 'Peking lapdog', a 'traitor', I had 'jumped ship', and so on. But I was not the only one. Sir Sze-yuen Chung, who had served on the Legislative and Executive Councils and had been the Senior Member for many years, was similarly insulted and denounced.

Among friends, things were seen differently. The world was not divided into two warring camps, them and us — St George and the Chinese Dragon. In Hong Kong there was more at stake: to make sure that whatever the outcome of the bitter war of words between Britain and China, Hong Kong in 1997 would keep its freedoms, its elections, its laws and its lifestyle. Looked at objectively, the assembly of Hong Kong Affairs Advisers with its bishops and Vice Chancellors was something of a guarantee that this would be so, not for the advice they were to give but as a defence against any departure by China from what had been agreed. However, the Western world and its media were still obsessed with the idea of Red China, Communist China. No matter where one travelled, the question was always couched in the same terms: 'What will you do when the Reds take over?' Few believed that there would be a life for Hong Kong after 1997 and that the 'Reds' were not going to 'take over'. The time would come when they would see how wrong they were.

My becoming an Adviser was no doubt seen as something of a public relations coup for China. But looked at another way, in securing our agreement to becoming Advisers and in formally appointing us, China had, in fact, created a brake on any attempt to change her previous undertakings. She could hardly renege when faced with the combined strength of the Advisers. We formed a bulwark against rule from Beijing. Some of my retired former colleagues in England did not see it this way. They were distant in years and space from the scene, ignorant of the details, and had the memory of Tiananmen lingering in their minds; they were also possibly unaware of the careful diplomacy and persuasion, particularly of the previous Governor, Sir David Wilson, which had secured agreement that the last legislature to hold office would have its life extended for two years after the reversion of sovereignty, and of Sir Edward Youde, under whose governorship the basic composition of the Legislative Council had been decided. Nevertheless, these erstwhile colleagues hatched a plot and circulated a letter demanding the withdrawal of my pension!

The Advisers travelled to Beijing on 1 April 1993. The check-in at the airport was blocked by yelling students who had come to barrack their Vice Chancellors. I was hemmed in between this shouting, pushing mob and the check-in counter, and photographs of these struggles were flashed round the world. Subsequently, on his return, one Vice Chancellor gave a defence of his decision to join the team of Advisers in an open forum before the students. In Beijing we received our certificates of appointment from Lu Ping and Zhou Nan in one of the halls of the Great Hall of the People, in the full glare of publicity. Later that evening, the BBC pressed for an interview, which began: 'Now, Sir David, you have been called a defector . . . .'

That evening we were divided into groups and asked for our views on the Hong Kong situation by Lu Ping and Zhou Nan. Nearly all of us spoke about the need to get on with projects such as the airport, whose delay was affecting the economy. I went on to say that the rather extreme language of criticism of Christopher Patten was counter-productive and should be moderated. Subsequently, steps were taken by China to make progress on land issues, cable TV, the Joint Liaison Group and the airport. Whether the soundbites against the Governor diminished in volume, I cannot recall. I believe they did.

The appointment of so many eminent public figures in Hong Kong as Advisers was clearly intended to demonstrate that outside the Legislative Council and the war of words between Britain and China, there was a substantive body of people who wanted an end to the dispute, who knew China better than the British government, and who were prepared to trust China's promises that after 1997 Hong Kong would enjoy the promised high degree of autonomy and that the way of life they now enjoyed would continue.

At about this time a more colourful and homely expression gained currency. The director of the Hong Kong and Macao Affairs Office referred to the 'second stove', using a Chinese metaphor indicating a split family, as a picturesque way of warning that measures would be put in hand to meet with any eventuality if there were no agreement with Britain. It was another way of saying 'You go your way and we'll go ours'. The Basic Law prescribed the setting up of a Preparatory Committee in 1996 to take responsibility for preparing the establishment of the Special Administrative Region and — ominous words — to 'prescribe the specific method for forming the first government and the first Legislative Council' of the Hong Kong SAR. In July 1993 Lu Ping announced the formation of a Preliminary Working Committee to set about organising this formal Preparatory Committee, but also to be ready, if an agreement could not be reached, to arrange for the appointment of a Provisional Legislature to take office in place of the one which would not survive without such an agreement.

Even at this late stage, the realities of 1997 had not sunk in. There were those who, having gone out on a limb, still did not believe that China meant what she said. They were living in a world of make-believe. What happened next was a more direct challenge to my integrity.

Visiting the Outward Bound Alumni Club 1985.

The Executive Council with Director Lu Ping at the 35th anniversary
of the founding of the People's Republic. From left: Sir Chung Sze-yuen,
Sir Roger Lobo, Sir Michael Sandberg, and Sir Philip Haddon-Cave. (See p. 153)

The United Kingdom Embassy in Beijing, view from the garden. (See p. 159)

The Business and Professional Federation on an early visit to Beijing. (See p. 163)

I am sworn in as Acting Governor by Sir Allen Huggins Chief Justice on the death of Sir Edward Youde. (See p. 179)

A delegation of Girl Guides meets Vice Minister Ji Pengfei.

My wife Jane, as Chief Commissioner of the Girl Guides, receives her MBE from the Governor Sir David Wilson.

The nuclear power station at Daya Bay. (See p. 176)

Greeting the children of the Government House staff, New Year 1987. (See p. 182)

'Sir David Wilson arrived with helmet, sword and feathers flying.' (See p. 192)

Dragon View, our house, had an uninterrupted view of mountains and sea. (See p. 201)

At Dragon View with Dr Raymond Wu and Li Chu-wen, former Deputy Director of the New China News Agency. (See p. 201)

The Chancellor of Oxford University, Roy Jenkins, and Vice-Chancellor, Peter North visit the Forbidden City. (See p. 201)

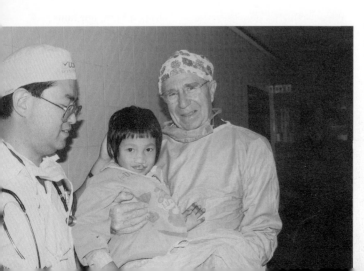

I became Chairman of Operation Smile, China Medical Mission. (See p. 201)

With the professors: (from left to right) Wong Siu-lun, Joseph Cheng Yu-sek, Lau Siu-kai and Lee Ming-kwan. (See p. 201)

My wife, Jane, in Beijing meets Vice-Premier Chen Muhua, Premier of the All-China Women's Federation. (See p. 201)

With two old Executive Council friends, Sir Chung Sze-yuen (middle) and Sir Lee Quo-wei. (See p. 225)

I always enjoyed talking with Director Lu Ping of the Hong Kong and Macao Affairs Office. (See p. 237)

From Dragon View we watched the bridge pushing across the channel linking Lantau to Hong Kong. (See p. 238)

A witty carton of Christopher Patten driving a mechanical grab at Dragon View. (See p. 248)

31

Defamation and the 'Second Stove'

Sunday was a quiet day at Dragon View; our domestic helpers usually went to early church and then on to meet their friends. Most unusually, on Sunday, 30 January 1994, instead of the clang of the ship's bell at the gate at the bottom of the steep flight of steps leading to the house, the front door gong chimed. We opened the door and immediately a camera started fast-ratchetting and two roughly dressed European men confronted us. I exclaimed angrily and asked them what they wanted, and attempted to wrestle the camera away from the shorter of the two. My wife intervened. I asked again and the reply came back sinisterly, 'Don't you know? You'll know soon enough.' There was no more explanation. They took themselves off.

Two days later, on 1 February, the first edition of a much-heralded new English-language daily, the *Eastern Express*, appeared with the banner headline, 'How Akers-Jones Obtained a Bargain Home'. There followed the photograph taken at the front door and an article on the front page, with more photos and 'story' on the inside pages, full of innuendo and damaging and smearing inaccuracies. The house had doubled in size and a later article bumped up the number of bedrooms from three to six! Various chartered surveyors, without knowing the property, had given their weighty opinions as to its value. At the same time the previous owner, whom we had not known when we bought the house, reiterated that the price had not been a 'friendship price'.

Among all top stories which were then worrying Hong Kong, the question of 'How Akers-Jones Obtained a Bargain Home' was a strange piece of news with which to launch a newspaper. Was there more to it than that? It was stranger still because the owner of this new daily, C. K. Ma, had invited me, the previous year, to become a member of the board of his charitable trust. Moreover, I had received a Lunar New Year card of good wishes from him only a few days previously! This extraordinary attack had come out of the blue, and there had been no attempt to check the facts with us before publication. Someone had decided that this was to be the lead story of the first edition of the new paper. No other newspaper followed up the story and the feedback from all I met was one of disgust. The paper began its brief career at a time when the leading English daily, the *South China Morning Post*, had changed hands and there was rumoured concern in government circles that its editorial policy would change to become more pro-China and anti-government. A counter-balance was thought to be needed. The *Eastern Express* started with a great fanfare and carried a large picture of the proprietor with the Governor, but before long, the editor left and it ceased publication.

From the end of 1994 there was no further serious attempt at bridging the gap between the two governments. The Patten electoral reform package had been put to the Legislative Council and an attempt to amend it defeated by one vote. Its passage was secured by one unexpected abstention at the last hour by a previous supporter of the reform package. Moreover, the voting was not left to the elected and non-official members, as there were still three government officials sitting in the legislature — the Chief Secretary, the Attorney General and the Financial Secretary. Without their guaranteed 'Yes' vote, the motion to introduce the changes would have failed, even taking into account the last-minute abstention. It was a hollow victory which, to use two contemporary metaphors, wrecked the through train and lit the fires under the 'second stove'.

Jonathan Dimbleby describes in *The Last Governor* the tense atmosphere in Government House as the Governor and his assistants, Edward Llewellyn and Martin Dinham, received up-to-the-minute reports on these shifting loyalties from the Legislative Council chamber, and he goes on to describe the jubilation and champagne which greeted the result of the vote. Reading his description, which came out after 1997, it seems almost unreal that they could have been so overjoyed and could have attached so much importance to the outcome of a vote for a change to the constitution when, as China had made it plain, it was doomed to fail. The legislators to be elected under the new rules in 1995 would survive only until 1997, when they would cease to hold office and a caretaker legislature would be sworn in.

Perhaps there were those in London who thought that China would not dare to do this, or they may even have thought that fate would intervene and bring about a change in the Chinese leadership. The people of Hong Kong knew better. China would not change its position; people had come to accept this and were indifferent to the complicated manoeuvrings between Britain and China and in the Legislative Council. There were more important things to think about; 1997 was just round the corner, and being used to the unpredictable, they knew that somehow their lives would go on.

Accounts of the five years between the arrival of Governor Christopher Patten and 1997 concentrate on the jousting between the two governments and tend to ignore the fact that in Hong Kong, outside the hothouse of politics, life went on as usual. We were constantly being asked from overseas either whether we were all right or whether it was going to be all right when China 'took over'. We were and it was. Just as during the period leading to the agreement between the two governments there had been both a dialogue taking place between officials of the government in Beijing and individual visitors and delegations from Hong Kong, so, too, in these five years there was more or less open house in Beijing and access to the leaders for anyone who had something useful to say. In April the Business and Professional Federation, to which I was an adviser, paid such a visit. We met Zhu Rongji, who was then Minister of Finance and the Economy, the Foreign Minister, Qian Qichen, and the director of the Hong Kong and Macao Affairs Office, Lu Ping .

The leaders spoke of the progress of the reforms in China, the state of the economy and so forth. We in our turn briefed the leaders about current concerns, particularly about the need to get on with infrastructure development such as the port and the airport, without which the economy would suffer, but also about passports and the concerns being shown by the civil service about their pensions and their job security after the transfer. With over a billion people to govern, it is remarkable how China's leaders always had time to fit in these meetings and for Hong Kong visitors to be well received. They returned to Hong Kong with greater trust and confidence in the eventual outcome of the long journey back to the Motherland.

People in Hong Kong had mixed feelings about the future. They were naturally proud that China was regaining what she had lost during the nineteenth century, that a colony in China would come to an end and be reunited with the mainland, that dignity and honour would be restored, but these were nebulous things to do with national pride. Their immediate concerns were about where the next meal was coming from and there was, naturally, nervousness about what would happen when the British, who had given them, law, language, administration, prosperous lives and an open society, hauled down the flag.

Meanwhile progress was being made on the airport and on the bridges, road, and railways leading to it. From where we lived we had a grandstand view. We could watch the world's assembled dredger fleet surging past to dump, far out to sea, loads of liquid mud from the future airport platform, while others hastened in the opposite direction laden with loads of sand from the sea bed to reclaim the airport from the sea. We watched the piers for great bridges rise above the islands and their stranded cables reaching down to grapple on and hoist aloft the giant steel boxes assembled and welded in China, setting differences aside, to form the bridge to carry the road and railway. This was the real Hong Kong, where the crash and bang of jackhammers and the rise of new buildings never ends.

32

Elections and the Second Stove Lights Up

Despite the outrage of China and the warnings from those in Hong Kong who knew better, Legislative Council elections were held in 1995 under the revised legislation of the Patten plan. This created new large constituencies and gave two votes to a large segment of the electorate, as well as creating an electoral college which was substantially different from the one described in the Qian–Hurd letters. The Democrats walked away with a majority of the seats and remained the largest single party in the legislature until the end of the century. They positioned themselves as critics of the government, and where the purse of the man in the street was affected, took a populist and some might say profligate line along with other councillors. Rents of public housing and fees and charges for government services were frozen, while constructive suggestions to help the government overcome the problems of falling revenues were lacking. These policies were partly responsible for the huge budget deficit Hong Kong was to experience in later years.

While sharing the same enthusiasm as Christopher Patten for accelerating the pace of democracy, the Democrats and their allies fell out with the Governor over the Court of Final Appeal. This, and not a court in Beijing, was to replace the British Privy Council as the final judge in litigation in Hong Kong. It was another and important pillar of the one country, two systems formula, and was another earnest of China's intention to uphold the autonomy of the Special Administrative Region with its legal system based upon the common law. But the agreement went further: not only would the power of final judgement be vested in the Court of Final Appeal in Hong Kong, but the court could, as required, invite judges from other common law jurisdictions to sit on the court. An argument then took place in Hong Kong as to whether this meant that there could be more than one foreign judge at any one time, with the chairman of the Democratic Party, Martin Lee, himself a barrister, playing a lead role. Representations were made through the Joint Liaison Group, but eventually it was settled that there would be only one. It in any case could be seen as a major concession to the Democrats to allow the court to invite a judge, say, from Australia, to sit on a court in a region of China!

Nevertheless, this agreement to limit the number of judges from other common law jurisdictions to one at any one time was dubbed an act of betrayal by the Democrats, and they introduced a motion of no confidence in the Governor in the Legislative Council. The motion was defeated and the legislation was passed. 'Gesture politics' was how the Governor described it, but nevertheless it signalled a significant falling out with the Governor, who still had two years of his term to pass before 1997, and was symptomatic of the general political malaise at that time.

Meanwhile the 'second stove' was lit and the Preliminary Working Committee was established by the Chinese government to make arrangements for the Preparatory Committee. In August 1996, the nomination rules were decided for the formation of the committee of four hundred to elect the first Chief Executive and the Provisional Legislature which would take over the reins after the handover. Later that year applications to become a member of the Preparatory Committee were invited, and I applied. Each of us had to be nominated by five people. My nominees were Leung Chun-ying, who subsequently became senior member of the Executive Council and who was also deputy chairman of the Preparatory Committee; Allen Lee Peng-fei, chairman of the Liberal Party and an elected Legislative Councillor who had known me for twenty years; Vincent Lo, chairman of the Business and Professionals Federation; Howard Young, whom I had known since he joined the first course at the

Outward Bound School in 1971 and who was a rising star in the Swire Company; and Tsui Tsin-tong, the chairman of a business company of which I was a non-executive director, and whom I had first met when he was chairman of the Tung Wah group of hospitals. I was elected from among a total of over five thousand nominees, and thus became a member of the four hundred who were to elect Hong Kong's first Chief Executive.

The candidates for the post of Chief Executive, who themselves were nominated, were well-known public figures: a retired Judge, Simon Li Fook-sean; the retired Chief Justice, Sir Ti-liang Yang; Peter Woo Kong-ching, chairman of a leading company and son-in-law of Sir Y. K. Pao; and Tung Chee Hwa, chairman of Orient Overseas Lines. Thus there were two judges and two leading businessmen. Voting by the four-hundred-member selection committee took place in two stages. We assembled in the Hong Kong Convention Centre at a meeting presided over by the Chinese Foreign Minister, Qian Qichen, and Director Lu Ping, head of the Hong Kong and Macao Affairs Office. We were each given an impressive red envelope which contained a voting paper on which to place a tick against the preferred candidate. We were seated in order of the number of strokes in the Chinese writing of our first names. My Chinese name contains eighteen brush strokes and consequently I was one of the last to be called. At this first round of voting Judge Simon Li was eliminated.

Outside the hall there was a small group of noisy protestors, armed with echoing bullhorns, who burnt a black paper coffin to signify the death of democracy. One man, one vote democracy would take many more years to arrive, but Hong Kong, at least, was replacing the Queen's appointed Governor with someone about whom there had been widespread public debate, someone who had explained himself to the people, and someone in whose final selection four hundred representatives of commerce and industry, religions, the professions, social interests and politics were to participate. Although there were those who wanted a precipitate rush to what they would advocate as only truly democratic, that is, a popularly elected Chief Executive, yet seen objectively, Hong Kong was making a start, a break from colonialism.

In the weeks that followed before the second and final stage of elections, the candidates explained their policies to the public and were cross-examined by the election committee in open forum. Voting took place on 11 December, using the same procedure. During the previous two weeks public support had swung behind Tung Chee Hwa, and he romped home with over three-quarters of the votes, thus becoming Hong Kong's Chief Executive in waiting.

For him it was not an easy time. He met the Governor, they took a photo call on the steps of Government House, then with hunched shoulders the Governor retreated into Government House and closed the doors while Tung Chee Hwa left to prepare for 1 July 1997.

The next job was to elect the Provisional Legislature. The passing of the legislation to put in place the 'Patten method' for replacing the remaining small colonial legacy of appointed seats in the Legislative Council had thrown the process of transition to Chinese sovereignty into disarray. Instead of those elected to seats in the Legislative Council continuing with their work until 1999, they were to step down, ignominiously, in 1997, to be replaced by caretakers until new elections could be held. The most that could be said was that political wrangling had made the people of Hong Kong slightly more alive to and interested in the processes of government. To some it had the opposite effect: 'A plague on both your houses,' they might have said as they turned away.

Just before Christmas, on Friday, 20 December 1996, the four hundred members of the election committee assembled at the Kowloon railway station to board a string of motor coaches to take us into China to elect the Provisional Legislature. A few eggs were thrown as we glided off with police outriders and a green wave of traffic lights for the half-hour ride to the border, crossing by the pre-stressed bridge whose construction I had negotiated twenty years before.

The following morning, the four hundred electors assembled in the Shenzhen Town Hall in front of a huge red curtain and the five-star emblem of China. One hundred and thirty candidates had been nominated for the sixty seats and, what was most surprising, thirty-four of these were already members of the existing Legislative Council! We were handed a ballot paper in Chinese, listing the candidates in the order of the number of strokes in writing of their family name. It was easy to make mistakes, and I had prepared a checklist of names of those for whom I was to cast my vote. We filed to the platform and posted our ballot papers into a box in front of television cameras.

There had been much talk of voting alignments among the four hundred. In the end the results were not quite as predicted. Out of the sixty elected, thirty-three were existing Legislative Councillors, including the President of the Council; this therefore made up a substantial proportion of the transitional Legislative Council. Five were members of a political party of independent views, the Association for Democracy and People's Livelihood, and eleven were holders of foreign passports. The media divided Hong Kong superficially into pro-Beijing and democrats, but in the event the elected members of this Provisional Legislature could in no way be described as lickspittle shoe-shiners of China. Many of those who had voted for the original Patten proposals now changed their affiliation. They switched trains to cross the border into the future.

Back in Hong Kong, the Governor referred to these proceedings as a 'bizarre farce', and in Westminster, the British Foreign Secretary, Malcolm Rifkind, challenged the government of China to submit its legality to the scrutiny of the International Court of Justice in The Hague. This futile suggestion ignored the fact that the Provisional Legislature had been elected as a result of a decision by the National People's Congress of China, and that its function was only to prepare laws which would be passed after the return of sovereignty to China. With just so much huffing and puffing, Hong Kong moved another step closer to transition.

33

Countdown

Following the election of the Provisional Legislature to take over the reins on 1 July, after the handover and until the fully constitutionally elected Legislative Council could take office, the six months leading to 30 June 1997 were a curious interregnum. It seemed strange and lacking in concern that we should be carrying on just as normal, as though the great change of rulers were not about to take place. It was as though we ought to feel differently on 1 July, as though we should now be walking on tiptoe, and, if the international media were to be believed, fearfully approaching the fateful day when, overnight, we would change from British colony to Chinese territory. Hong Kong in fact carried on as though nothing was going to happen. What else could we do? The streets of Hong Kong were as crowded as ever, the Stock Exchange showed no signs of nervousness, and in a fever of buying, property prices climbed to absurd heights. A square foot of floor space in central Hong Kong was almost worth its weight in gold and quite modest apartments were selling for a million pounds and more.

The stand-off between the Governor and the Chief Executive designate, Tung Chee Hwa, continued in its absurdity. The offices of the future Chief Executive, insensitively selected by the government in the crowded heart of the business district, were insecure, demeaning and wholly unsuitable, and other accommodation had to be found. The civil service were at pains not to render any assistance to the incoming government. Meanwhile I regularly received faxes and e-mails of articles in the *New York Times* and *Washington Post*, all depressing, derogatory and offensive to China, Hong Kong and Tung Chee Hwa.

About that time, Lord Howe, the former British Cabinet Minister, and Bob Hawke, former Prime Minister of Australia, were guests of the Australian Chamber of Commerce in Hong Kong. Geoffrey Howe warned Hong Kong not to export revolution to China and advised the media to act with restraint. This was sound advice, but the media had little time for past heroes and treated it with derision and disdain. Not only Hong Kong but the world was changing, and there could be no better evidence of this changed world than seeing Russia play Yugoslavia before a packed stadium in Hong Kong at the Chinese New Year football match, something that would have been unheard of only a few years previously.

March, in Hong Kong, arrives as though winter had never been. Autumn leaves at last fall to the ground, pushed off their perches by the eagerness of new spring growth. The paths in the woods behind our house were covered with these newly fallen leaves, and across the water dividing us from the islands we could see through cool, grey, mists the great bridges leading to the new airport nearing completion. The sea in front of us was busier than ever. Brightly coloured barges loaded with containers were towed slowly past, motorised barges steered from the bow surged in competition with one another, giant catamarans built in Australia thrust with foaming jets on their journeys to and from Pearl River ports, heavily laden carriers of coal moved their long, uncluttered decks to the power station. It was economic growth as usual, and before the handover this was reflected in a budget surplus of HK$20 billion.

At this eleventh hour, there was public and media debate about a proposal to replace laws for the maintenance of public order by new laws to regulate the unfettered freedom to demonstrate and to prevent infiltration by foreign political organisations. Until then the laws in this area had been fairly brief and simple, but now we were dealing with a different situation and laws were needed to replace and improve colonial legislation originally intended to deal with secretive Triad societies. The laws were being debated at a particularly sensitive time and it was easy to create fear in the population that this was the beginning of the heavy hand of China reaching down to snuff out Hong Kong's freedoms. The outcome of the public debate was that compromises were reached and reassurances given and the legislation passed. Not until three years after the handover, and a thousand demonstrations later, with new organisations popping up almost every day, were there calls for further relaxation.

In 1988, shortly after retiring, I had been invited to be the chairman of the National Mutual Insurance Company. The Australian parent company wished to expand further by obtaining one of the few licences being granted to foreign insurance companies to sell life insurance in a very limited way within China, and I had made frequent visits to Beijing on behalf of the company. I got to know many officials in the People's Bank of China and the People's Insurance Company. On these visits I had time to see how Beijing was changing and to hear directly from ministers and vice ministers how the Chinese economy was performing. The chairmen of the People's Bank and the People's Insurance Company were both world-class table tennis players and I spent exciting hours watching them compete, and later presented them with their prizes.

I was fortunate because there were few expatriates with my mixture of interests and background who were able to obtain first-hand impressions of China's leaders, not on one but on many occasions. I was able to learn at first hand how China was absorbing the experience of other nations faced with similar problems of unemployment and the development of social security, and to hear its leaders talk frankly about the problems they faced. The visits had another effect. They made me increasingly confident that nothing untoward was going to happen to Hong Kong in 1997, that China was too preoccupied with her own problems and that we would be left to solve our own, and that 'one country, two systems' was not simply a polite and reassuring cliché.

Our lives, too, were threatened with change. After ten years overlooking the sea and islands we learned that the road in front of our house was to be widened and that everything, house, garden, swimming pool, and giant trees would be demolished and destroyed. We were shocked and saddened, but eventually resigned to the fate which so many families had had to face when confronted by the juggernaut of development. It was ironical that forty years previously it had been my job to resume land and prepare to move a village for the widening of another section of the same road which was to run through an up-and-coming new town!

When the news was out, we were visited by journalists and camera teams. It was a story that kept them occupied in their less exciting moments many times over during the following years until, after many delays, in 2001 we eventually had to move. The press, at the beginning, portrayed this as Patten's Revenge, and there was a witty cartoon of Christopher Patten driving a mechanical grab flying the Union Jack advancing on the house, with my wife in her Girl Guide uniform and myself cowering fearfully in the corner!

On 17 February 1997 Deng Xiaoping died. This was the man who had met MacLehose in 1979, who had first explained the solution to the problem of Hong Kong, who had expounded the famous formulas 'one country, two systems' and 'Hong Kong people ruling Hong Kong' which were to be the beacons guiding Hong Kong, and who had spoken firmly and emphatically to the iron lady, the British Prime Minister Margaret Thatcher. It was Deng who, significantly, at the end of the power struggle following the deaths of Mao and Zhou, had first appeared in public in shirt sleeves, to the roars of the crowd, at a football tournament between Hong Kong and Beijing. And behind Deng at this same match, in full view of the Hong Kong television cameras, was sitting the president of the Hong Kong Football Association, Henry Fok Ying-tung, who later became a Deputy to the National People's Congress in Beijing.

In Hong Kong, queues of people formed to pay their respects, to sign a condolence book and to make three solemn bows before a flower-framed photograph. The passing of a leader who had risen from the beginning of the Chinese Communist Party and the era of the Long March marked another transition for China. It had been his well-known wish that he would see Hong Kong returned to China, and it was sad that he who had done so much to bring this to an acceptable conclusion without bloodshed or recrimination did not live to see the day.

With only four weeks to go to handover, June began with a brief burst of sunshine, and then the weather turned for the worse for the rest of the month with heavy rain and thunderstorms. There were dense black clouds, warnings of landslides and flooded streets, and this drenching rain reached its climax on the day when, after 156 years, the colony came to an end.

This was to be a very different occasion from the ending of other colonies where at a joint ceremony, with varying degrees of pomp and celebration, sovereign power was handed over to an independent government. In Hong Kong, the flag at Government House was pulled down quietly for the last time, folded and presented to the Governor in a brief, emotional ceremony attended only by his family and staff.

On the day of the handover, 30 June, we left home for two nights' stay in a hotel in central Hong Kong, for with such heavy rain and floods, there could be no guarantee that we would reach the crowded events of the next two days in time from the New Territories. That morning we enjoyed a breakfast party to celebrate the birthday of a friend, Shelley Lee, who was now a senior member of the public service and who had been personal assistant to Lord MacLehose when he was Governor. At the breakfast were Lord MacLehose and Lady Youde, who had come from England, and Sir Lee Quo-wei, former Executive Councillor who had just been awarded the Grand Bauhinia Medal (one of the first twelve honours of the Special Administrative Region and a sign that the Hong Kong government's way of honouring and thanking people was to continue). It was a great gathering of old friends, with much chatter and excitement.

In the late afternoon we and four thousand other invited guests were screened for security and taken to a farewell performance at a parade ground formed by reclamation of H.M.S. *Tamar*, the Royal Navy dockyard basin. The new headquarters for the Chinese Navy had been relocated from the central business district to Stonecutters Island, in the west of the harbour. The Provisional Legislative Council, since it was a body with no legal standing, had no part in these proceedings, although, curiously, some individuals were invited because they were members of both the outgoing and the incoming councils! The Chief Executive was also absent because he had to meet President Jiang Zemin and members of the Chinese government who were arriving from Beijing and were due to land by special arrangement at the new airport. He would be sworn in after midnight.

The *Tamar* performance and ceremony was little different from those we had witnessed for the departure of other Governors, and indeed, compared with some, it was on a modest scale. There was no great pageant of a hundred and fifty years of change and achievement. His Royal Highness Prince Charles the Prince of Wales, the Governor, members of Executive Council and other notables sat beneath a canopy; the rest of us were seated on raised benches in the drenching rain. Green and yellow umbrellas were provided, and by skilfully locking them with the row in front most of the rain could be made to cascade from one pale green concave to another, but after an hour or so, shoes were filled with water and everyone was soaked. There was no cover for the massed bands, the soldiers, sailors and airmen marching and counter-marching, the pipers and the kilts, the lion and dragon dances, the colourfully costumed dancing children, and the singers of sentimental songs; indeed, in a special effort the downpour increased to a torrent for the lone piper's mournful lament and the floodlit lowering of the flag. Music and speeches were drowned by the rattle of rain on four thousand umbrellas. Prince Charles then bravely stood, dripping and drenched, to take the salute at the final march past. Inside the Convention Centre, ladies emptied the water from their shoes into rubbish bins, gradually we dried off, and dinner was served. This was the culmination: the two governments had at last come together, and the British and Chinese diplomats, the officials and political leaders who had contributed to the writing of the Agreement, all dined together.

From the dinner tables we moved to the Grand Hall for the transfer of power and authority to the Chinese people's government. Chinese and British delegates were seated in a curved dais. Fanfares were played by Chinese and British trumpeters, the British in red, gold-buttoned uniforms and bearskins, the Chinese in smart, white, well-tailored uniforms.

President Jiang Zemin and Prince Charles spoke, with firm promises of autonomy from China, good wishes and praise from Prince Charles. At midnight the British and Hong Kong flags were lowered and folded and the Chinese and Bauhinia flag of the Special Administrative Region slowly raised. With great precision, the flag parties marched off in step in their separate directions; the 'captains and the kings' departed, the Prince and the Governor going immediately to the Royal Yacht *Britannia*, which inched soundlessly and slowly away from the quay and, escorted by H.M.S. *Chatham*, moved off into the rain-drenched night, past the old gun emplacements at the narrow entrance to the harbour and into the darkness of the South China Sea.

For a brief interval we were in the hands of the Chinese central government. Within an hour or so our own Special Administration Government was sworn in by President Jiang, including the Chief Executive and his principal officials, many former colleagues among them, the Executive Council, and the Provisional Legislative Council. Then came the judiciary, including the Chief Justice Andrew Li, whose mother had been godmother to our son, in a dignified sober black gown, and the judges, many expatriates among them, in their scarlet robes and short bob wigs, to the bewilderment of President Jiang. However, since Britain did not recognise the Provisional Legislature, the British Prime Minister, Tony Blair, presumably to show disapproval, did not attend these proceedings. Here was a sad end to a chapter of British history and a sorry comparison with the end of other colonies.

Our evening was not finished. It was 2.30 in the morning and raining still. We wandered about trying to locate the BBC who wanted a valedictory message from Anthony Lawrence, a veteran BBC correspondent, and me before closing down.

At daybreak the People's Liberation Army in troop carriers and trucks entered Hong Kong across the border, driving through border towns lined with flag-waving villagers to their downtown barracks. Then, strangely, they disappeared and have scarcely been seen since. Their headquarters, a tall building on the waterfront which had formerly been the headquarters of the British forces, still faintly bore the name 'The Prince of Wales Building' for several more months.

The next day there followed a celebration of the establishment of the Special Administrative Region. Against a painted background of scenes copied from the wall paintings of Xian, there were reassuring speeches repeating the obligatory time-honoured messages and performances by crowds of costumed children. Then we listened to a concerto written for the occasion by Chinese composer Tan Tun which incorporated both ancient bronze chimes and the cello playing of Yo Yo Ma. In the afternoon we trooped up the slope of Hong Kong Island to a modern building for the crowded opening of the representative office of the Foreign Affairs Ministry, headed by Commissioner Ma Yuzhen, the popular former Chinese Ambassador in London. In the evening Jane and I were joined by Betty Churcher, Director of the Australian National Gallery, of whose council I was an international member, and we watched a rather uninspiring procession of illuminated barges circling the harbour. This was not quite the end; on the morning of 2 July the Hong Kong Affairs Advisers, whom I had joined to cries of 'traitor', but whose term of office and usefulness had now ended, were formally thanked for their help by the Foreign Minister Qian Qichen and stood down.

34

Settling Down

Despite all the gloomy predictions, and the fear expressed by the foreign media and political commentators that the 'Reds' would take over, the PLA would march in, communist rule would follow, and everything built up over a century and a half of being a colony would collapse or be removed, the streets of Hong Kong did not look any different in those days after the handover than they looked before. There were no horseback victory parades such as had accompanied the Japanese arrival after defeating the British forces in 1941: there was not a soldier in sight. There was no gloating over the extinction of the Crown Colony. In fact it was a British 'business as usual' atmosphere that prevailed. Everyone went about their daily lives as though nothing had happened. Now, as I write at the beginning of the new century, I can say that the pledge to Hong Kong by Deng Xiaoping of 'no change for fifty years' looks more believable than when he first uttered it. Hong Kong's capitalist system is still alive. But its economy is suffering, not only from the problems faced by the rest of the world's economies, but from its own special problems, such as the hollowing out of industry and its migration to the mainland, the link with the US dollar, and so forth.

Of course Deng's statement was hyperbole even then; no society can remain frozen. Change was on the way. Early in 1997 there were warning signs that all was not well with Asian economies, and in the months and years which followed Hong Kong could not ring-fence itself from the economy of its neighbours. The rot began in Thailand. Banks had overborrowed and overlent and there was no possibility that the Thai currency could remain pegged to the dollar. The baht was allowed to float and went into free-fall. The Malaysian, Indonesian, Taiwan and Korean economies were all affected in varying degrees and responded in their different ways. The Japanese economy, which had been the pit prop to the economies of the region, had been stagnating already for some years and could not be looked to for help.

Since the crisis of confidence about the future in 1983, Hong Kong's currency had been linked to the US dollar. The link had provided stability throughout the following years of political strain, and now was not the moment to let go this sheet-anchor. Moreover, Hong Kong had been enjoying a period of growth and property prices had soared to levels bordering on the absurd. With a stock market heavily influenced by the property sector, the market index, too, had reached an unsustainable level. Prices came tumbling down, but the link with the dollar had to be defended. To remove it at time of crisis would have led to a flight of capital and would have destroyed overseas investor confidence which had taken long to build and which was the very thing Hong Kong needed to see it through the years of transition and adjustment to the larger economy of China.

Hong Kong had formidable reserves and deployed these to fight off attacks on the link. It was painful, and because of the dollar link, Hong Kong, among the nations of Asia, became a very expensive place. Tourism dropped away, hotel rooms were vacant, retail shops were boarded up and restaurants had empty tables. But the government held out, using determination and skill to defend the Hong Kong dollar and at one time acquiring shares in the market in order to ward off an attack through manipulation of the futures market.

It was not long before more trouble came from an unusual quarter. We have our supermarkets and shops, greengrocers and butchers, but the majority of housewives and their domestic helpers still go to the market to buy fresh vegetables, meat, live fish and live poultry. There are markets built to serve each district, and in the streets surrounding the markets are hawkers, who claim a patch of pavement or roadside gutter to sell vegetables and fruit to undercut the licensed stallholders in the markets, and against whom a hawker control organisation wages a long and unsuccessful war. Live chickens and fish are sold in the market, and frozen foods are scorned and spurned by gourmet households who can tell at once whether they are eating frozen or fresh food. Meat, too, principally pork, reaches the market stalls within hours of being killed. Not long after the changeover, chickens started to die and 'bird flu' was diagnosed.

Worse was to come. The belief that the virus would not affect humans proved false, and the virus crossed over to the human population and caused a number of deaths. Then followed the wholesale slaughter of chickens, ducks, geese, and quails, indeed anything that had wings. Well over a million and a half domestic birds were killed, mainly by stuffing them into large black plastic bags and gassing them. It was a ghastly but necessary measure to put a stop to the spread of a virus which showed a capacity to mutate, which had killed people and which could have given rise to a pandemic. Markets, cages and farms were disinfected and given a thorough clean-up, but it was weeks before there was a return to normality. It was an unexpected shock and challenge to the government coming on top of the Asian financial crisis and was dealt with decisively. (The experience gained from this epidemic among poultry subsequently stood the government in good stead when a different strain of the flu virus struck in 2001. Similarly, this led to the slaughter of the entire population of poultry, a halt to imports and the closure of markets.)

The rainshadow of the handover continued. There was a futile attempt to go to the courts to declare the Special Administrative Region, the Provisional Council and all its works illegal. But the SAR and the Provisional Council had been created and confirmed by the sovereign power, China. The Court of Appeal was quick to dismiss this absurdity.

For a few days in August, Jonathan Dimbleby's book and television series *The Last Governor* were the talk of the town. Dimbleby had been able to interview and televise the Governor even before his arrival in Hong Kong, and thereafter had virtually unrestricted and unprecedented access to Government House and the Governor during the rest of the Patten governorship. The book is a frank revelation of opinions and emotions and conduct of affairs. Some of the Governor's open views of personalities during that period as recorded by Dimbleby must have come as a surprise to them. I am mentioned in the book three times, each with some irritating inaccuracy. The television documentary takes one into the Governor's study during the crucial debate on the electoral reform package, into his limousine after meeting President Clinton and into the Ambassador's residence in Beijing while the Governor was telephoning London. Dimbleby interviewed me once in 1992 and said he would keep up the practice, but I saw him no more. After 1997 Christopher Patten retreated to France to write his book *East and West* and Hong Kong got on with tackling the problems caused by the collapse of the Asian economies.

'It will all be over by Christmas,' a phrase used at the beginning of the 1914–18 war, was used of the Asian financial collapse, but its effects dragged on, like that war, for years and not months, and one economic problem drifted into another. In former economic downturns Hong Kong could rely on improvements in the world economy to lift exports and set the wheels of industry turning faster, but Hong Kong's industry had migrated to China. Now the exports from Hong Kong factories were exports from China, and although the container port benefited, this did not provide much employment for former factory workers. The people of Hong Kong were reminded frequently that they had overcome problems in the past and would do so again, but this time it just did not seem to happen.

Hong Kong, too, was caught up in the fever which gripped the world over the new technology. New IT companies were launched with nothing but a persuasive idea and no assets behind them and suffered a predictable fate. Telecommunication companies went through a dizzying series of swaps, mergers and takeovers; talk now was in terms of tens of billions of dollars and huge sums of money were borrowed and lent. But those very technologies which had been hailed as bringing in a new age of prosperity were castles in the air. Profit, earnings, asset value, these old-fashioned words were found to be not so old-fashioned after all. The inevitable happened, and thousands of investors who found their savings had vanished grumbled, but did not take to the streets to demonstrate.

The eruption in property prices and the related boom in the stock market before 1997 led to a rush to cash in on the huge profit to be made by investing in property. Almost as suddenly, investors found that their property had dropped like a stone in value, leaving them, in the bland and comfortless phrase, with 'negative equity' on their hands and a mortgage to fund on a property which was not worth the money.

Finding land for housing and the coordination of supply with demand, not only for the public housing programme but also for private property developers, had never been never easy, and the limit on land disposal between 1985 and 1997 imposed by agreement with China took away a valuable element of flexibility from the planners. This was a long period to be hamstrung. Moreover, private developers were reluctant to make huge investment decisions until they could be absolutely sure of the future. As a result, overall housing production dropped. More important, the supply of flats for the public housing programme also decreased dramatically in the mid-nineties. Then, as a result of pressure and serious warnings from the Housing Authority, the planners and engineers had a rush of blood to the head and produced land in such quantities in 1995–6 that, after the three years that it takes to build, public housing production in 1999 and 2000 reached about 60,000 units a year, or housing for about 200,000 people.

At the same time, private property developers also recovered their confidence and began to build. This resulted in a gross oversupply of apartments for sale just when prices had plummeted. Potential home buyers preferred to hang on to their money rather than invest in such an uncertain market. The Chief Executive, Tung Chee Hwa, in his maiden speech to the Legislative Council in 1997 had declared a policy aim of producing 85,000 flats a year, but actual production far exceeded this figure. Housing demand and supply and consumer confidence were in disarray, and property developers were left with uneconomic developments on their hands.

Whenever something like this happens there is call for a review of policy and administration. Since then, housing policy has gradually changed, returning a major responsibility for property development to private business and substantially reducing the future commitment of the government, which, with over three million people in its care, is one of the world's biggest landlords. But projects, once started, proceed to an inexorable conclusion, and in this case the result was a huge overhang of housing in the market. Property development and housing were thus another vexatious problem haunting the handover years. Could anything more go wrong? It did.

On 2 July 1998, President Jiang Zemin had flown from Beijing to open the replacement airport at Chek Lap Kok. The old airport, Kai Tak, was in the east, and Chek Lap Kok in the west. The roads and bridges were all complete and the airport express railway line from downtown Hong Kong through a newly completed Western Harbour Tunnel was up and running. It had been decided to move everything overnight from the old airport to the new in a fleet of trucks, and for the waiting planes to take off from Kai Tak at intervals of a few minutes throughout the night to be ready at the new airport for business the next day, immediately after the opening ceremony.

The move went like clockwork and the ceremony took place with the usual fanfare (although neither Lord Wilson nor Sir David Ford, who had had such a hand in the decision to build the airport, were present). President Jiang flew back to Beijing in good order. But then things started to malfunction: passengers were directed to the wrong gates for their planes, escalators, baggage handling, lavatories, and signboards were in disarray, and even the tried and tested electronic equipment of the air cargo terminal would not function properly. It was all put right very efficiently and quickly and compared favourably with the opening of other international airports, but it was a further blow to Hong Kong's pride.

The sale of land by auction and the award of contracts to the lowest tender rather than by picking winners or cronies for the job are sensible axioms of Hong Kong administration. But the system has its weaknesses, which now came to the fore. The fall-out from the Asian financial crisis reached as far as the contractors for major housing developments. In order to build huge apartment blocks on soft ground, the piled foundation needs to reach down a hundred meters or more until the piles touch bedrock. Here was an opportunity to cut costs on contracts, which were now uneconomic, by reducing the length of the piles which were out of sight and underground. This criminal venality was revealed when the tower blocks began to lean slightly, and corruption was uncovered: somebody had to have been paid off. The 'short pile' scandal was nipped in the bud, but it gave watchdog legislators an opportunity to demand that heads should roll and exposed a weakness in the political structure. Who was accountable? Who was to blame?

The political structure described in the Basic Law does not provide for ministerial appointments; it speaks of the executive being accountable to the legislature, but this is a generalised responsibility. It does not pinpoint politically appointed individuals or members of a cabinet with specific responsibilities for a portfolio, who can be called to account and, if need be, asked to resign. A lively debate ensued about who was accountable in the political structure, which then petered out because no one had the answer. Because of the autonomy granted to Hong Kong under the rubric 'Hong Kong people ruling Hong Kong', it could be resolved only by removing the remaining legacies of colonial administration, by bringing about a rearrangement of the political structure and removing, like a bit of cabbage stuck between the teeth, a vestige of the colonial system.

The drafters of the Basic Law concentrated on the composition and election of Legislative Council, and had not dealt with the role and function of Executive Council, nor explicitly with the role and relationship of the civil service, who were caught in the middle between an elected legislature and an elected Chief Executive, and an Executive Council which gave its advice privately and confidentially to the Chief Executive. The poor civil servants were called upon more and more to perform a political role for which they were not equipped, and without a direct link with or much support from the Chief Executive or members of his Executive Council. In a matter of a few years, Legislative Council had become a fully elected body. No members were now appointed by a Governor, and the remaining handful of civil servants who had been a stabilising element in the old council were no longer there. The presiding officer was chosen by the members and no Governor, with colonial authority, any longer called members to 'Order'.

Moreover, there was now another weakness. In the past there had been a friendly working relationship between the executive and legislative bodies, who shared a common office. The shuffle of appointments after the arrival of Christopher Patten in 1992 meant there were no longer councillors who sat on both councils. Political parties, who saw themselves quite rightly as guardians of the public interest, became increasingly critical of the government, and as they went up in public perception, Executive Council went down, figuring less prominently in public affairs almost to the point of invisibility. The media, too, was changing and was less inclined to take the government side.

There was a clear and discernible empty space in the political structure. At a time when the systems in Hong Kong were under great strain and when the unexpected seemed to be the order of the day, there was no defined intermediate authority to be accountable and responsible when things went wrong. The call for heads to roll fell on empty air.

Apart from these negative things, who was to speak and be responsible for promoting and explaining, on a day to day basis, the policies and programmes of the government? Hong Kong soldiered on for many years without grappling with this problem. The government came under increasing pressure and criticism from the public and the media, while lacking nominated spokesmen or 'ministers' to speak out and defend the government's position. I made a number of speeches outlining what I thought should be done, and chaired a committee in the Business and Professional Federation (BPF) which prepared a detailed proposal which it submitted to the government.

In the annual address to the Legislative Council in 2001, when there were increasing calls for change, the Chief Executive indicated that he was going to change the system. This blank space in the Basic Law would be filled in, much along the lines of the recommendation of the BPF to appoint 'ministers' in all but name, to be supported by civil servants who would be Permanent Secretaries.

The Chief Executive was as good as his word. At the end of June 2002, just before the fifth anniversary of the SAR, he announced the appointment of a new 'ministerial' system. Members of Executive Council were given portfolios to oversee, some civil servants were promoted and appointed to Executive Council, and some members were brought in from the private sector. All are now served by Permanent Secretaries from the civil service. This change filled the lacuna in the Basic Law, and hopefully when the new system settles down it will introduce a new dynamic into the corridors of power in which each has a clearer idea of his responsibility and a more decisive government will emerge.

There was another sensible change in the constitutional framework made during this period which was possible without offending the Basic Law, and which must be mentioned for the sake of completeness. Hong Kong now had too many layers of government. There were two regional municipal councils and nineteen District Boards. The two elected municipal councils seemed superfluous, and were in a sense in competition with the Legislative Council. (It is an interesting comparison that one of the changes that took place in the government of Singapore after independence was the abolition of the municipal council.) After public consultation, the middle tier of representation, the municipal councils, was abandoned. It sank without trace and no one now ever talks of it. I, who previously had worked so hard to balance an unbalanced structure and to set up the Regional Council in the New Territories as a stopgap measure, now, with a full-fledged Legislative Council, was able to support this rationalisation and its removal.

35

Weather Report

resident Jiang Zemin addressed the 15th Party Congress of the People's Republic of China on 12 September 1997 as follows: 'China is in the primary stage of socialism. Correcting the erroneous concepts of the past is a new endeavour. We have done what was never mentioned by Marx, never undertaken by our predecessors and never attempted in any socialist country. We can only learn from practice, feeling our way as we go.' Chairman Deng put it more colourfully when he said it was like crossing a river feeling the stones with your feet.

Since these words were spoken, the speed of change has been nothing short of phenomenal. China, with over a billion people to govern, has changed gear, introducing fundamental changes to its economic structure, introducing four modernisations – in industry, science and technology, agriculture, and the military – and opening its doors to the world, calmly and quickly.

Now that the changes introduced by Deng in 1978 have been operating in China continuously for twenty-four years, foreign investment, particularly from Hong Kong or funnelled through it, has poured in to harness China's labour force in order to make the goods demanded by the markets of the West and to join in the building of cities and towns, highways and power stations. The financial markets have opened and the stock exchanges of Shenzhen and Shanghai are quoted in Hong Kong. China is always in the news and almost every day there has been some new development and excitement.

Flights to mainland cities have become a commonplace and there are tens of flights from Hong Kong to Shanghai; fast ferries and an electrified railway line make 250 million trips by people every year out of Hong Kong to every part of China, and more and more visitors come from the mainland to Hong Kong. Other Chinese travel further afield. Students from China flock in their thousands to the universities of the West, and those who do not follow on with a career in the West are bringing back to China new experiences and knowledge, as well as fluency in English and other languages. In one month alone, half a million visitors from the mainland visited Hong Kong.

The agreement as to how Hong Kong was to fit into China after the return of sovereignty allowed it to continue to develop physically, economically and socially and set the parameters of political development for at least ten years after 1997. Hong Kong people would govern Hong Kong with a high degree of autonomy, and it would retain its capitalist system. But in the years it took to reach an agreement with China about the future of Hong Kong, no one predicted the remarkable pace of change in China itself. Mentioning it would have been met with disbelief, and even accusations of going soft on China. Hong Kong failed to comprehend the full effect that this was going to have on Hong Kong.

In 1997 Hong Kong embarked on its journey as a Special Administrative Region within China with many factors in its favour. The economy was healthy and resilient and, unlike surrounding territories, because of its huge foreign exchange reserves, it was able to resist being detached from its anchor in the US dollar. The economy had its armoury of special characteristics: the utilities, business and industry were not subsidised; the rate of taxation was low and limited in its range; there was regulation of business without interference; and the government's finances were managed with puritanical rigour. The judiciary was independent; we shared a common law system with many other jurisdictions; and we had our own Court of Final Appeal. Hong Kong made no contribution to the coffers of the central government of China, nor any contribution towards defence, as it had to Britain in colonial days. An effective commission against corruption was independent and had far-reaching powers. There was free and open daily discussion of affairs, and protests against perceived injustice were a regular safety valve. And we retained our independent membership of world financial, economic and trade organisations.

These characteristics are all embedded in the Basic Law. What previously went without saying is now provided for by law: Hong Kong has by law to provide an appropriate environment to maintain Hong Kong as an international financial centre; the law requires it to avoid budget deficits and keep budgets in pace with the growth rate of the economy; Hong Kong keeps the money it earns; it must retain its status as a free port and safeguard the free flow of capital. There is much more on these lines to demonstrate the special nature of the Administrative Region.

When the negotiations were concluded in 1984 to preserve this strange hybrid, it seemed that there was plenty of time: thirteen years to go before the return to China. This was an illusion. The years passed all too quickly in making the arrangements and putting into place the laws to solidify the political structure. Attention was focused on these issues, more particularly during the final five years. There was not the motive of the driving excitement and imperative of looming independence, as in other colonies, for local politicians to take a hard and questioning look at aspects of the social order, so as to make a start, even before the handover, on putting right things which badly needed attention.

The colonial government possibly overdid the policy of non-intervention, of leaving Hong Kong to develop on its own lines without interference and without trying to adjust to the world around us. It was left too long and too late before it was realised that after more than a century and a half of British rule a knowledge of English was restricted to a comparatively small elite, and that we lacked sufficient men and women familiar with the new technologies which our developing economy needed. It was up to the incoming government and Hong Kong's new Chief Executive to begin to overhaul the education, health and social service systems, to introduce crash courses in English on a widespread scale and bring native-speaking English teachers into some of our schools. And the new government finally had to grit its teeth and, despite uninformed opposition, introduce measures to deal with worsening air pollution, which at times was so bad that Kowloon was barely visible from Hong Kong.

Hong Kong, with its population of nearly seven million and growing, is challenged now perhaps more than it has ever been by its lack of natural resources, by the migration of its industry to China and by the changes in the global economy. In the past twenty or so years its economy has become intertwined with, and dependent on, the mainland. Hong Kong is the largest investor in China and China is the largest investor in Hong Kong. Hong Kong has factories, hotels, shopping malls, and residential and commercial property in China. It trades the stocks of Chinese companies, and red chips mingle with blue chips.

Nevertheless, Hong Kong has advantages which will be difficult to replicate in mainland China, for it will take many years for China to adopt and implement a system of law which can synergise and march easily with the legal systems of the West . Concentration in China now is on growth and on gradually reducing the role of the state in the economy. This is not easy and will be a fairly prolonged process as the huge numbers of unemployed and displaced persons are accommodated. China has an ageing and a continually growing population. So China, too, has problems of her own to cope with. Hong Kong has its laws and legal system which have international understanding and backing; it has its freedom and all the safeguards provided by the Basic Law, and the central government of China has been entirely scrupulous in the manner in which it has observed its international obligations under the agreement with the United Kingdom.

There were those who predicted a doomsday scenario for Hong Kong because of 1997. In an astonishing turnabout, in 2001 the *Fortune* Global Forum met in Hong Kong! It will, however, require the patience of a few years before the results of decisions which have been taken and are being taken every day to begin to show. Science parks are near completion and the first tenants are moving in. Small and medium enterprises are being helped to improve; innovation is being encouraged. New reclamations will transform the Hong Kong waterfront. New railways are already being built, and the first will open in 2003. In Kowloon a new centre for theatres and galleries will take shape. Tourism will get a substantial lift when Disneyland is complete in 2005. Most of these improvements will take time to implement and their contribution to increasing employment and opportunities will be gradual, but certain.

Hong Kong's vision is to become the world city of Asia. As the months of the new century pass, its integration with the growing economy of southern China will strengthen. The twin city of Shenzhen which stretches along our northern boundary already has a population approaching seven million, and all the towns of the Pearl River delta are developing, including the urban renewal and expansion of Guangzhou, and are being linked together by motorways and railways. The two economies of Hong Kong and Shenzhen are moving towards a level when the controls at the entry points will be open day and night and there will be a free flow of people for employment between them. People, increasingly, will live in the suburbs north of the boundary and commute to Hong Kong, as do the workers in other great cities of the world.

Will Shanghai be a threat? This is the wrong question. There is room and a need for both Hong Kong and Shanghai: Hong Kong serving the huge, populous region of southern China, and Shanghai serving a great region of growth stretching inland to Chongqing.

I have written elsewhere in these pages of Hong Kong's continuing tendency to look outward to the rest of the world and to pay insufficient official heed to developments on its doorstep in China. But Hong Kong has always been dependent to a greater or lesser degree on the economy and the politics of China. In 1949 with the success of the People's Liberation Army over the forces of the Guomindang, it was a political decision which halted the PLA at the border, for they could very easily have swept in and over Hong Kong. During the years which followed, Hong Kong relied very heavily on cheap and regular supplies of food from China. Since the beginning of economic reform in 1978, Hong Kong's industry would not have survived if it had not been able to move to China.

Hong Kong has been sustained in these years by China's indirect contribution to its economy. This has been taken for granted and has tended to leave intact an outward-looking attitude which is slow to change.

Hong Kong today is facing questions which it has never previously had to face. During the colonial period it never had to ask 'What is my identity, who am I?' Our interpretation of the phrase 'one country, two systems' concentrated on the superiority of our system and its proud possession of the rule of law, on our freedom, our administration, our simple tax structure and our economic well-being, so much so that we failed to evaluate the significance of what was happening north of the boundary in Shenzhen and of the changes taking place in the rest of Guangdong and throughout China. We have been absorbed by the challenges faced by our one system and have neglected the fact that, although we are a Special Administrative Region, we are one of the cities of one country. As I write, the Chinese economy continues to grow at 7 per cent overall and Hong Kong's economy grows at 1.5 per cent. Compared with the days when unemployment in Hong Kong was negligible, it is now over 7 per cent. This is a serious and hitherto unknown problem.

As part of the means to meet these challenges, we cannot be passive onlookers to the transformation in China as though the effect it would have on Hong Kong were not something to concern us. Only recently have we begun to enter into serious discussion about finding a solution to the shared problem of air and water pollution. We have to find a means so that the undoubted benefits of our system of law and financial management and our service economy can become more useful and more used by business enterprises in China. And we have to be more proactive, more aggressive in pursuing ways to link our transport infrastructure with that of China so that it facilitates not only the transport of goods but the movement of people, and enables further investment by Hong Kong in those areas of the neighbouring province that are relatively less developed. We must develop transport links which stretch out like a fan with Hong Kong as a hub, and we must build the bridges to Zhuhai and the west. Like other world cities we need our commuter express trains, and we need to entice Chinese enterprises to set up their offices in Hong Kong, with its access to and knowledge of overseas markets, to use Hong Kong as a base for their overseas investments, and to see Hong Kong as a useful avenue to the world.

To say that China needs Hong Kong and cannot live without Hong Kong is overstating the case. However, Hong Kong has to face up to the situation that those attributes and aspects of our society which we regard as unique protectors of our way of life and prosperity are also moving into China. Lawyers, accountants and professionals of all kinds are gradually shifting the emphasis of their work into China.

Despite gradually losing its pre-eminence in many areas, it is Hong Kong's opportunity and destiny to become the focal point of a huge metropolitan area stretching from Guangdong, eighty miles to the north of Hong Kong, to encompass the whole of the Pearl River delta. It will need far-reaching and speedy decisions if Hong Kong is to succeed in this and not be left by the wayside.

Finally, if Hong Kong is to become truly international it must shed its fear of immigration of people from around the world to work and students to study. Only then will we become the world city of Asia and one of China's great cities with our own special characteristics.

This is the vision. Will Hong Kong rise, as it has in the past, to those great challenges? I believe it will.

Envoi

I n 1793, in the midst of the French Revolution, Lord Macartney led a great and grand fleet of ships from Britain on an embassy to China. His objective, which he failed to achieve, was to put an end to the privations and indignities suffered by British merchants trading in Canton and Macao and to establish a permanent diplomatic presence accredited to the Imperial Court in Peking. The fleet sailed first south-eastwards, crossing the Equator to Rio de Janeiro, and then on a long haul across the southern Atlantic and round the Cape of Good Hope. It sailed across the southern Indian Ocean, through the Sunda Straits, north-eastwards following the coast of Indo-China, called at Macao, and finally went up river to Tientsin. My wife Jane and I were curious to see the place where this first serious effort by the British to establish relations with China had come to such an ignominious conclusion.

Travelling from Beijing, it had taken seven days for Macartney and his entourage to cover the distance to Jehol (modern Chengde), beyond the Great Wall, where the Emperor was relaxing for the summer. It took us all of five hours in a tourist coach. Macartney travelled in a horse-drawn carriage, lurching, bumping and grinding over the narrow, rocky and dusty summer track and winding through the low mountains north of the wall until he reached the yurts, the conical tents, of the Manchus, the summer residence of the Emperor and his court.

Chengde is a place of Buddhist temples and a fine lamasery (a Tibetan or Mongolian monastery for lamas). We toiled up the slope, passing through numerous worshipping halls to reach the crimson walls of the temple at the summit which towered up like a smaller version of the Potala in Lhasa. There, out of breath and with aching knees, we climbed the many steps of the staircase across the wall to the quadrangle of shrines set in the top, each with carmine pillars, blue bracketed roof and yellow tiles, until we reached Buddha glinting gold in the gloom. There from the roof we could look across Chengde to the forests and mountains beyond. This was the place to which Macartney had travelled across the oceans and all the weary way from Beijing. He brought with him gifts demonstrating the latest achievements of the West, including an elaborate planetarium, and, as an afterthought, a personal gift from himself, a resplendent decorated sprung coach which, spurned, was left on the quayside, drenched with rain and gathering dust.

The summer residence of the Emperor (to call it a palace conveys a wrong impression) lies in a wooded, walled park, large enough to hunt in without going outside the wall. The residence itself is a series of grey-roofed and grey-walled pavilions and chambers connected by roofed corridors, reaching down to a willow-fringed lake around which are spaced elegant pavilions.

It was in one of these chambers that we came across the following inscription on a brass plaque: 'Not forgetting the national humiliation the Emperor signed the Beijing Treaty here on October 28 1860 (September 15 by the Lunar Calendar). It was in the West Warm Chamber that the Emperor Xian Feng was forced to sign the Beijing Treaty with Britain, France and Russia which ceded Kowloon to Britain.' It goes on to recall that at the same time 100,000 square kilometres to the north were ceded to Russia.

Macartney, having come so far, could not find it in himself to perform the requisite prostration of the kowtow before the Emperor, kneeling and knocking his head upon the ground. This kowtow is given as the superficial reason for his unseemly departure. Eventually, after many exchanges, the Chinese courtiers accepted that Macartney would go down on one knee when the Emperor passed, or when documents representing the Emperor were presented. This was a reasonable compromise. The real reason for Macartney being hurried away was the Manchu court's obsession with self-sufficiency, its feeling of insecurity and fear of foreign cultural invasion, and fear of losing control of its empire in China. It was paranoid about the consequences of opening up to the world, and said in so many words that China had no need of anyone. The embassy was told to go home, taking its gifts with it.

China became a member of the United Nations in 1971 and now, as I write, has become a member of the World Trade Organisation. Hong Kong and Macao have been reunited with their motherland. This, and the opening to the world, marks the end of a long and eventful journey and many 'national humiliations', and at the threshold of the new century, a fresh start for Hong Kong, the beginning of a new journey.

* * * * * * * * * * * *

This has been a personal account of years of excitement, interest and enjoyment, of struggle and challenge in an extraordinary place where we have been fortunate to have lived and worked. What better way to sum it up than in these words from Shakespeare's *As You Like It* – recalling a curious medieval belief.

Sweet are the uses of adversity,
Which like the toad, ugly and venomous,
Wears yet a precious jewel in his head.

* * * * * * * * * * * *

The End

Index